Sue Kay & V
addition

American Inside Out

Student's Book

Intermediate

MACMILLAN

1 Friends

1 Write down the names of three people who are important to you: a friend, a relative, and somebody famous.

2 Ask other people in the class about their lists. Find out as much as you can.

1 Marisol
2 Rolando
3 Shakira

Fame

1 Discuss these questions:

a) Who are the five most famous people in your country?
b) Who do you think is the most famous man in the world?
c) Who do you think is the most famous woman in the world?

2 Look at photographs 1–6.

a) Do you know who these people are?
b) What do you know about them?

1
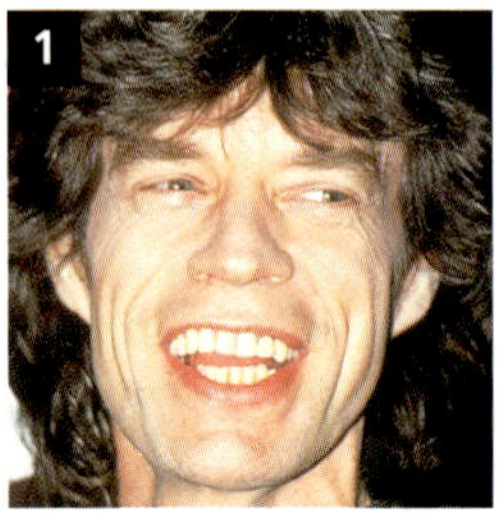

2

3
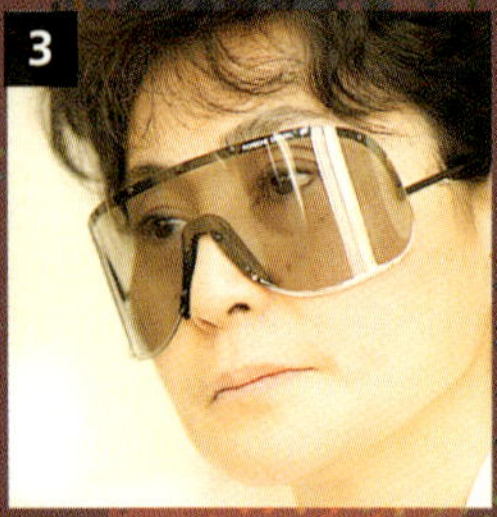

4

5

6

LANGUAGE TOOLBOX

He/She looks like …
This one could be …
Maybe it's (Bob Marley)'s son/daughter/mother.
Maybe it's …
It's hard to say, but …

3 Each of the famous people in the photographs in 2 is related to one of the people below. Match each of the famous people with his/her relation and say how the two people are related.

Test your knowledge of question forms

1 These are the answers from an interview about one of the people in the photographs. Write the questions.

a) She was born in London, but she has dual nationality because her mother's from Nicaragua.
b) No, she's living in Ibiza now.
c) Not long. She moved from London with her two daughters about a year ago.
d) Yes, she says she's very happy there. She and her daughters like the outdoor life. And her mother's a Spanish speaker, so she feels more comfortable in a Latin country.
e) Yes, she's very talented. She's a painter. And she has a jewelry business. She also models occasionally.
f) She doesn't have much spare time. But she likes to read and to listen to music.
g) She likes all kinds—pop, classical …
h) She says she doesn't. But don't tell her father.
i) I don't think she sees them very often. Her mother's in New York, and her father is often on tour.
j) She loves Brazil. Her children love it there too.
k) I think her father named her. Her mother wanted her to have a Spanish name.

2 01 Listen to the interview. Are your questions the same as the ones on the recording? Who was being interviewed?

Pronunciation

1 02 Look at tapescript 02 and listen to the questions. Underline the strongest stress in each question.

For example:
Where were you born?

2 Work with someone you don't know very well. Use questions similar to the ones from the interview. Begin your question with the following cues to find out as much as you can about each other.

Have you …? What's your favorite …? Who …? Do you enjoy …? Are you good at …?
Can you …? How long have you …? Do you ever …? Are you interested in …?

Close-up

Question forms

Work with a partner and discuss the following:

a) In each of the following questions, which word is the *subject*? Which is the *auxiliary*? Which is the *main verb*?

1 Has she been to New York?
2 Did you have a good flight?
3 Is John staying at the Waldorf?
4 What do you do?

b) In a question, does the subject usually come before or after the auxiliary?
c) What tenses are used in a)?
d) Match the tenses to the auxiliaries.

continuous tenses	*have/has/had*
perfect tenses	*do/does/did*
simple tenses	*am/is/are/was/were*

Language Reference p. 8

e) Three *modal auxiliaries* are *can, could,* and *would*. What others can you name?
f) *Which, when,* and *how* are *question words*. There are five other important question words. What are they?
g) Where does a question word usually go in a question?

1 Which person is the *subject* and which is the *object* in this sentence?

Mark Chapman shot John Lennon in December 1980.

2 What are the answers to these two questions?

1 Who did Mark Chapman shoot?
2 Who shot John Lennon?

a) Is *who* the subject or the object of each question?
b) Which question uses an auxiliary?

3 The words in these sentences have been mixed up. Put the words in the correct order. Add *did* when necessary.

a) who Arantxa Sánchez trains?
b) band play Bob Marley which with?
c) Mick Jagger with songs who writes?
d) marry Yoko Ono who?
e) appear $1 million ad Claudia Schiffer in who car a paid to?
f) for the World Ronaldo play in Cup who 1998?

Match the questions to the answers in the box.

John Lennon   Keith Richards   The Wailers   Citroën   Brazil   Her father

4 Use the words in the box to make five true sentences.

a)	Elton John	died	Evita in the movie of the same name.
b)	Madonna	wrote	*Candle in the Wind* at Princess Diana's funeral.
c)	Edith Piaf	played	*La Traviata* in 1853.
d)	Frank Sinatra	sang	*Je Ne Regrette Rien.*
e)	Verdi	performed	in 1998.

5 Write two questions for each of the sentences in 4.

For example:

a) Who performed … *Who performed* Candle in the Wind *at Princess Diana's funeral?*
Which song … *Which song did Elton John perform at Princess Diana's funeral?*

b) Who … Which part …
c) Who … Which famous song …
d) When … Which American singer …
e) When … Who …

Prepositions

1 Sentences in English can end with a preposition, for example: *Where do you come* *<u>from</u>?* Which prepositions are missing from these questions?

a) Who do you usually have lunch ___________ ?
b) What are you learning English ___________ ?
c) What do you spend the most money ___________ ?
d) Who does your teacher remind you ___________ ?
e) When you go out with your friends, what do you talk ___________ ?
f) What kind of music do you like listening ___________ ?

2 Work with a partner. Ask your partner the questions in 1.

Using questions

1 Many questions are formed using the same few structures. Match the questions to the most appropriate answers.

Do you have/ Have you got	a)	Do you have any children?	Yes, plenty, thank you.
	b)	Do you have a pen?	Sure. What do you want?
	c)	Do you have a minute?	Yes, here you are.
	d)	Do you have enough potatoes?	Yes, three.
Is that…?	a)	Is that your father?	Yes, I'm sorry. Is he bothering you?
	b)	Is that my pen?	Yes. We'd better get a taxi.
	c)	Is that your dog?	Yes, it is. I'm sorry, it looks just like mine.
	d)	Is that the time?	Yes. That's the day he joined the army.
Would you like to…?	a)	Would you like to go out for coffee?	It's always been my dream to do that.
	b)	Would you like to call me tomorrow?	Certainly. How long will it be?
	c)	Would you like to live in the country?	O.K. What time would be good for you?
	d)	Would you like to wait here for a minute?	Good idea. Where should we go?

Language Reference p. 8

2 Which of the questions are *asking for information*? What are the others doing? Imagine the situations.

Tic-Tac-Toe

1 Work in two teams. Team A: Look at page 140.
Team B: Look at page 143.

2 Use the questions to play *Tic-Tac-Toe*. The object of the game is to get a line of three *Os* or three *Xes* before the other team.

a) Draw a Tic-Tac-Toe grid on a separate piece of paper.
b) Decide whether your team is *Xes* or *Os*.
c) Take turns asking and answering questions. When a team member answers a question correctly, he/she chooses a square on the grid and writes *X* or *O*.

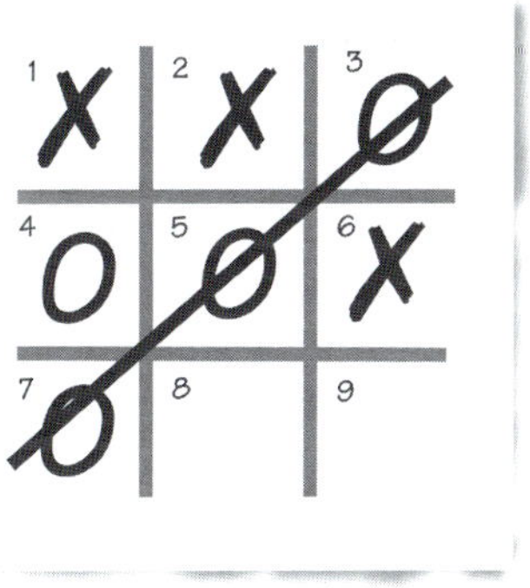

Language Reference: Questions

Question forms have many uses. Here are a few examples:

Asking for information:	*Where's the nearest post office?*
Asking for permission:	*Is it O.K. if I leave work early tonight?*
Making requests:	*Could you pass me the salt?*
Making offers:	*Can I help?*
Extending invitations:	*Would you like to go out for dinner?*
Making suggestions:	*Should we go to the movies?*
Showing friendly interest:	*How are your children?*

Yes/No questions

1 When *be* is the only verb in the sentence, we put it before the subject in the question.

Affirmative: ***You were** in my class last year.*
Question: ***Were you** in my class last year?*

2 We usually put the auxiliary before the subject in the question.

Present continuous
***You're** working for IBM.*
***Are you** working for IBM?*

Past continuous
***You were** thinking about Jack again.*
***Were you** thinking about Jack again?*

Present perfect
***She's** been to Mexico recently.*
***Has she** been to Mexico recently?*

Past perfect
***He'd** already left when she arrived.*
***Had he** already left when she arrived?*

Simple present
***He speaks** English well.*
***Does he speak** English well?*

Simple past
***She played** football yesterday.*
***Did she play** football yesterday?*

Note: Because there is no auxiliary in the affirmative of simple tenses, we use the auxiliary *do* to form questions.

3 We use these *modal auxiliaries* with the simple form of a verb: *can, could, will, would, shall, should, had better, may, might,* and *must.* We use the modal auxiliaries *have* and *ought* with *to* plus the simple form of a verb. We usually put modal auxiliaries before the subject in a question.

can ***You can** swim.*
***Can you** swim?*
will ***She'll be** here tomorrow.*
***Will she be** here tomorrow?*

Questions with question words

Questions with question words begin with *when, where, who, why, how, which, what,* and *whose.* We usually put the question word at the beginning of a question.

Do you smoke?	***How much** do you smoke?*
Are you going?	***When** are you going?*
Has he seen you?	***Where** has he seen you?*
Are you tired?	***Why** are you tired?*

When the question word is the subject of the sentence, we do not use *do, does,* or *did:*

Affirmative: *Mark Chapman shot John Lennon in 1980.*
Subject question: ***Who shot** John Lennon?*

This happens most often with *who* but can also happen with *which* and *what.*

***Which** company **bought** Rolls-Royce in 1998?*
***What happened** next?*

Questions ending with prepositions

Many verbs can be followed by a *dependent preposition.* We usually put the preposition at the end of a question.

He spent all his money on cars and clothes.
*What did he spend all his money **on**?*

Friends for Life

1 Tina and Will met when they were both studying at the same college. Three years later, a student magazine contacted them and asked them to participate in a survey to find out how many people had stayed friends.
Look at the photographs of Tina and Will. Do you think each of the following statements is true or false?

a) Tina and Will had similar interests when they were in college.
b) They chose similar careers when they graduated.
c) They have similar lifestyles now.

2 Read what they both say about their friendship and find out if you were right.

That Was Then This Is Now

TINA I first met Will when I was looking for someone to share the house I was renting. I put an advertisement in the local student newspaper, and he was one of the people who answered it. When we met, we hit it off right away, and I told him he could move in.

Living with Will was fun. We soon found out that we had a lot in common and quickly became close friends. We always had really good discussions about everything that was important to us at the time—politics, the environment, literature, and other less important things like cooking. We also liked the same music, and that's important when you're sharing a house. We had a few arguments a couple of times about the housework. Will thinks I'm messy, but I think life's too short to worry about things like that.

When we graduated three years ago, we went our separate ways, and since then our lives have been very different. I went back to my hometown and got a job as a production assistant for art exhibitions. I like my job because I'm helping young people to get involved in the arts. I'm living with my parents because I'm not earning very much. Will thinks I'm crazy because money is very important to him now, but I get a lot of personal satisfaction from my job. He's earning a lot of money, but he doesn't have time to spend with his family and his friends. I don't see him very often now. When he comes for the weekend, we have fun, but our lifestyles are so different now that we don't have very much to talk about.

WILL Tina and I got along very well at college. When we first met, we clicked right away, and we ended up sharing a house for nearly three years. We had the same attitude about the important things in life. The only thing we argued about was the housework. I'm a Virgo, so I'm very neat, whereas Tina's the opposite. I don't think she ever found out where we kept the vacuum cleaner!

When I graduated, I moved to the city and got a job with a finance company. I have to work long hours, and I don't really enjoy what I'm doing, but I make really good money. I'm very ambitious, and I want to get to the top of my profession. I enjoy spending money on CDs, clothes, a nice car, and going out to good restaurants. Tina's working really hard too, but she's not earning much. I don't understand why she's doing it. I think she's taking a vacation—it seems very idealistic to me. Anyway, it means that our lifestyles are very different now, so we've drifted apart. We haven't had a fight or anything. We still talk on the phone, and when I go to visit her, we have a good time. I know she'll always be there for me.

(Adapted from *The Independent*, April 9,1998)

Together at college

Tina now

Will now

Vocabulary

1 Tina and Will use several expressions to talk about their friendship. Complete as many of these expressions as you can from memory. Compare them with a partner. Then look at the article again to check.

a) Two expressions that mean "we liked each other immediately."
We clicked … *We hit it …*

b) An expression that means "we had similar interests."
We had a lot …

c) An expression that means "we enjoyed each other's company."
We got along …

d) An expression that means "we got to know each other very well."
We became close …

e) An expression that means "we argued."
We had a few …

f) Two expressions that mean "we became more distant from each other."
We went our separate … *We drifted …*

g) An expression that means "I know I can count on her when I need a friend."
She'll always be …

2 The following is a summary of Tina and Will's friendship. Put the lines of the summary in the correct order.

( ) met. They became close	(*2*) off immediately when they first
( ) separate ways, and they've drifted	( ) fight, and they say that they are still
( ) friends and got along	( ) there for each other.
(*1*) Tina and Will hit it	( ) apart. They haven't had a
( ) in common. Now they have gone their	( ) well. They had a lot

Anecdote

1 03 Listen to Balvir telling Tim about a close friend. Which of the following topics do they talk about?

Balvir and Tim

- ☐ How did you first meet?
- ☐ What was your first impression of her?
- ☐ What do you like about her?
- ☐ What don't you like about her?
- ☐ What do you have in common?
- ☐ How do you differ?
- ☐ Why did you become such close friends?
- ☐ Will you be friends for life?
- ☐ What does she look like?
- ☐ What is she like as a person?
- ☐ What special talents and abilities does she have?
- ☐ What kind of clothes does she wear?
- ☐ What's her job?
- ☐ What's her family like?
- ☐ What are her hobbies and interests?
- ☐ What do you do and what do you talk about when you're together?

2 Listen again and write down what they said about the topics.

3 Think about a close friend. You are going to tell a partner about him/her. Choose from the list in 1 the things you want to talk about. Think about what you will say and what language you will need.

4 Tell your partner about your friend.

You've Got a Friend

Vowel sounds

1 04 There are many vowel sounds in English. Look at these words and the phonetic symbols for their vowel sounds. Listen and repeat each word.

a) call /ɔ/	e) good /ʊ/	i) soon /u/	m) I'll /ɑi/
b) come /ʌ/	f) got /ɑ/	j) winter /ɪ/	n) down /ɑu/
c) again /ə/	g) can /æ/	k) take /ei/	o) boy /ɔi/
d) friend /ɛ/	h) need /i/	l) cold /ou/	

2 Look at each of these words from *That Was Then, This Is Now* (p. 9). Say it and decide which word in 1 has the same vowel sound.

a) hit	d) means	g) off	j) fun
b) time	e) have	h) house	k) clothes
c) same	f) put	i) lot	l) went

3 Think of other words you know that have the same vowel sounds as the vowel sounds of the words in 1.

4 05 You are going to listen to the Brand New Heavies perform the song *You've Got a Friend*. Check the words from 1 as you hear them. Which word isn't in the song?

Carole King, American singer, songwriter, and pianist, entered the music scene in the early 1960s. Her music is strongly influenced by rhythm and blues. She wrote *You've Got a Friend* and sang it on her best-selling album, *Tapestry*, released in 1971. Many music groups have recorded this song.

The Brand New Heavies perform Carole King's classic *You've Got a Friend*.

5 Look at the lyrics. The lines have been cut in half. The lines are in the correct order in column A, but they are mixed up in column B . Listen and match the two halves of each line.

		A	B
VERSE 1	1)	When you're down	loving care
	2)	And you need some	even your darkest night
	3)	And nothing, no,	and think of me
	4)	Close your eyes	and troubled
	5)	Oh, and soon	is going right
	6)	To brighten up	I will be there
CHORUS	1)	You just call out	be there, yes I will
	2)	And you know	summer, or fall
	3)	I'll come running,	is call
	4)	Don't you know that winter, spring,	wherever I am
	5)	All you've got to do	a friend
	6)	And I'll	yeah, to see you again
	7)	You've got	my name
VERSE 2	1)	Ain't it good to know that	if you let them
	2)	People can	be so cold
	3)	They'll hurt you	let them
	4)	Take your very soul	you've got a friend
	5)	So don't	and desert you

Vocabulary

1 One of the lines is "Ain't it good to know that you've got a friend." What does *ain't* mean? Is it correct English?

2 Read the following lines from different pop songs. Rewrite the underlined words in more formal English.

a) I wanna hold your hand.
b) I'm gonna be by your side, gonna be loving you forever, every day of my life.
c) It ain't me you're looking for, babe.
d) See, baby, if the road you choose don't work out for you, you know I'll be your rescue.
e) I can't get no satisfaction.
f) You gotta roll with it.

3 Try to match the singer or band in the box with each song line in 2.

Oasis   The Beatles   Bob Dylan   Destiny's Child   the Rolling Stones   'N Sync

Check your answers on page 141.

4 Collect other examples of "pop song English" and bring them to class.

Destiny's Child

You've Got Mail

1 These e-mail messages were sent to a magazine for English language students.

a) Which ones do you think are the most and least interesting? Why?
b) Are there any messages that you would be interested in answering?

Delete | Print | Forward | Reply | Done

Hi! I like to skateboard, surf, go in-line skating, ski, swim, and play baseball. I LOVE animals. I have five hamsters and a dog. I had eight fish, but they died. I also had a turtle, but my neighbor's dog killed her. I also like playing computer games and listening to Nirvana and Bush, and I have my own band, called Turbulence.

Ben, New York

LIFE IS A DARING ADVENTURE. I'm a woman of 44, with two grown children, a piano, a dog, and a few survival strategies. Interested in everything, but mostly in people and different lifestyles.

Ana, Colombia

HEY YOU! READ THIS NOW!! Good! Now that I have your attention, I can tell you that I'm a 19-year-old girl who loves to dance, talk, exercise, and go horseback riding. I'm interested in everything from football to ballet. I promise that if you write to me, you will get a response. SO WHAT ARE YOU WAITING FOR?!

Francine, Canada

Hi! I'm a 20-year-old male who would like to write to females from all around the world because girls are easy to talk to and a beautiful girl is nature's greatest creation!

Emilio, Peru

Hi. This is Paulo writing! I'm 25, and I'm looking for a serious pen-pal about my age. I'd prefer a gal, but even guys are accepted. I live in Brazil and I'd like to correspond in English. If you're interested, I have brown hair and green eyes, and I'm five feet, eight inches tall. I love alternative music such as Sonic Youth and some pop too like Shakira, and of course rock (U2). But I hate techno. I also love movies, theater, arts...well, I'll tell you the rest if you write. Well, hope to hear from you soon.

Paulo, Brazil

2 Write an e-mail with a message about yourself.

3 This is a letter written by one of the people in 1. Read it and decide who wrote it. You will correct the mistakes in spelling and capitalization later.

4 Find ten spelling mistakes and ten letters that should be capitals and write the words correctly.

5 Write a letter introducing yourself to a pen-pal.

Dear ....
thank you for your e-mail message and your adress. I am writting to you to tell you more about myself and also to send you a photograph. That's me on the left. The one in the middle is my older brother, olivier, and that's my sister sonia on the right. I get along very well with my sister, but my brother and I have nothing in common—he's very serious and boreing. He just spends all his time on the computer and never goes out.

I like going out—especialy to dance. On saturday nights I work in a nightclub to earn some money because i'm a student. I'm studying english and spanish at college, but I'm not sure why. I mean, I don't know what I want to do when I graduate

Anyway, I love travelling, and languages will be usefull for that. Last summer I studyed english at a school in chicago (my parents are divorced, and my dad lives there now), and next summer I want to go to spain to learn flamenco and go horseback riding on the beach.

What else can I tell you? I'm single. I had a boyfriend for six months, but we broke up because he was to jealous. I want to get maried and have children one day, but not yet!

As I told you in the e-mail, I'm interested in just about everything—even football! How about you? Please write soon and tell me what you're interested in.
Appologies for my bad spelling.
Love ...

2 Relax

Think about some of the things you did yesterday. Write each one under a heading: working, studying, or relaxing.

How much time did you spend working or studying, and how much time relaxing? Was this a typical day? Compare with a partner.

The Little Book of Calm

1 Look at the photograph. How do you think the woman is feeling? Look at the book she's reading. What do you think it's about?

The Little Book of Calm is only 4 in. x 4 in. It contains only 1,000 words but has sold over two million copies and has made its author into a multimillionaire.

Sally

Barbara

Robert

Pete

2 According to *The Little Book of Calm*, a relaxed person:

a) spends time alone.
b) takes a short nap during the day.
c) goes for a walk in the country or in a park.
d) gets some physical exercise.
e) goes running.
f) floats in water.
g) takes a leisurely hot bath.
h) takes a different route to work or college.
i) drinks hot water.
j) gets a massage.
k) goes dancing.
l) drinks milk.
m) changes his/her routine.

The four people in the photos read *The Little Book of Calm*. Do you think they liked it? Why/Why not?

3 06 Listen to each speaker. Were you right? What activities from 2 did each one mention?

Close-up

Adverbs of frequency

1 Listen again and read tapescript 06. Underline all the words and expressions that tell you how often people do things.

For example:
…I never have time for a nap during the day. I get a massage from time to time, but I hardly ever take a leisurely bath…

2 Work with a partner. Match each of the words and expressions you have underlined in the tapescript with the word or expression below that has the most similar meaning.

often	regularly	sometimes	not very often	don't ever

3 Ask your partner questions to find out how often he/she does any of the things recommended by *The Little Book of Calm*. Does your partner do any other relaxing activities?

Do you ever…?	Yes. Every day/often /once a week/sometimes… Yes, but not very often/hardly ever. /No, never…

4 Where would you put *often* and where would you put *every morning* in this sentence?

Bob (a) walks to work (b) .

Language Reference p. 16

5 Does each adverb or adverbial phrase below usually go in position (a) or position (b)?

frequently	from time to time	always	hardly ever	never	now and then
occasionally	once a month	usually	once in a blue moon	once in a while	
sometimes	twice a year	normally	once every two weeks	rarely	

6 Put the adverbs in **bold** into these sentences.

a) I eat in restaurants. **once in a blue moon**
b) I go to the hairdresser's. **once every six weeks**
c) I argue with my brothers and sisters. **hardly ever**
d) I check my e-mails. **every day**
e) I listen to classical music. **now and then**
f) I forget where I put my keys. **sometimes**
g) I'm late for appointments. **often**
h) I go for a walk. **once or twice a week**

7 Do you think these sentences are true for your partner? Rewrite them, changing the adverbs as necessary.

For example:
Vera eats in restaurants two or three times a week.

Now ask your partner questions to check if the sentences you have written are true.

For example:
How often do you go to the hairdresser's?
Do you ever listen to classical music?

8 Work with a partner. Ask your partner questions to find out how similar or different you are.

How often do you Do you ever	receive e-mails dream in color go to the gym surf the Internet rent videos get headaches look at yourself in the mirror write letters go to the theater

Language Reference: Adverbs of frequency

Adverbs

always, often, frequently, usually, normally, generally, sometimes, occasionally, rarely, not often, hardly ever, never

The most usual positions are:
Before the main verb:
*I **sometimes** have time for a nap.*
*I **rarely** read the paper.*

After the verb *to be:*
*He's **always** late.*
*She's **hardly ever** home when I call.*

After the first auxiliary:
*I've **often** wondered why he hates her so much.*
*He's **never** sent a Valentine's Day card.*

Adverb phrases

two or three times a week, every morning, once a month, from time to time, once in a while, now and again, once in a blue moon, etc.

The most usual position is at the beginning or end of a clause.
*I get a massage **from time to time**.*
*I have an English class **twice a week**.*
***Once a month** I go dancing with my friends.*

Note: *always, usually,* and *normally* are not used alone to tell you how often something happens. How often do you go out? ~~*Always.*~~ ✘
Every night. ✔
Do you ever play tennis? ~~*Yes, usually.*~~ ✘
Yes, once or twice a week. ✔
Do you often get headaches? ~~*Yes, normally.*~~ ✘
Yes, frequently. ✔

Sally Sees Herself As She Really Is

1 Read the article and find out:

a) how Sally changes her mind about how she sees herself.
b) what she thinks of *The Little Book of Calm*.

(Adapted from *The Weekend Telegraph*, November 15, 1997)

I was under the impression that I was a pretty relaxed person until I watched the video of my sister's wedding. As I watched myself, I realized that I am not the cool, calm, sophisticated woman I thought I was. In fact, I'm the opposite. I fidget. I talk nonstop, fiddle with my hair, scratch my nose, wave my hands around like a lunatic, and bite my nails, and I never sit back and relax on a seat; I sit on the edge of it, ready to jump up and go somewhere else.

So it was no surprise when a friend gave me *The Little Book of Calm* for my last birthday.

I read the blurb on the back cover. "Feeling stressed?" it asked. "Need some help to regain balance in your life? *The Little Book of Calm* is full of advice to follow and thoughts to inspire. Open it to any page, and you will find a path to inner peace."

So I opened it to any page and read the advice: "Wear white." Wear white! I haven't worn white since my first child was born. This is not good advice for someone who has to deal with young children and their dirty fingers every day.

I turned to another page. "Take a lesson in calmness from children. Watch how children live every moment for the pleasure of the moment." Do you know my children? When one of them is screaming, "Aargh! he's pulling my hair!" and the other is screaming, "She stole my candy!," the feeling I get is not calmness.

"Make an appointment with yourself to deal with worries at a specific time in the future." Make an appointment! I already have too many appointments. I don't need another appointment to worry about.

"Get up early and watch the sunrise." Well that's nothing new. I wake up at the crack of dawn every day, thanks to the children. I haven't slept past six in years.

"For every ninety minutes of work, take a twenty-minute break." Yes, I like that. But there's a problem. Who's going to tell my children "Don't bother Mommy now; she's taking a break"?

"Use a soft voice." With fighting children? I don't think so. In fact, my voice is getting louder every day. I decided to try once more. "Rediscover milk." No problem. I love milk, and I drink it all the time...with a shot of strong Italian espresso coffee in it, of course. ■

2 Is each of these sentences true or false?

a) Before seeing the video, Sally thought she was a calm person.
b) She wasn't surprised when she saw herself on video.
c) She discovered that she's the kind of person who never keeps still.
d) She read *The Little Book of Calm* from cover to cover.
e) The advice in *The Little Book of Calm* changed her life.

3 Have you ever seen yourself on video? What were the circumstances? Were you surprised at how you looked? How did you feel about it? Ask a partner.

Vocabulary

1 Find an expression in the article that has a meaning similar to each group of underlined words. Compare with a partner. Then look back at the article to check.

a) I never stop moving. (line 6)
b) I talk constantly. (line 6)
c) I touch my hair. (lines 6–7)
d) Arrange a time to give your attention to your worries. (lines 29–30)
e) I wake up very early in the morning. (line 34)
f) For every ninety minutes of work, rest for twenty minutes. (lines 36–37)

2 Complete these sentences with words and expressions from 1 above. Sometimes you will need to change the grammar of the expressions.

a) Nobody can ever get a word in because you…
b) Our flight leaves at 8:05, so we need to get up…
c) Did you remember to call the dentist and…
d) You look tired. Why don't you…
e) Sit still! Stop…
f) Carla, you'll break that if you keep…
g) In this job, you'll have a lot of new problems to…

3 How well do you know your partner? Read the questionnaire on the right and choose A) or B) according to which you think is true for your partner.

4 The more B) answers you have, the more relaxed you are. Find out who's the most relaxed person in the class.

HOW RELAXED ARE YOU?

1	A	I start worrying about Monday on Friday night.
	B	I find it easy to forget work and relax on the weekend.
2	A	I'm always fidgeting.
	B	I find it easy to keep still.
3	A	When I visit people's homes, I sit on the edge of the seat for the first hour.
	B	When I visit people's homes, I sit back and relax right away.
4	A	I'm always fiddling with something.
	B	I don't need to have something in my hands.
5	A	I bite my nails.
	B	I never, or almost never, bite my nails.
6	A	I worry all the time.
	B	If I have a problem, I deal with it. If I can't do anything, I don't worry about it.
7	A	When I make an appointment, I start worrying that I'm going to forget it.
	B	When I make an appointment, I write it down.
8	A	I hate waiting in lines. I'm too impatient. If I can, I cut in.
	B	I accept waiting in lines because it's fair.
9	A	I lose my temper two or three times a week.
	B	I hardly ever lose my temper.
10	A	I usually arrive at appointments too early or too late.
	B	I usually arrive at appointments on time.

Close-up

Present tenses

1 The article *Sally Sees Herself As She Really Is* uses three different present tense structures: the simple present, the present continuous, and the present perfect. Look at the sentences below. Which tense is each one in?

a) I bite my nails, and I never sit back and relax on a seat.
b) I haven't worn white since my first child was born.
c) "Aargh! he's pulling my hair!"
d) I wake up at the crack of dawn every day.
e) I haven't slept past six in years.
f) My voice is getting louder every day.
g) Don't bother Mommy now, she's taking a break.
h) I love milk, and I drink it all the time.

Language Reference p. 19

2 Work with a partner. Look at the sentences in 1 and match each one to one of the following uses:

- shows that a situation is true all the time
- shows that an activity is in progress and is temporary
- shows that something that started or happened in the past is true and/or important now

3 Look at the four paragraphs below. Put each verb in parentheses in an appropriate present tense. Who or what are the paragraphs about?

A I (1) ________ (wake up) three or four times every night. I (2) ________ (give up) smoking and I (3) ________ (not/stay) out late in two weeks. I (4) ________ (not/want) to go to work, and I (5) ________ (hurry) home every night. I'm the happiest man in the world.

C I (1) ________ (finish) college, but I (2) ________ (not/know) what I really (3) ________ (want) to do, so I (4) ________ (work) here until I decide. I (5) ________ (wear) a uniform and a very silly hat. I sometimes (6) ________ (serve) 100 people in one day, and at the end of the day I (7) ________ (smell) like french fries. I (8) ________ (work) here for less than a week, and I'm already absolutely exhausted.

B I (1) ________ (sleep) a lot during the day and often (2) ________ (stay out) all night. I (3) ________ (visit) all the neighbors' yards, but I (4) ________ (walk) softly so nobody (5) ________ (hear) me. I (6) ________ (wash) at least twice a day, and I (7) ________ (eat) as often as I can. I (8) ________ (use up) several of my nine lives already.

D I'm 28, so I (1) ________ (get) too old for this job, but I (2) ________ (make) a lot of money, and I (3) ________ (invest) it wisely. I (4) ________ (travel) to some very exotic locations since I started 12 years ago, and I (5) ________ (work) in at least ten capital cities, including Paris, Rome, London, and Tokyo. I (6) ________ (eat) very healthily, and I (7) ________ (drink) a lot of water. In fact, I (8) ________ (be) on a diet for 12 years.

4 On a piece of paper, write three true sentences about yourself. Use a different present tense for each one. Fold the piece of paper and give it to your teacher. Then take another student's piece of paper and guess who it belongs to.

Language Reference: Present tense structures

The simple present

We use the simple present mainly to talk about things that are true all the time.

1 Habits and routines

*I **bite** my nails, and I never **sit** back and **relax** on a seat.*
*I **play** football with my friends every Sunday.*

2 Facts and situations we see as more or less permanent

*I **love** milk.*
*The sun **is** 96 million miles from the earth.*

The present continuous

We use the present continuous to talk about present situations that we see as temporary.

1 Activities in progress

*Don't bother Mommy; she**'s taking** a break.*
*I**'m learning** two foreign languages right now.*

2 Changing situations

*My voice **is getting** louder every day.*
*I**'m starting** to understand English much better now.*

The present perfect

We can use the present perfect to talk about a present situation that is connected with the past.

1 A present situation that started in the past

*I **haven't worn** white since my first child was born.*
*I**'ve worked** here for less than a week.*

2 A past event that caused a present situation

*I can't finish the work. My computer **has crashed**.*
*Where's my cell phone? Oh, no, I**'ve left** it in the taxi.*

In this case, we usually use the present perfect only in very formal situations. However, we usually use the simple past in all other situations:

*My computer **crashed**.*
*I **left** it in the taxi.*

Books, Movies, and Music

1 Find out how many people in the class:

- are reading a novel now
- enjoy reading biographies and autobiographies
- still listen to the first records, tapes, or CDs they ever bought
- have a favorite place to read
- prefer watching a movie to reading a book
- have recently been to a concert
- have recently seen a movie they didn't enjoy.

2 07 Listen to seven dialogues. What are the people talking about in each one: a book, a movie, or a piece of music?

3 Listen again. Which words and expressions helped you? Write each one under a heading: books, movies, or music.

4 Find words connected with books, movies, and music and add them to the three lists.

reggaestorylinepaperbackhiphopbluesnovelopera
shortstorypremiereplotdancemusicalsciencefictionhorror
classicalsubtitlesstereosystembandorchestrasoundtrackdirector

5 08 Listen to these musical excerpts from movie soundtracks. What type of movie do you think each one is from? Choose from the list below.

romantic comedy   gangster   horror   comedy   war
science fiction   western   thriller   love story   action

6 Work in groups. Think of some more movies of each of the types above. Which types of movies do people in your group like the best?

A Good Read

Adjectives with *-ed* and *-ing*

1 Choose the correct form of each adjective in bold in the article on the right.

2 Look at the replies in 1 and answer these questions:

a) Which adjective ending do you use to say how people feel?
b) Which adjective ending do you use to describe the people or thing that causes the feeling?

3 How do you choose a book?

We asked several people the question, "How do you choose a book to read?" Here are their replies:

1 "I judge the book by its cover. If the cover looks **interesting/interested**, I buy the book. Sometimes I'm lucky, and the book is good, and sometimes I'm **disappointing/disappointed**."

2 "I always read book reviews in newspapers and magazines, and when I read about a book that sounds **interesting/interested**, I write it in my diary."

3 "I don't take any risks. I always read books by authors I know. I get really **exciting/excited** when one of my favorite authors comes out with a new book, and I buy it immediately. This way I'm never **disappointing/disappointed**."

4 "I read the first page, and if it's **boring/bored**, I don't buy the book. If I want to turn the page and continue reading, I buy the book."

5 "It's easy. I never read fiction, but I'm **fascinating/fascinated** by biographies of famous people. I find strong women in history particularly **inspiring/inspired**."

6 "I tend to choose books written by women. They have a better feeling for characters and the relationships between them, and that's what I find **interesting/interested** in a book—although, I've just finished a book by a man, and it was wonderful!"

How Are You Feeling?

1 Tell your partner how you're feeling today. Explain why. Choose words from the box if appropriate.

tired	happy	exhausted	excited	worried	bored
relaxed	nervous	disappointed	confused	cheerful	

2 Choose three other adjectives and say what makes you feel like this.

3 Choose three of the topics below and tell other students what you think about them. Use some of the words from 1.

For example:
I think the political situation in my country is very confusing.
I'm very worried about the political situation in my country.

- the political situation in your country
- the nightlife in your city
- winter
- karaoke
- English grammar
- auto racing
- giving a speech
- getting exercise
- surfing the Internet
- finding out about other cultures
- traveling by air

Anecdote

4 Think about a movie you have seen or a book you have read recently. You are going to tell a partner about it. Choose from one of the lists below the things you want to talk about. Think about what you will say and what language you will use.

- ☐ Where did you see the movie? (at a theater? at home?...)
- ☐ When did you see it?
- ☐ Why did you choose this movie?
- ☐ What did you know about it beforehand?
- ☐ Who did you see it with?
- ☐ Do you know who directed the movie?
- ☐ Who were the actors?
- ☐ What type of movie was it?
- ☐ What was the plot?
- ☐ Did it have a happy ending?
- ☐ Did you enjoy the movie more or less than you expected?
- ☐ Would you recommend this movie?

- ☐ What was the last book you read?
- ☐ When did you read it?
- ☐ Why did you choose this book?
- ☐ Who wrote it?
- ☐ What did you know about it beforehand?
- ☐ Have you read any other books by the same author?
- ☐ Who were the main characters?
- ☐ What type of book was it?
- ☐ What was the main story?
- ☐ Did it have a happy ending?
- ☐ Did you enjoy the book more or less than you expected?
- ☐ Would you recommend this book?

5 Tell your partner about the movie or the book.

Net Reviews

1 Have you ever looked for information about a movie on the Internet?

2 What do you think the classic movie *Casablanca* may be about?
Look at this Web page and match the headings to the information.

a) cast
b) keywords
c) memorable quotes
d) plot summary
e) review
f) type of movie
g) date of release
h) title and main details

WEB MOVIES

1

Casablanca
Directed by Michael Curtiz
Based on a novel by Murray Burnett and Joan Alison, *Everybody Goes to Rick's*

2

Romance/Adventure/Drama/War

3

Humphrey Bogart: Rick Blaine
Ingrid Bergman: Ilsa Lund Laszlo
Paul Henreid: Victor Laszlo
Conrad Veidt: Major Strasser
Sydney Greenstreet: Señor Ferrari
Peter Lorre: Ugarte
Dooley Wilson: Sam
John Qualen: Berger

4

November 1942

5

Casablanca is a classic movie starring Humphrey Bogart and Ingrid Bergman. Set in Casablanca during World War II, it tells the story of exiled nightclub owner Rick Blaine and his former love, Ilsa, who meet again after many years. She has come to Casablanca with her husband, Victor Laszlo, a Resistance leader, who is trying to avoid the Nazis. Rick has transit papers that would help Victor escape, but Rick and Ilsa decide to use the papers so that they can leave Casablanca together.

6

sacrifice
classic
love triangle
police
piano
"As Time Goes By"
cafe
politics
escape

7

- Berger: We read five times that you were killed, in five different places.
  Victor: As you can see, it was true every single time.
- Ilsa: Play it once, Sam. For old times' sake.
  Sam: [lying] I don't know what you mean, Miss Elsa.
  Ilsa Lund: Play it, Sam. Play *As Time Goes By*.
  Sam: [lying] Oh, I can't remember it, Miss Elsa. I'm a little rusty on it

8

A romantic classic that gets better each time you watch it. Although the plot is familiar, the acting is always a superb new surprise. Bogart deserved the Oscar he was awarded as Best Actor. Bergman is radiant and should have gotten an award too.
Full of intrigue and heroic and dastardly characters, and featuring one of the best songs ever written, the movie brings back the romance and style of the 1940s while it reminds us of the horrors of war in any generation.

3 Read these comments made by Internet users about *Casablanca*. What rating out of ten do you think each person gave the movie?

real movie **REVIEWS**

TITLE **Casablanca**

IMAGES

"I must say I enjoyed this movie, even though I usually yawn during old movies. The story is pretty good." Jim, New York.

RATING 7 10

"It is fascinating to see how an old black-and-white movie can still be so good. *Casablanca* has really become one of the best movies of all time—a beautiful movie, full of sensitivity and emotions." Vera, Rio de Janeiro.

RATING 10

I guess it was a good movie in its day. It just seems so old and dated, and I couldn't wait for it to be over. The characters talk too much, and there isn't much action. I guess I don't like black-and-white movies in general." Angel, Miami.

RATING 10

"When my friend rented the movie, I didn't want to see it. I hate old movies. But I was pleasantly surprised. The acting is just wonderful, and the story held my interest from beginning to end. Actually, I was in tears when Ilsa... Well, I don't want to spoil it for anyone."
Jack, Toronto

RATING 10

"A few questions came to me during the movie—who in their right mind would leave Humphrey Bogart for Paul Henreid? I mean Rick Blaine for Victor Laszlo? I don't know. I've never been in a situation like this, so who knows what I would do. But if you don't like sad endings, don't bother to see this movie." Beatriz, Oaxaca.

RATING 10

A Movie Review

Writing

LANGUAGE TOOLBOX

It's directed by...
It's a romantic comedy/an action movie/a thriller...
It's based on a book by...
(Will Smith) plays the part of (Muhammad Ali)...
The movie takes place in/was filmed in...
What I liked/didn't like about it was...

Write a review of a movie you have seen. Include the following information:

- the title of the movie
- the type of movie
- the name of the director (if you can remember)
- any other information, such as whether it is based on a book, where it was filmed, etc.
- the main actors and which characters they play
- a summary of the plot (in the present tense)
- what you particularly liked or didn't like about the movie

3 Dating

Choose three or more of these "firsts." What do you remember about them? Tell a partner.

- first home
- first friend
- first hero
- first dance
- first crush
- first date
- first English lesson
- first kiss
- first vacation
- first broken heart
- first regret
- first trip abroad

Twenty-First Century Dating

1 Read these excerpts from an article on how two couples began their relationship. What do you think happened before they first met or spoke to each other?

Couple 1 "Then Tom and I had our first 'date'—we talked for 11 hours, and that phone call changed the course of our relationship. Now we've decided to meet."

Couple 2 "It was love at first sight for Joel Emerson and Lisa Bunyan, which was lucky because they met for the first time on their wedding day!"

2 Work with a partner. Find out how the two couples met.

- Student A: Look at page 139 and read about couple 1.
- Student B: Look at page 140 and read about couple 2.

When you finish reading, close your books and tell each other about the two dates.

Vocabulary

1 Complete the sentences. Refer back to *Twenty-First Century Dating*, pages 139 and 140, if you need to.

a) I don't believe in _______ at first _______ .
b) Somewhere in the world, there's a Mr. or Ms. _______ for everybody.
c) People usually don't marry the man or woman of their _______ .
d) _______ women enjoy their independence, whereas _______ men tend to want to get married.
e) A man should _______ to a woman. It isn't natural for a woman to ask a man to marry her.
f) A marriage is more likely to succeed if both partners have been involved in _______ before getting married.
g) If the bride and _______ are in love, then it doesn't really matter what their parents think.
h) It's better to save money than spend it on an expensive _______ in some exotic place.

2 Do you agree with the statements above? Discuss with your partner.

Listening

1 09 Listen to the two interviews about the relationships one year later. Have the relationships survived? What problems did each couple have? Listen and find out.

2 Listen again. Which of the following sentences belong to Tom and Kathy's story and which belong to Lisa and Joel's?

a) They arranged to meet at the airport.
b) She was very nervous.
c) They've been married for a year now.
d) He looked just like his photo.
e) They've just celebrated their first wedding anniversary.
f) She went right back home.
g) His mother hasn't spoken to him since the wedding.
h) They've moved away from their hometown.
i) She hated his shoes.
j) They've decided not to tell where they live now.

Close-up

Present perfect and simple past

1 Look at these two sentences and answer the questions.

1 Kathy and Tom had an e-mail relationship for six months.
2 Joel and Lisa have been together for one year.

a) Do Kathy and Tom still communicate by e-mail?
b) Are Joel and Lisa still together?
c) Which tense is each sentence in?

2 Here is some more information about Tom, Kathy, Joel, and Lisa. Look at the tenses of the verbs. Check (✓) the situations that are still going on now.

a) Kathy has been single since she returned from Denver.
b) Tom went traveling in Europe for a few months.
c) Joel and Lisa haven't been back to their hometown for six months.
d) Joel has been a marketing consultant since he left college.
e) Kathy has been looking for the man of her dreams for a long time.
f) Tom has had his own shoe-manufacturing business since 2001.
g) Kathy hasn't used the Internet since she met Tom.
h) Lisa played the piano for ten years.

since and *for*

1 Fill in the chart on the right.

2 Write five sentences about yourself, using the time expressions from the chart: four that are true and one that is untrue. Then read your sentences to your partner and see if he/she knows which sentence is untrue.

since		*for*
yesterday	→	one day
1995	→	
	←	five minutes
my last birthday	→	
	←	ten years
I was born	→	
	←	two weeks
New Year's Day	→	
	←	an hour

Language Reference: The simple past and the present perfect

The simple past

We use the simple past to talk about events and situations in the past. We use it to say when the event or situation happened.

*I **saw** John in the supermarket.*
*He **lived** in Italy when he **was** a child.*
*Christina **went** to work on the bus until she **passed** her driving test.*

The present perfect

The present perfect has several uses, but it always shows a connection between the past and now. In this unit, we use it to talk about situations that started in the past and that continue now.

*We**'ve known** each other for 20 years.*
*I**'ve had** this watch since my 18th birthday.*

since and *for*

We use *since* to identify the point at which a period of time began. We normally use it with perfect tenses.

*They've been married **since** 1999.*
*I haven't seen him **since** April.*
*She's lived in Brazil **since** she was 18.*

For is used with a period of time.

*They've been married **for** five years.*
*He was in the army **for** 18 months.*
*I'll be at work **for** another hour if you want to call me.*

Remember our first dinner together, when we sat on soapboxes and ate off an old peach crate?

How We Met

1 Read Karen's account of how she met David and answer the questions.

a) When did they meet?
b) When did fate bring them together again?
c) Where did she see him again?
d) How long have they been together?

David and Karen

A **KAREN, 18, AND DAVID, 21**

I met him on a train last summer. He was gorgeous. We talked a lot, and when I got off, he helped me with my luggage. Unfortunately, I was too shy to ask him for his phone number. But fate brought us together again. A few months ago, I saw him again at a party, and he recognized me right away. The attraction was magnetic, and now we've been together for three months, two weeks, and three days.

2 Read Emma's account of how she met Paul. Complete the account with appropriate time expressions.

Paul and Emma

B **EMMA, 32, AND PAUL, 35**

(1) ________ , I went to the police station to report a burglary. I was really upset, and the policeman who interviewed me was very kind and understanding. He calmed me down, gave me a cup of coffee, and then drove me home. (2) ________ , he called and asked me out, and we have been together (3) ________ .

3 Read about Sukwinder and Rajvir. Put the verbs in parentheses in the correct form.

Rajvir and Sukwinder

C **SUKWINDER, 63, AND RAJVIR, 70**

I first (1) ________ (see) Rajvir near our house in Simla, India, when I was 16. I (2) ________ (like) him, but we didn't really talk. I told my father that I liked him, and he (3) ________ (go) to visit his family. Then we (4) ________ (get) engaged. We couldn't get to know each other before we were married, so the first time I was alone with my husband was after the marriage. We (5) ________ (be) married for 43 years, and we (6) ________ (not/have) an argument yet.

4 Read about Elena and Rudy and complete the account with appropriate verbs. What do you think happened to Rudy's letters?

Elena and Rudy

D **ELENA, 86, AND RUDY, 87**

I (1) ________ Rudy when I was 23, and it (2) ________ love at first sight. We (3) ________ out together for over a year. We (4) ________ to get married, but my mother was against it because Rudy is a Christian Scientist, so I (5) ________ seeing him. I (not) (6) ________ from Rudy for a long time, although he says he (7) ________ lots of letters. I (8) ________ other boyfriends, but I never got married. I (not) (9) ________ anyone else. It was 60 years later, when all my other boyfriends had died, that I (10) ________ to wonder if Rudy was still alive. So I (11) ________ to a magazine for retired people. Four days after my letter was published, I (12) ________ a letter from Rudy. He came to see me, and after two days he (13) ________ . We (14) ________ married when Rudy was 85 and I was 84, and we (15) ________ happily married for two years. I (not) (16) ________ at another man since the day Rudy came back into my life.

5 Which of these stories do you think is the most romantic?

6 Think about couples you know: friends or family. What do you know about how they met? Tell your partner.

Dream Date

The schwa

The schwa is the most common sound in English. Its phonetic symbol is /ə/. You hear it in words like around /əraund/, student /studənt/, restaurant /rɛstərɑnt/, banana /bənænə/. It is never stressed.

1 10 Listen to the silly "lines" below. Look at the words with a schwa sound.

a) What's ə nice girl like you doing in ə place like this?
b) Yə know, I'm not just ən interesting persən; I have ə body too.
c) I'm in advərtising. Would you like tə be in our next photo shoot?
d) Do yə believe in love ət first sight, or do I have tə walk past you əgain?
e) A: Do yə have ə boyfriend?
B: Yes.
A: Want ənothər one?
f) Your fathər must be ə thief, because he stole thə stars frəm thə sky ənd put thəm in yər eyes.
g) I just moved next door, ənd I wəs wondering if yə could recəmmend ə good restərant nearby. Would yə like tə join me?

2 Work with a partner. Which are the silliest lines? Which ones do you like least? Choose four lines and practice them.

3 Do you know any similar lines in your own language? Translate them into English and mark the schwas.

Vocabulary

1 What qualities do you look for in your ideal partner? Choose the six most important qualities from the list below.

good-looking modest reliable generous broad-minded witty cheerful
sincere rich intelligent hardworking outgoing easygoing faithful kind

Find someone else in the class who has chosen the same qualities.

2 Read the descriptions of different types of people below.

The kind of person who:
a) thinks only of his/her own needs and never thinks about other people.
b) thinks he/she knows everything.
c) refuses to consider new ideas or other people's opinions.
d) is not up-to-date with modern ideas and values.
e) says he/she believes one thing and then behaves in a way that shows he/she is not sincere.
f) forgets things, often because he/she is thinking about something else.
g) is easily offended.

big	centered
over	faced
two-	minded
old-	sensitive
absent	headed
narrow-	fashioned
self-	minded

Match words from the two lists to form compound adjectives that fit the descriptions.

3 Many people believe that the identity of their ideal partner is written in the stars. You are going to read an article about an ancient Chinese form of astrology that divides people into nine personality types.

Read the article once and decide which description best describes you.

KI ASTROLOGY

According to the ancient Chinese, everything goes around in nine-year cycles.

There are nine *Ki* personality numbers, and each one is associated with an element: water, soil, fire, tree, or metal.

1 (water)

You seem to be friendly and outgoing, but you also have a very private side to your personality. You're a deep thinker, and you enjoy your own company. Your cool manner is attractive, but it can frighten people off and leave you feeling isolated.

You don't enter into relationships lightly, and when you do, you take them very seriously. You're not the romantic type, but you can be very passionate.

Famous ones: Johnny Depp, Quentin Tarantino

Compatible signs: 3, 4, 6, 7

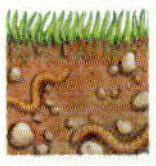

2 (soil)

You love helping people, and it's important to you that others are happy. You would give your neighbor the shirt off your back if he/she needed it. You hate arguments, and you tend to avoid confrontation. You're best in groups rather than alone.

You're capable of great unconditional love, but you tend to choose partners who will take advantage of your generous nature.

Famous twos: Tom Cruise, Marilyn Monroe

Compatible signs: 6, 7, 9

3 (tree)

You're loud, talkative, active, and fun. However, you're easily bored and tend to flit from one thing to the next. Some people think you're too honest, and you frequently offend people.

Your dynamic nature makes you attractive to the opposite sex. You want exciting relationships, but you also need your independence.

Famous threes: Robert De Niro, Eddie Murphy

Compatible signs: 1, 9

4 (tree)

You're a good listener, and you have a good understanding of other people's problems. However, you're not very good at making decisions about your own life, and you tend to change your mind easily. You appear to be easygoing, but you can be stubborn and impulsive at times.

On the one hand, you're an idealist who is looking for true love, and on the other, you're often attracted to partners for exterior qualities like power or status.

Famous fours: Yoko Ono, Marlon Brando

Compatible signs: 1, 9

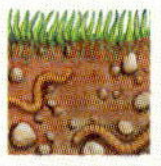

5 (soil)

You have a strong personality, and people often turn to you for advice. You like to be the center of attention, and it is important for you to succeed in everything you do. But you don't always think before you act, and you don't always learn from your mistakes.

In relationships you're caring and committed. However, because you like to experiment, you can be unfaithful.

Famous fives: Elizabeth Taylor, Bob Dylan

Compatible signs: 6, 7, 9

6 (metal)

You're a born leader who loves to be in control. You work hard to achieve your ambitions, and you usually succeed. You are active and sociable, but you hate to be criticized. You're a good speaker and very charismatic.

You're faithful in relationships, but you like to be the boss. You tend to be attracted to softer partners.

Famous sixes: Madonna, Michael Jackson

Compatible signs: 1, 2, 5, 8

7 (metal)

You always seem to be happy. You're witty and good with words, but a good listener too. People enjoy your company, and you make people feel at ease. Sometimes you say what people want to hear, even if it is not what you really think.

You love the excitement of romance. However, you tend to get bored quickly, and your relationships do not always last very long.

Famous sevens: Michelle Pfeiffer, Melanie Griffith, Tina Turner

Compatible signs: 1, 2, 5, 8

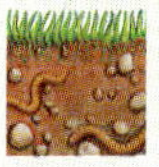

8 (soil)

You are rather old-fashioned and do not like change. You tend to be very private and difficult to get close to. You have a strong sense of right and wrong, and when you decide to do something, nothing can stop you.

Once you find someone, you tend to put all your energy into making the relationship work. You have a strong sense of family and commitment.

Famous eights: Steven Spielberg, Jackie Onassis

Compatible signs: 6, 7, 9

9 (fire)

People are attracted to your magnetic personality. You seem strong and in control, but underneath you're easily hurt. You can be oversensitive at times. You need time by yourself, and you can't stand routine.

You're attractive to the opposite sex, and when you're in love, you're passionate, romantic, and giving.

Famous nines: Jack Nicholson, Eva Peron

Compatible signs: 2, 3, 4, 5, 8

Now turn to page 141 and follow the instructions to calculate your *Ki* astrology sign. Did you guess correctly?

Criticisms and generalizations

1 How are the following ideas expressed in the article?

a) You often scare people. (Personality 1)
b) You usually choose partners who treat you badly. (Personality 2)
c) You often lose interest in things and give up. (Personality 3)
d) Sometimes you won't listen to reason. (Personality 4)
e) You sometimes have other relationships behind your partner's back. (Personality 5)
f) You usually choose partners who do what you tell them to do. (Personality 6)
g) You usually abandon your partners when you lose interest in them. (Personality 7)
h) You don't usually share your feelings. (Personality 8)
i) You are sometimes too sensitive. (Personality 9)

2 Rewrite the following sentences using *tend(s) to be* or *can be*. Do you agree with the statements?

Language Reference p. 30

a) Women are more sensitive than men.
b) People of the older generation are narrow-minded.
c) Very good-looking people are bigheaded.
d) Women are more faithful in relationships than men.
e) People from hot climates are more outgoing than people from cool climates.

I'm Not Crazy About Him

1 11 Meg and Rose are sisters. Meg met Rose's new boyfriend, Jake, for the first time yesterday. Listen to the conversation. What did Meg think of Rose's new boyfriend?

2 Listen again and read the conversation at the same time. Underline anything that is different from the recording.

Meg and Rose

Rose: What do you think of Jake?
Meg: He's all right.
Rose: You don't like him, do you?
Meg: Well, he was unfriendly.
Rose: Oh, he's just shy, that's all.
Meg: Shy? You must be joking. Five minutes after meeting me he asked to borrow five dollars! That's not what I call shy!
Rose: O.K., that was rude, but he's broke.
Meg: Well, I'm poor myself, and I'm trying to save up for my vacation.
Rose: All right, all right, I'm sure he won't ask you again. He's good-looking, though, isn't he?
Meg: Yes, I guess so—but he knows it. I think he's really bigheaded.
Rose: You're just jealous.
Meg: No, I'm not. I don't want him. He's mean, bigheaded, and stupid.
Rose: What do you mean stupid? You're stupid too.
Meg: Shut up!
Rose: No, you shut up!
Meg: Mom!

3 What expressions do the two sisters use to avoid saying things directly? Refer to tapescript 11 if necessary.

Language Reference p. 30

4 Make the following critical comments less direct.

For example:
He's short-tempered. *He isn't particularly patient.*

a) She's insensitive.
b) He's bigheaded.
c) They're stupid.
d) She's lazy.
e) She's mean.
f) They're narrow-minded.

Language Reference: Criticisms and generalizations

When we need to say something critical, there are certain expressions we can use that sound more diplomatic. We use the same expressions to make generalizations.

can be... (at times)

*You seem to be easygoing, but you **can be** stubborn and impulsive **at times**.*
*Because you like to experiment, you **can be** unfaithful.*
*You **can be** oversensitive **at times**.*

a little, rather, and *kind of*

We can use *a little, rather,* or, more informally, *kind of* to make the adjective less absolute.
*You can be **kind of** stubborn at times.*

tend(s) to...

*You hate arguments, and you **tend to** avoid confrontation.*
*You **tend to** be attracted to softer partners.*
*You're not very good at making decisions about your own life, and you **tend to** change your mind too easily.*

not particularly/exactly...

- He was unfriendly. → *He **wasn't exactly** friendly.*
- He's poor. → *He's **not particularly** well-off.*
- She's lazy. → *She's **not particularly** hardworking.*

We sometimes use *not exactly* to express sarcasm.
*You're **not exactly** Ms. Einstein yourself.*

A Boyfriend's Worst Nightmare

1 Work in groups. What could a boyfriend's worst nightmare be? Write as many possible circumstances as you can think of. Now read the article.

My girlfriend has had a Canadian pen-pal named Eddie since she was in her early teens. That's O.K. I also exchanged letters and e-mails with Catarina from Brazil until I went to college. But then I got involved in the excitement of college life and lost touch with her.

But my girlfriend is more loyal to hers. Or maybe her little pen-pal has a special place in her heart.

As they got older, their lives changed, but they still continued writing to each other. She's a successful journalist now, and he has a very good job at the University of Vancouver. He is six feet tall, dark, and handsome. I am not tall. Or dark. And I'm not particularly handsome. I know what he looks like because my girlfriend talks about him… a lot.

I also know that he's 27, he's an academic, and he plays ice hockey. So he's both athletic and extremely intelligent. And tall, dark, and handsome, as I said before.

Several years ago, before I got together with my girlfriend, he was passing through Seattle and stopped for a visit. When my girlfriend's mother met him, she liked him so much that she decided he was the ideal husband for her daughter.

So, bearing all this in mind, when my girlfriend ran toward me a few weeks ago with a letter from him in her hand and said, "Guess what… Eddie has a job in Seattle for three years," I wasn't exactly over the moon.

As the day of his arrival got nearer, I got more and more jealous. My girlfriend asked me, "Why are you getting so stressed out about him? Yes, he's good-looking, interesting, intelligent, and athletic. But it's you I love, and it's you I'm with." Believe it or not, this didn't make me feel any better.

Finally, the day arrived when I was to meet the famous pen-pal. My first thought when I saw him was, "Tall, yes. Dark, yes. Handsome, yes. Intelligent, definitely. Charming, probably. It can't get any worse than this."

(Adapted from *The Independent on Sunday,* October 12, 1997)

2 What do you think happened next? Write the last paragraph of the story.

3 Turn to page 143 and read the end of the story.

4 How does the ending compare to your version? When was the last time you had a weight lifted from your mind?

Vocabulary

1 Refer to the text and answer these two questions:

a) Why did the writer stop writing to his pen-pal? What happened?
b) What happened to his feelings as the day of Eddie's arrival got nearer?

2 Here are some more examples of this use of *get*. Invent ways to complete the sentences and then compare with another student.

For example:
I got angry because *he kept me waiting for half an hour.*

a) I got depressed because…
b) I got bored because…
c) I got confused because…
d) I got upset because…
e) I got involved in crime because…

3 Read the ends of the expressions—the parts you invented—to other students. See if they can guess which sentences they belong to.

4 Adrenaline

1 Which of the following would make you feel:

- angry?
- excited?
- scared?
- nothing?

talking to someone you are really attracted to / galloping on a horse / climbing to a high point and then looking down / taking off in an airplane / riding on the back of a motorcycle at high speed / being stuck in a traffic jam / giving a speech in front of an audience/going on a roller coaster / finding out that you have been robbed / being stopped by the police / watching your country's soccer team in the World Cup finals / taking an exam

adrenaline

Adrenaline is a substance that your body produces when you are angry, scared, or excited. It makes your heart beat faster and gives you more energy. *That was my first big game in months, and the adrenaline was flowing.*

2 Tell your partner about any of the situations you have experienced personally. Which experience gave you the biggest "adrenaline rush"?

My Name Is Mike, and I'm a Sky Diver

1 Have you gone skydiving? Would you consider jumping from an airplane with a parachute on your back?

- Yes, for charity.
- Yes, for fun.
- Yes, for money.
- No way!

2 Read about Mike and answer these questions:

a) Why did he start skydiving?
b) How did he feel on his first jump?
c) What caused his accident, and why has he continued to go skydiving?

www.deadmike.com

I just did my first jump since the accident that almost killed me just over a year ago. As I was lying in the hospital, thinking that I would never go skydiving again, I wasn't happy to be alive. Instead, I was wondering how I could possibly live without it.

It all started one night after another typical nine-to-five day. I was sitting at home thinking, "There has to be more to life than this," when a commercial came on TV: "Try skydiving," it said.

The next day, I called my local skydiving school and signed up for my first jump.

I spent a day training and then I was ready for my first jump. Or almost. First, I had to sign a waiver. It said that I understood I was taking part in an activity that could end in serious injury. I suddenly realized that I was about to do something voluntarily that would put my life at risk. As I signed the document, I wondered if I were completely insane.

I will never forget my first jump. Five of us walked to the runway and got into a plane barely big enough to hold three people. I was beginning to get nervous, but the others were talking and joking, and I started to relax. It was a beautiful, cloudless day, and the sun was just going down. It took us about 20 minutes to get to 11,000 feet, and then the instructor opened the plane door—the view took my breath away. Suddenly, it was time to jump, and as I pushed myself away from the plane—I don't know what I was thinking—my mind went blank.

Words cannot describe the rush of adrenaline I experienced while I was free-falling.

At 5,500 feet I pulled the cord, and the parachute opened immediately. Suddenly, everything was silent and peaceful. Twice I shouted, "This is absolutely incredible," though I knew there was nobody to hear me. It was the most amazing four minutes of my life.

From the first jump, I was hooked. I started spending every spare minute I had skydiving. At work, I sat in front of my computer and imagined ways of making more money so that I could jump more often. It became my reason for living, and nothing else mattered. I was addicted to skydiving.

Things were going really well. I was spending every spare minute jumping from a plane.

Then disaster struck on my 1,040th jump. Another sky diver collided with my parachute at 80 feet. I fell and hit the ground at about 30 mph, face down. I broke both legs, my right foot, my left elbow, my right arm, my nose, and my jaw. I lost 10 pints of blood, 19 teeth, and 25 pounds of fat. I was lucky to survive. People who have never experienced skydiving will find it hard to understand that my only motivation to get better was so that I could do it again. All I can say is that for me, skydiving is life, and life is skydiving.

3 The sentences below summarize Mike's story. Correct the details that are wrong.

a) Mike was reading a newspaper one night when he saw a commercial for skydiving.
b) He called the skydiving school immediately and signed up for a jump.
c) After a day of training, he was sure he was doing the right thing.
d) His first jump was unforgettable. It was a beautiful morning, and he was relaxed.
e) After an hour's flight, he jumped out of the plane, and his parachute opened immediately.
f) After his first jump, he didn't think he would do it again.
g) During his spare time, he thought about skydiving a lot.
h) On his 1,040th jump, he had an accident when his parachute didn't open.
i) He nearly died and thought that his skydiving days were over.
j) The only reason he wanted to get better was so that he could go skydiving again.

Vocabulary

1 Complete as many of these questions as you can from memory. Look back at the text on page 33 to check.

a) What couldn't you l_________ without?

b) Why do you think people t_________ p_________ in dangerous sports?

c) Have you ever p_________ your life at r_________ voluntarily?

d) When was the last time a view t_________ your br_________ a_________ ?

e) Do you know anybody who is a_________ to a sport like Mike is?

2 Work with a partner. Ask each other the questions.

Grading adjectives

1 Find pairs of adjectives in the box that have similar meanings.

For example:
angry *furious*

angry	exhausted	incredible	awful	hilarious	bad	fabulous
excited	furious	tired	thrilled	good	funny	strange

2 Put each adjective in 1 under a heading: very or absolutely.

For example:

very	absolutely
angry	*furious*

Language Reference: Gradable and absolute adjectives

Gradable adjectives

We can use adjectives like *good*, *small*, or *nice* with adverbs like *very*, *fairly*, and *pretty*.
For example: ***very** good*; ***fairly** small*; ***pretty** nice*.
We cannot use adverbs like *absolutely* and *totally* with these adjectives.

Absolute adjectives

We can use strong adjectives like *incredible* with adverbs like *absolutely* and *totally*.
For example: ***absolutely** perfect; **totally** unique.*
*When Mike did his first jump, he shouted, "This is **absolutely** incredible."*

Stress

1 12 Complete the following dialogues. Then listen and check.

A

A: ______ ______ ______ skydived?
B: ______, ______ have.
A: ______ ______ **good**?
B: **Good?** ______ ______ ______ **incredible!**

B

C: ______ ______ ______ ______ surfing?
D: ______, ______ have.
C: ______ ______ **scared?**
D: **Scared?** ______ ______ ______ **terrified!**

2 Listen again and notice how each word in **bold** is emphasized in the sentence.

3 Practice the dialogues with a partner.

4 Work with a partner. Make up and practice a similar dialogue, using gradable and absolute adjectives.

A Sporting Life

Vocabulary

1 Put the sports into categories according to what you think they have in common. Think of different categories.

For example:
Swimming, surfing, sailing, and scuba diving are all water sports.

aerobatics | badminton | baseball | basketball | bungee jumping | cycling | football | horseback riding | ice hockey | ice skating | judo | karate | mountain climbing | sailing | scuba diving | skydiving | snowboarding | soccer | surfing | swimming | table tennis | tennis | volleyball | weightlifting | windsurfing

2 What verb would you use with each sport: *do, play,* or *go?*

For example:
go *swimming*
play *tennis*
do *weightlifting*

3 Can you add any sports to the list in 1?

4 In small groups, discuss the following questions:

a) Which of these sports do you take part in or watch?
b) Which of these sports are shown on television a lot?
c) Do you think any of these sports are unsuitable for women? Why?

5 13 Jane Couch made UK sports history when she won the first official female boxing match in November 1998.

Listen to the interview. Which of the questions on the right does the interviewer ask? Take notes on Jane's answers to the questions.

How did you get interested in boxing?
Were you interested in sports in school?
How long did it take you to get in shape?
Do you know how many professional female boxers there are?
What did your friends and family think about it?
Is it easy for a woman to be a professional boxer?
What do your critics say?
What do you think are the most important skills to have as a boxer?
How do you relax?
How do you get ready for a match?
Have you ever been seriously hurt in a match?
Do you think you've changed since your success?
How did you feel before the match last week?
When's your next big fight?
Where will it be?

Close-up

Past experience

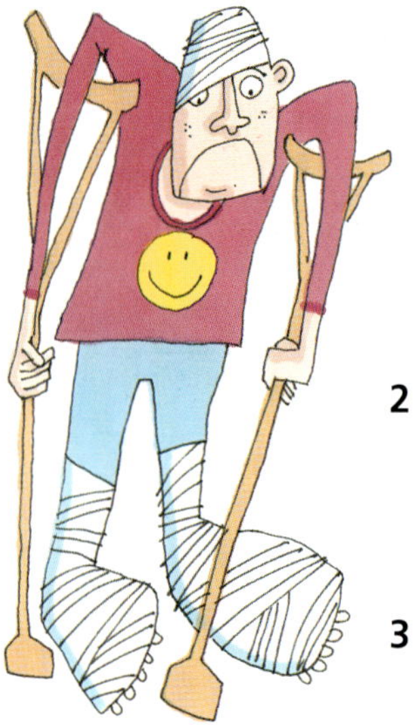

1 The grammar in the following sentences is correct, but the sentences don't make sense. The endings have been mixed up. Rearrange the sentences so that they make sense.

a) Have you ever ridden a snake?
b) Have you ever been asked to the top of a mountain?
c) Have you ever met a desert?
d) Have you ever driven a television program?
e) Have you ever climbed to make a speech?
f) Have you ever crossed a famous person?
g) Have you ever appeared on a Ferrari?
h) Have you ever caught a horse on the beach?

2 Work with a partner. How do you think your partner would answer each question?

a) Yes, I have.
b) No, never…but I'd like to.
c) No, never…and I wouldn't like to.

3 Discuss your answers. How well do you know each other? Ask more *Have you ever…?* questions.

4 14 Listen to five people being interviewed about their past experiences and complete the chart below.

Have you ever…	Y/N	What were you doing?	What happened?
a) gotten injured playing a sport?	______	______	______
b) been in a dangerous situation?	______	______	______
c) broken a bone?	______	______	______
d) been really frightened?	______	______	______
e) thought you were going to die?	______	______	______

5 Work with a partner. Compare your notes. Then ask each other the questions from 4. Find out as much as you can.

6 Look at the questions in **bold** in 4. Three tenses are used: the simple past, the past continuous, and the present perfect. Match the names of the tenses to the questions.

7 Look at tapescript 14. Find other examples of the three tenses.

a) Which tense is the most useful for introducing a new topic of conversation?
b) Which would you probably use if you wanted to say exactly when something happened?
c) You want to tell a story. Which of these two beginnings do you prefer?

1 It was late summer. People were sitting in street cafés, enjoying the sunshine, and watching the world go by.
2 It was late summer. People sat in street cafés, enjoyed the sunshine, and watched the world go by.

Language Reference p. 38

8 The diagram below shows three timelines—one for each of the three tenses you're studying: simple past, past continuous, and present perfect. Which timeline goes with which tense, and why? Discuss with a partner.

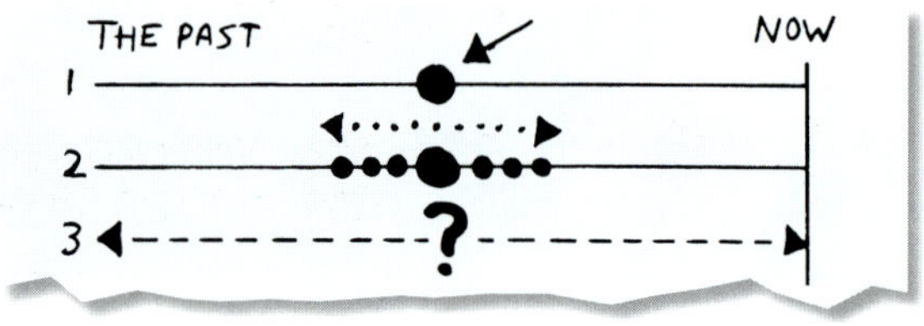

Language Reference p. 38

9 Complete these dialogues with the words in parentheses. Use the simple past, past continuous, or present perfect. Sometimes more than one form is possible.

A

A: (1) ___________ (you/read) *The Grapes of Wrath* by John Steinbeck?

B: Yes, (2) ___________ (I/read) it last year when (3) ___________ (I/travel) around the U.S.

A: What (4) ___________ (you/think) of it?

B: (5) ___________ (I/love) it.

C

E: Nice car.

F: Thanks. (1) ___________ (we/buy) it last week.

E: How much (2) ___________ (it/be)?

F: $35,000. But (3) ___________ (we/not/pay) for it yet.

B

C: So (1) ___________ (you/lose) your laptop again.

D: Yes. Can you believe it? (2) ___________ (I/leave) it in a taxi this morning.

C: (3) ___________ (you/call) the taxi company?

D: Yes, but they can't get in touch with the driver.

D

G: What (1) ___________ (you/do) at the time of the robbery?

H: (2) ___________ (I/watch) TV.

G: Which program (3) ___________ (you/watch) that night?

H: I don't remember.

G: No? (4) ___________ (you/ever/be) arrested?

H: (5) ___________ (that/be) a long time ago. (6) ___________ (I/change).

10 On a sheet of paper, write six true sentences about yourself.

a) I haven't ... since ...
b) I ... in years
c) I didn't ... yesterday
d) I was ... + **ing** when ...
e) I've ... several times
f) I wasn't ... + **ing** when ...

11 Fold the paper and give it to your teacher. Then take someone else's paper from your teacher and guess which student it belongs to.

Good news—the results of your tests suggest that you haven't gone permanently blind.

Language Reference: Talking about past experiences

The present perfect and the simple past

English often makes a distinction between *time up to now* and *finished time.*
For example:

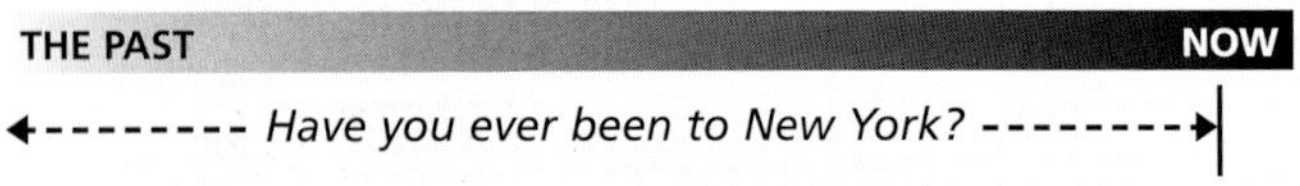

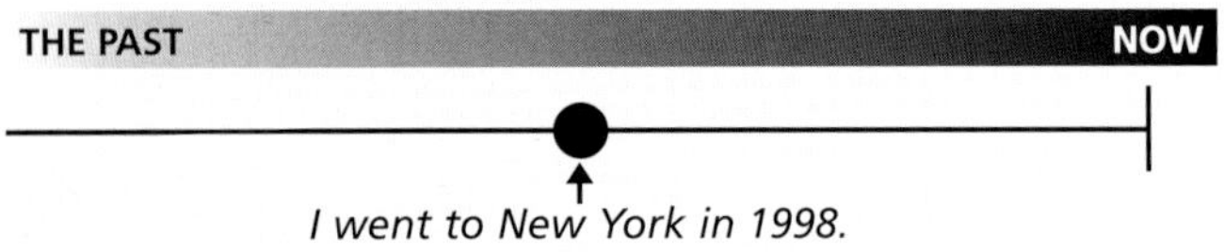

The present perfect is used to locate an action in time up to now. The simple past is used to fix an action in finished time.

Time expressions

Choosing between the present perfect and the simple past is often a question of the *time expression* you need to use.

1 Some time expressions describe time up to now: *since I was six; yet; for the last few days.* With these time expressions, we use the present perfect.
2 Some time expressions describe fixed points in the past (finished time): *in 1984; when I was six; yesterday; before I left school; last week; at 6:00; two minutes ago; last semester; at Christmas time.* With these time expressions, we use the simple past.
3 With some time expressions, we can use either the present perfect or a past tense form: *this year; this week; recently; already; ever; never.*

The present perfect as a conversation opener

You can use *Have + ever…?* to establish the topic of a conversation or introduce a story.
***Have** you **ever been** to Tuscany?*
***Have** I **ever told** you about the time I went skiing with my brother?*
You will find more information about the present perfect in Units 2, 3, and 6.

The past continuous and the simple past

The past continuous is almost always used in contrast with the simple past. We can use it to describe something that was in progress when the main events in the story happened. Here Mike talks about the first time he thought of trying skydiving.
*I **was sitting** at home when a commercial **came on** TV.*

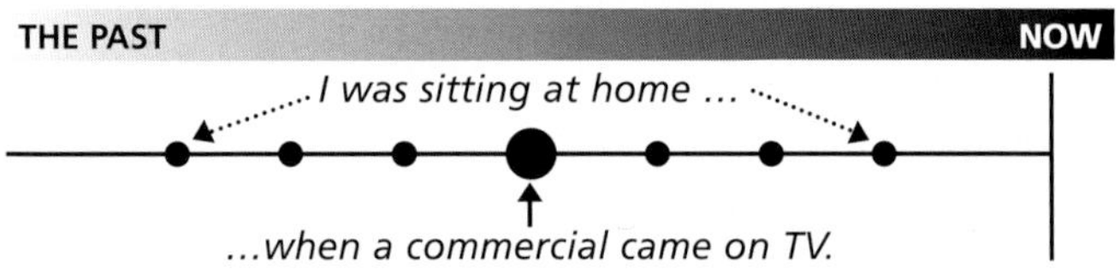

The past continuous and the simple past are also contrasted in more complex ways. Notice the way they are used together in this passage from the same text.
*I **was beginning** to get nervous, but the others **were talking** and **joking,** and I **started** to relax. It **was** a beautiful, cloudless day, and the sun **was** just **going down.** It **took** us about 20 minutes to get to 11,000 feet, and then the instructor **opened** the plane door—the view **took** my breath away. Suddenly, it **was** time to jump, and as I **pushed** myself away from the plane—I don't know what I **was thinking**—my mind **went** blank.*

Anecdote

1 Think back to a moment when you felt a rush of adrenaline. You are going to tell your partner about it. Choose from the list below the things you want to talk about. Think about what you will say and what language you will need.

- ☐ Where were you? At home? In a car? At a sports event?
- ☐ Did it happen recently? How old were you?
- ☐ Who were you with?
- ☐ What were you doing?
- ☐ What happened?
- ☐ How did you feel?
- ☐ What were the consequences?
- ☐ Would you like to have the same experience again?

2 Tell your partner the story. Give as much detail as possible.

LANGUAGE TOOLBOX

Stories are often told in five stages.

1 **Introduction**
Have I ever told you about the time I was attacked by a lion?
2 **Background**
I was on vacation with Jan…
We were traveling around Africa on my motorcycle…
3 **Problem**
Suddenly I heard a sound in the jungle …The next minute I saw…So there we were, up a tree…We were beginning to get nervous…
4 **Resolution**
Then I had an idea…Finally I was able to get the motorcycle started…I drove off at a hundred miles an hour…I didn't stop until I got to Nairobi…
5 **Comment**
I often wonder what happened to Jan…

The Adrenaline Game: Truth or Dare?

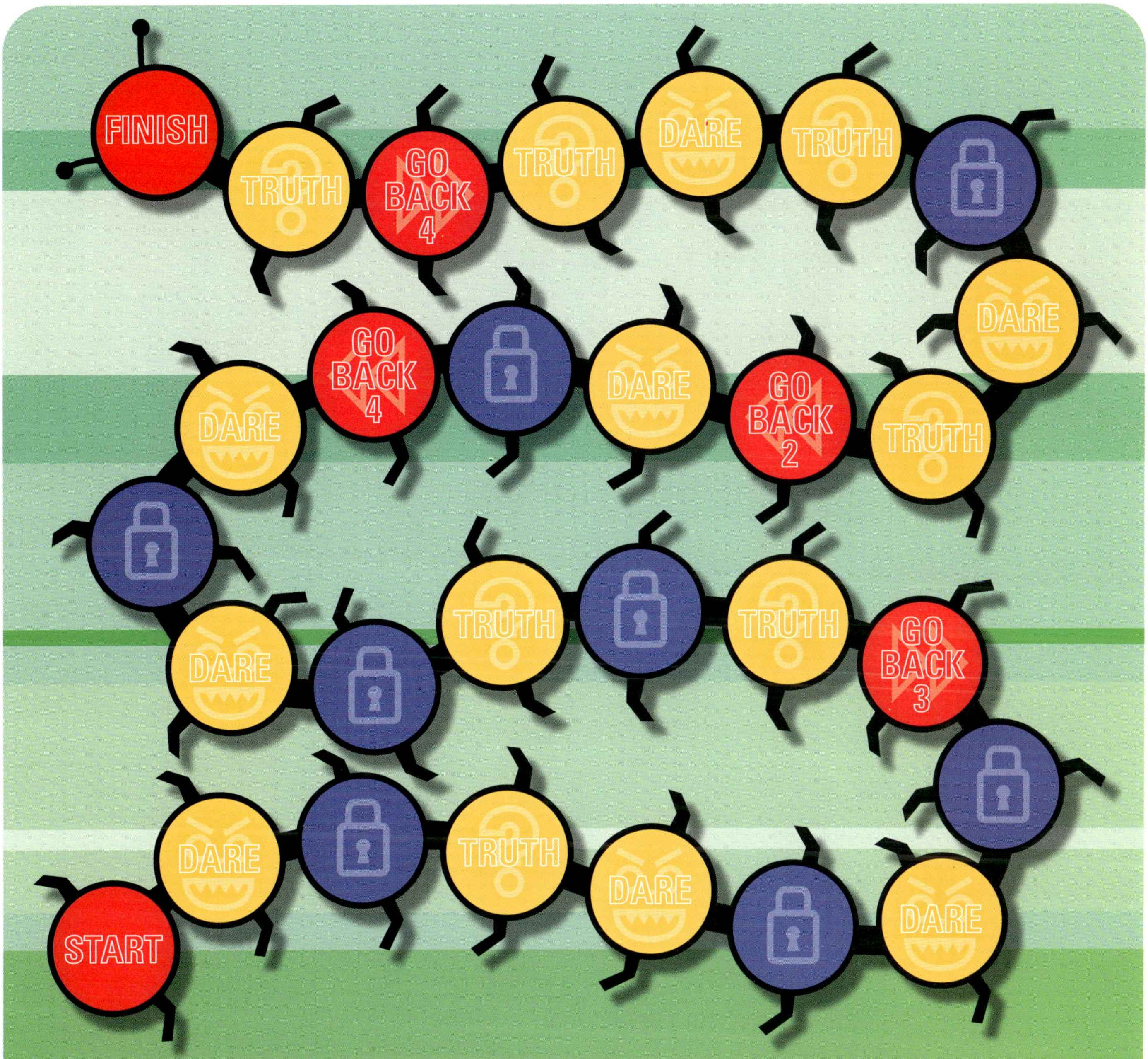

RULES OF THE GAME

Work in teams of three or four.

BEFORE THE GAME

Each team prepares ten TRUTH questions and ten DARES. Here are some suggestions:

TRUTH
Have you ever ... ?
Did you ... ?
When was the last time you ... ?
How many times have you ... ?
When was the first time you ... ?
What were you doing when ... ?

DARE
Sing a song in English.
Imitate a famous person.
Say the alphabet backwards.
Make three animal sounds.
Demonstrate ballet dancing.
Show us everything in your pockets.

HOW TO PLAY

1 Each team throws the die. The team with the highest roll of the die starts.
2 Each team takes a turn throwing the die and moving the team's counter around the board according to the number on the die.
3 When a team lands on a TRUTH or a DARE square, the team members nominate a "victim" to answer a question truthfully or take a dare from the other team.
4 Each team must nominate a new victim each time until each team member has had a turn.
5 Teams cannot use the same TRUTH or DARE twice, unless they have used all their TRUTHS and DARES.
6 After hearing the TRUTH or the DARE, the victim can say "change" and take a DARE instead of a TRUTH, or vice versa. After saying "change," the victim cannot go back to the original TRUTH or DARE.
7 If the victim refuses to answer a TRUTH or take a DARE, the team loses the turn and moves the counter back to the square it was on at the beginning of the turn.
8 The winner of the game is the team that reaches the finish circle first.

Close-up

Comparisons

1 Find the names of twelve sports.

baseballboxingbungeejumpingsoccerfootballrockclimbing
skydivinggolfrunningscubadivingskiingsnowboarding

2 15 Listen and say which sports George, Katrina, Paul, and Eva are talking about. Which key words helped you to identify the sports?

3 Listen again. Complete these sentences to summarize what the people say about their experiences. You may need more than one word for each blank. Read tapescript 15 again to check.

a) ________ is slightly ________ than ________ . (George)
b) ________ is just as ________ as ________ . (George)
c) ________ was one of the ________ I've ever ________ . (Katrina)
d) ________ are by far the ________ . (Paul)
e) ________ is much ________ than ________ . (Eva)
f) ________ isn't nearly as ________ as ________ . (Eva)

4 Use the same structures to give your own opinions about different sports. Find other people in the class who agree with you.

Language Reference p. 40

5 Work with a partner. What rules do you know about comparative and superlative adjectives?

Language Reference: Comparisons

Comparative and superlative adjectives

1	fast	*faster*	*the fastest*
	cheap	*cheaper*	*the cheapest*
2	nice	*nicer*	*the nicest*
	safe	*safer*	*the safest*
3	big	*bigger*	*the biggest*
	hot	*hotter*	*the hottest*
4	slow	*slower*	*the slowest*
	few	*fewer*	*the fewest*
5	funny	*funnier*	*the funniest*
	easy	*easier*	*the easiest*
6	good	***better***	***the best***
	bad	***worse***	***the worst***

Comparative and superlative structures

useful → ***more/less*** *useful* → ***the most/least*** *useful*
exciting → ***more/less*** *exciting* → ***the most/least*** *exciting*
X is/isn't ***as*** *fast/nice/big/slow/easy/good/useful/exciting* ***as*** *Y.*
Snowboarding is ***similar to/like skiing****.*

Modifiers

Football is ***much/far/a lot*** *more popular than skydiving.*
Skydiving isn't ***nearly as*** *popular as football.*
The Seikan Tunnel in Japan is ***a little bit/slightly*** *longer than the Channel Tunnel.*
Brazil is ***by far*** *the biggest country in South America.*
Harrison Ford is ***one of*** *the most successful movie stars of all time.*

Like Romeo Loved Juliet...

1 Make lists of things that are:

- sweet
- deep
- strong
- high
- bright
- bigger than you

2 Work with a partner. Tell your partner about your list.

3 Complete the love letter.

4 16 Ronnie and Vic are in love. Listen to their conversation. How many of the images and comparisons in the conversation are the same as yours?

Darling,

You are sweeter than ___,

And my love is stronger than ___,

And it's deeper than ___.

I love you like bees love ___,

Like the sun loves ___,

Like fish love ___.

If I lost you, I'd ___.

I'm going to be as faithful as ___.

I'll never ___.

5 Kids

1 Write down the names of any children you know. Put each name in the appropriate category.

- babies: 0–1 years old
- toddlers: 1–3 years old
- young children: 4–7 years old
- older children: 8–12 years old
- teenagers: 13+ years old

2 Tell your partner about them.

3 Divide into two groups: *parents* and *children*.

- Parents: Discuss and list the qualities of a good child.
- Children: Discuss and list the qualities of a good parent.

Then compare your list with the other group.

A Child's Point of View

1 Read these children's definitions of a mother and choose the one you like the best.

A mom is a person who takes care of you and tucks you in at night. When you've make a mistake, she says it's all right.
Jan, age 13

Mothers are people who sit up worrying about you, and when you come home, they yell at you.
Gary, age 13

A mom is a woman who says "Go to bed," and when she says that, you keep quiet and she forgets about you.
Jennifer, age 9

A mother is a superwoman who can be in two places at once.
Judy, age 10

A mom is a person who cries when you do something bad and cries even harder when you do something good.
Robin, age 14

A mom is someone who always knows when there is something wrong, even if you don't tell her.
Lisa, age 14

Mothers are people who are mad when you're home and sad when you're away.
Vinnie, age 12

2 Write a similar definition for a father.

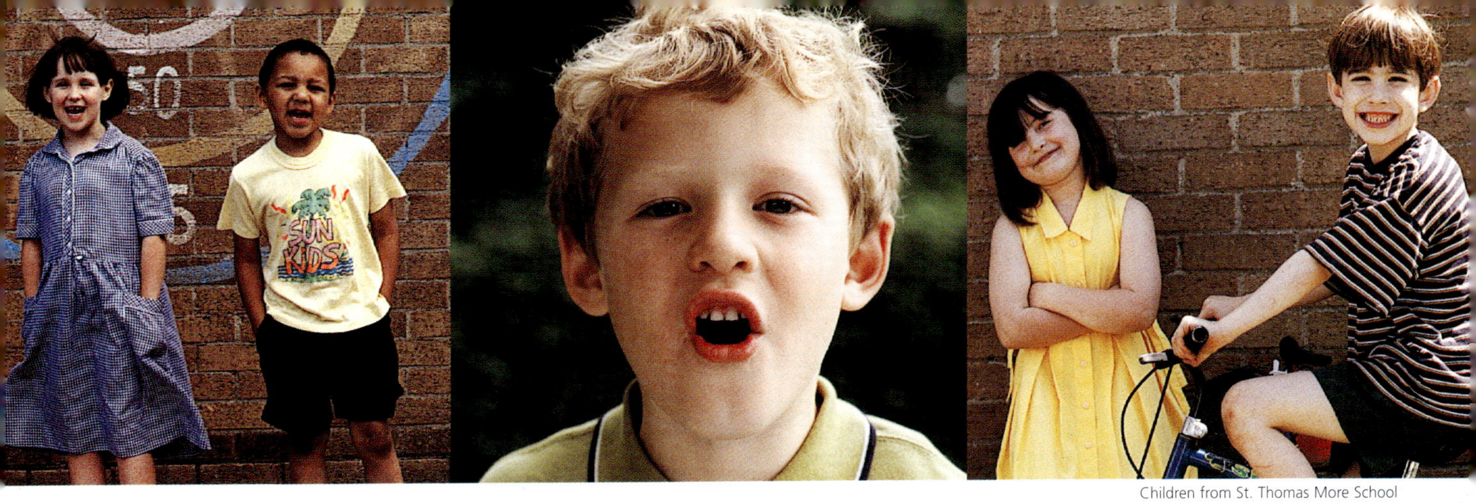

Children from St. Thomas More School

3 17 You are going to listen to these children defining five things from the list below. Which things do they talk about and in what order?

a) God	f) a vet	k) summer
b) a dinosaur	g) a police officer	l) a judge
c) an iceberg	h) a cell phone	m) a desert
d) the Internet	i) a robber	n) a jungle
e) the ozone layer	j) a museum	o) Halloween

4 Work with a partner. Imagine you are explaining other things from the list to a four-year-old child. Write down what you would say.

Close-up

Defining relative clauses

1 Work with a partner.

a) Underline the relative clauses in the sentences on the right.

b) Which word is the relative pronoun in each case?

c) In each sentence, change the relative pronoun to either *who* or *which*.

1 It's something that lived a very long time ago. It looks very scary.

2 A person that helps people in heaven.

3 It's something that crashes down on people.

4 A person that steals things at night.

2 Here are some typical children's jokes. Look at the pictures and complete each joke with an appropriate word.

a) Q: What do you call an _________ that has a machine gun?
A: Sir.

b) Q: What do you call a _________ who's very small?
A: Minimum.

c) Q: What happened to the _________ who stole a calendar?
A: He got twelve months.

d) Q: What do you call a Supreme Court _________ who has no thumbs?
A: Mr. Justice Fingers.

e) Q: What prize did the man who invented the _________ win?
A: The Nobel Prize.

Can you translate any of the jokes into your own language? Are they funny?

3 What do you know about education in the U.S.? Complete each sentence, using *who* or *that.*

a) A professor is a person…
b) A high school is a school…
c) Private schools are schools…
d) A degree is a title…
e) Undergraduates are people…
f) A scholarship is money…

You take the children's bath time too seriously, Norman.

4 Write similar sentences about the education system in your country.

For example:
"Selectividad" is an examination that you take to get into college in Spain.

Omitting relative pronouns

The relative pronoun is sometimes optional. For example, both of these sentences are correct:
He's the man that I saw.
He's the man I saw.

But in this sentence, the relative pronoun is necessary:
He's the man that lives next door.

Language Reference p. 46

Read these sentences and cross out the relative pronouns that are optional.

a) Jill Bennett is the woman who you want to speak to.
b) She's seen the car that she wants.
c) It was the degree in engineering that helped me get the job.
d) He's a man who likes his food.
e) It's a university that specializes in technical subjects.
f) What was the name of the movie that you wanted to see?
g) The teacher that I liked the best in school was Mr. Stevens.
h) He's the teacher who taught us math.

Where, when, and *whose*

You can also make relative clauses with *where, when,* or *whose.*

1 Complete each sentence, with *where* or *when* and a relative clause so that it is true for you.

a) My schooldays were a time in my life…
b) The town I grew up in is the kind of place…
c) The best vacation I ever had with my parents was…
d) I once had a fight with my brother/sister/best friend…
e) We used to play in a place…

Read one sentence to your partner and then tell him/her more about it.

2 Find out how many people in the class have these things in common with you and write down their names.

Find someone whose:

- car is the same make as yours. ____________
- birthday is in the same month as yours. ____________
- taste in music is the same as yours. ____________
- mother is the same age as yours. ____________
- shoe size is the same as yours. ____________
- favorite food is the same as yours. ____________

Definition Auction

Rules of the game

1 Work in teams. The definitions are for sale in a public auction. Some of them are true and some of them are false. Each team decides which definitions they think are true.

2 Each team tries to buy the definitions that they think are true by bidding (offering) more money than all the other teams. You have a total of $10,000 to spend at the auction.

3 The winner of the game is the team that buys the highest number of true definitions.

A midwife is a woman whose husband is between 50 and 60 years old.

A minor is a child who works in a mine.

A truant is a student who tells the truth.

A sophomore is a student in the second year of high school or college.

A pacifier is something you put in a baby's mouth to stop it from crying.

A bib is something that young children wear when they are eating.

A bully is a field where young bulls are kept.

A grind is a student who studies very hard all the time.

Language Reference: Defining relative clauses

Defining relative clauses give information that helps to define the topic of the sentence. They can be introduced by relative pronouns: *who, which,* and *that.*

who, which, that

We use *who* to refer to people, and *which* to refer to things or ideas. We can use *that* for either. *Which* is more formal than *that.* It is more common in written English than in speech.

An iceberg is an enormous block of ice ***that/which*** *floats in the ocean.*
A judge is someone ***who/that*** *decides how the law should be interpreted and applied.*

whom

Whom is sometimes used as a very formal alternative to *who* in sentences where it is the object.
Subject: ***He*** *did it.* → *He's the man* ***who*** *did it.*
Object: *I saw* ***him.*** → *He's the man* ***who/whom*** *I saw.*

Omitting relative pronouns

We can omit the relative pronoun when it is the object of the clause.

He's ***the man who/whom*** *I saw.*
→ *He's* ***the man*** *I saw.*

She's ***the woman who/whom*** *I helped.*
→ *She's* ***the woman*** *I helped.*

That's ***the company that/which*** *I worked for.*
→ That's ***the company*** *I worked for.*

when, where, whose

We can also use *when, where,* and *whose* in relative clauses.
Autumn is the time of year ***when*** *leaves fall off the trees.*
An art gallery is a place ***where*** *paintings and sculptures are displayed to the public.*
A widower is a man ***whose*** *wife has died.*

Children's Rhymes

Stress timing

1 18 Look at this popular children's nursery rhyme and listen to the recording. The boxes show the stressed syllables.

HUMP	-ty	DUMP	-ty		SAT	on a		WALL
HUMP	-ty	DUMP	-ty		HAD	a great		FALL
ALL	the king's	HORS	-es and		ALL	the king's		MEN
COULD	-n't put	HUMP	-ty	to-	GETH	-er	a-	GAIN

2 Say the rhyme along with the recording. Follow the stress and speed of the recording. Try to finish at exactly the same time as the recording.

3 19 Listen to another nursery rhyme. Work with a partner. Write the nursery rhyme. Use these words and any others you need. Then underline the stressed syllables.

Ann	fire	except	frying pan	under	little	fly	has
away	gone	house	Ladybug	home	crept	children	

4 Listen to the rhyme again and practice saying it at the same speed.

5 Work with a partner. Make up a four-line rhyme with a simple rhythm, using words from the box below or your own words.

Rome	home	comb	waiter	later	alligator	hat	fat	rat	far	car
deliver	river	shiver	wearing	sharing	staring	would	could	should		

First Memory: The Bicycle

1 You are going to read about one of Roald Dahl's childhood memories. Look at the picture and discuss the following:

a) What year do you think it is?
b) How old do you think the boys are?
c) What are they wearing?
d) How do you think their life was different from children's lives now?

Roald Dahl

Roald Dahl began writing after a "monumental bash on the head" received when he was a Royal Air Force fighter pilot during World War II. He became one of the best-known and most successful of all children's writers.

2 Quickly read *First Memory: The Bicycle* to find out Roald Dahl's "greatest wish" at that moment in his life.

Between the age of seven and nine, only two moments remain clearly in my mind. The first lasted not more than five seconds, but I will never forget it.

It was my first term, and I was walking home alone across the village green after school when suddenly one of the senior twelve-year-old boys came riding full speed down the road on his bicycle about twenty yards away from me. The road was on a hill, and the boy was going down the slope, and as he flashed by, he started back-pedaling very quickly so that the free-wheeling mechanism of his bike made a loud whirring sound. At the same time, he took his hands off the handlebars and folded them casually across his chest. I stopped dead and stared after him. How wonderful he was! How swift and brave and graceful in his long trousers with bicycle clips around them and his scarlet school cap at a jaunty angle on his head! One day, I told myself, one glorious day I will have a bike like that, and I will wear long trousers with bicycle clips, and my school cap will sit jaunty on my head, and I will go whizzing down the hill, pedaling backwards with no hands on the handlebars!

I promise you that if somebody had caught me by the shoulder at that moment and said to me, "What is your greatest wish in life, little boy? What is your absolute ambition? To be a doctor? A fine musician? A painter? A writer? Or the Lord Chancellor?" I would have answered without hesitation that my only ambition, my hope, my longing was to have a bike like that and to go whizzing down the hill with no hands on the handlebars. It would be fabulous. It made me tremble just to think about it.

[Excerpt from *Boy* by Roald Dahl, 1984]

3 Read Roald Dahl's first memory again and find four differences between the picture and the excerpt.

Vocabulary

1 Roald Dahl uses exaggerated language to bring the scene alive. Find the actual words he uses to describe the following:

a) The senior boy came riding very fast down the road.
b) As he passed me, he started back-pedaling.
c) I stopped immediately and watched him.
d) I will go riding fast down the hill.
e) My wish was to have a bike like that.
f) It would be very nice.

2 Underline all the words in Roald Dahl's first memory that you think are related to bicycles. Can you guess the meaning from the context? Compare with a partner.

Second Memory: The Great Mouse Plot

1 20 Read and listen to Roald Dahl's second memory. What was the terrible problem with the sweet-shop?

My second and only other memory of Llandaff Cathedral School is extremely bizarre. It happened a little over a year later, when I was just nine. By then I had made some friends, and when I walked to school in the mornings, I would start out alone but would pick up four other boys of my own age along the way. After school was over, the same four boys and I would set out together across the village green and through the village itself, heading for home. On the way to school and on the way back, we always passed the sweet-shop. No we didn't; we never passed it. We always stopped. The sweet-shop in Llandaff in the year 1923 was the very centre of our lives. To us, it was what a bar is to a drunk, or a church is to a bishop. Without it, there would have been little to live for. But it had one terrible drawback, this sweet-shop. The woman who owned it was a horror. We hated her, and we had good reason for doing so.

2 Which of the following drawings is the most accurate illustration of the boys' routine?

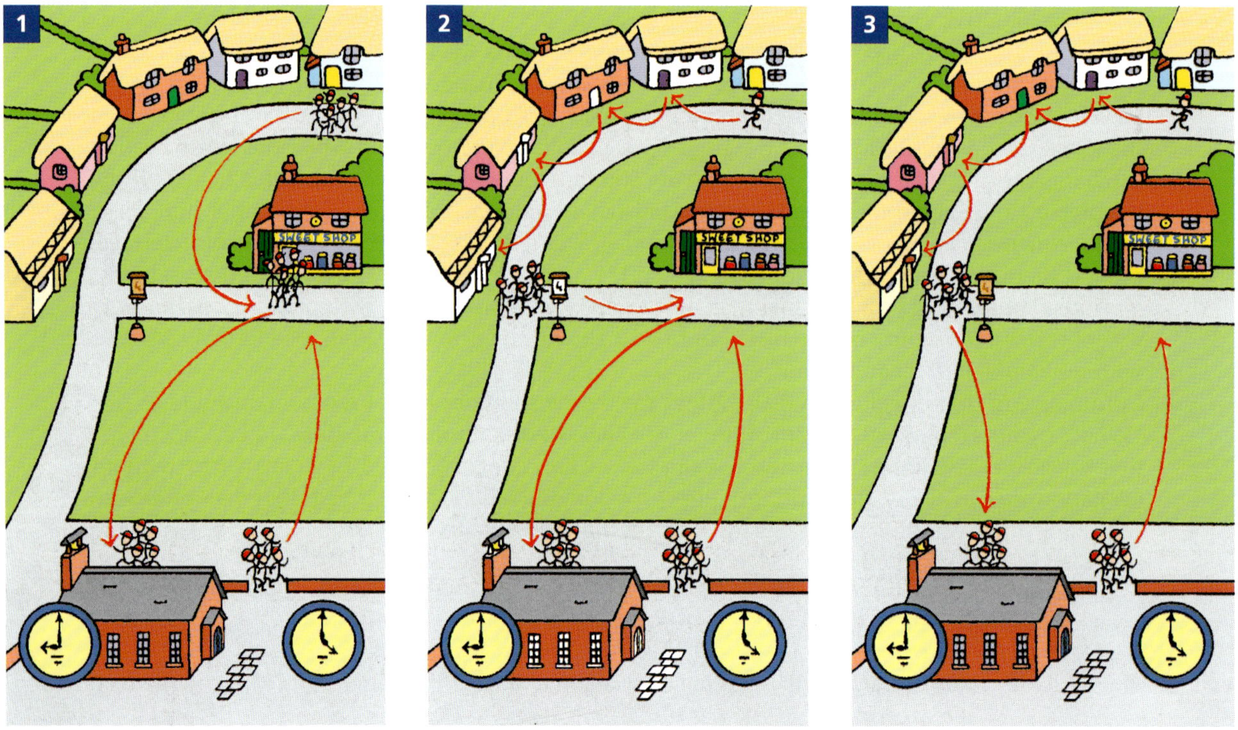

Close-up

Would and used to

1 Complete the sentences below without looking back at the second memory.

a) … I ________ start out alone but ________ pick up four other boys of my own age along the way.

b) After school was over, the same four boys and I ________ set out together across the village… heading for home.

2 Do the sentences in 1 describe:

a) repeated actions in the past?

b) situations in the past?

c) single events in the past?

Language Reference p. 49

3 The simple past, *would* + verb, and *used to* + verb are all possible ways to talk about the past.

The sentences below are all in the simple past. Read them and discuss these questions:

1 Which sentences could be changed to *would* + verb?
2 Which sentences could be changed to *used to* + verb?
3 What does this tell you about how to use these two structures?

When I was a child:

a) I was afraid of the dark.
b) I believed in ghosts.
c) I went on vacation to Disney World three times.
d) I broke my leg skiing.
e) I sucked my thumb when I was tired.
f) I started learning the piano.
g) I had long hair.
h) I went to the movies every Saturday.
i) I didn't like vegetables.
j) I lived right downtown.

Is each sentence true or false for you?

Anecdote

My son, Eric, won't be coming to school today; he's in terrible pain.

4 Think about your life at the age of eight. You are going to tell your partner about it. Choose from the list the things you want to talk about. Think about what you will say and the language you will need.

- ☐ Did your life use to be very different from how it is now?
- ☐ Where did you use to go to school? How did you get there?
- ☐ Do you remember any of your teachers?
- ☐ Were there any you particularly liked or disliked? Why?
- ☐ Who were your friends?
- ☐ What did you use to do before/after school or during recess?
- ☐ Did you ever do anything naughty? Were you caught and punished?
- ☐ What was your favorite game?
- ☐ What was your favorite kind of candy?
- ☐ Was there an older child you particularly looked up to?
- ☐ What was your greatest wish?

5 21 Why do the boys hate Mrs. Pratchett, the sweet-shop owner? If you would like to know what happens at the end of the story, read tapescript 21 and listen to the recording.

Language Reference: *would* and *used to*

would

We can use *would*… to talk about regular or repeated past actions. It sometimes suggests a feeling of nostalgia so is often used for personal reminiscences.

*Every day my pals **would play** football after school.*
*I **would visit** my grandmother on weekends.*
*We **would go** skiing at the same resort every year.*

We rarely use *would* with this meaning in the negative or question form.

used to

We can use *used to* like *would* for regular or repeated past actions and also for past states or situations.

*I **used to go** to the movies every Saturday.*	*I **would go** to the movies every Saturday.* ✓
*I **used to have** long hair.*	*I ~~would have~~ long hair.* ✗

We can use *used to* in negative forms and in question forms.

*Kids **didn't use to have** cell phones. Now they do, and I don't!*
***Did** you **use to like** school?*

6 News

Discuss these questions:

- What do you know about the people in these photographs?
- If you saw one of these photographs in a newspaper or magazine, would you read about it? Why/Why not?
- Who are the most photographed celebrities in your country?
- Is there any celebrity scandal in the news these days?

The Hunters and the Hunted

Read the Web page on page 51 and find the connections between:

Paparazzo	→	scooter
a photograph	→	a million dollars
Tom Cruise	→	a tunnel in Paris
Madonna	→	80 mph
Alec Baldwin	→	a black eye
George Clooney	→	a Vietnamese potbellied pig

Robert de Niro

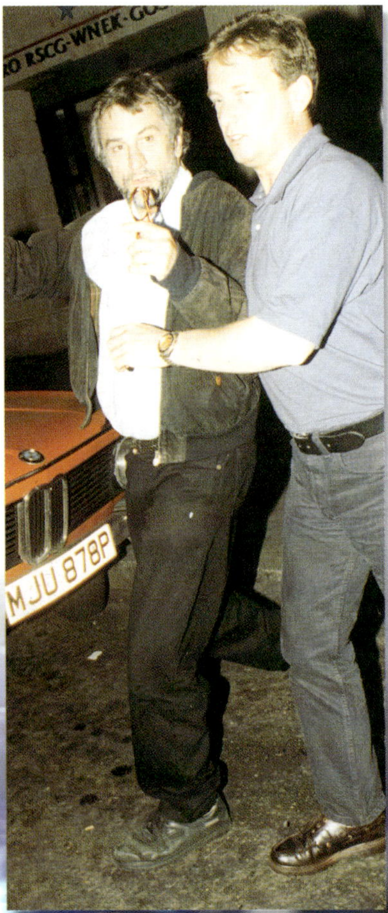

Jack Nicholson

Madonna

This page has been created to air concerns over the ever-growing problem of an aggressive breed of photographer known as "the paparazzi."

PAPARAZZI

The term "paparazzi" comes from a character called Paparazzo in the Fellini movie *La Dolce Vita* who rode around on a scooter, taking photographs of the rich and famous. These days paparazzi take photographs of famous people, hoping to get them in an unflattering or compromising pose. The photograph is then sold for an enormous sum of money, sometimes close to a million dollars, to the tabloid press.

Some people say that celebrities are public property and that this invasion of privacy is to be expected—"that's show business," they say. I think that this is true up to a point, but celebrities are being followed, harassed, chased, provoked, and spied on in their own homes. That's not show business—that's criminal.

Unnecessary risks

- Tom Cruise has been pursued at high speed through the tunnel in Paris where Princess Diana was killed.
- When Madonna was promoting *Evita* in Rome, she had to drive away at 80 mph with her baby in the car because she was being chased. The paparazzi didn't even give her time to strap the baby into the car.

Invasion of privacy

- Alec Baldwin gave a paparazzo a black eye when he filmed the actor and his wife, Kim Basinger, returning to their Hollywood home with their new baby. Baldwin was arrested and charged with assault, but he was later acquitted.
- Cindy Crawford has been filmed in her bathroom from over a mile away with a huge telephoto lens.
- When Princess Diana's father died, a paparazzo was waiting outside her hotel. She tearfully begged him to leave her alone, but the pictures were printed in the national newspapers the next day.

Provocation

The paparazzi go out of their way to make people angry so that they can get a better picture. The American actor George Clooney was walking down the street with his girlfriend when a paparazzo shouted, "Who's the fat girl?" The picture of Clooney's angry face was splashed all over the newspapers the next day. However, the actor got his revenge on the paparazzi when one of the photographers was hiding in his yard to get pictures of him and his girlfriend at home—the photographer was chased away by Clooney's pet Vietnamese potbellied pig.

The paparazzi are out of control. Some papers have recognized what is happening and have refused to buy pictures when it's obvious that a person's privacy has been invaded. Other papers should follow their example.

CLICK HERE TO VOICE YOUR OPINION

Vocabulary

1 Match words and phrases from the two columns to make seven expressions from the text on page 51. Do as many as you can from memory. Then look back at the text to check.

a) give	(someone) a black eye
b) charge	(someone) alone
c) follow	(someone) angry
d) go	(someone's) example
e) invade	out of your way to do something
f) leave	(someone's) privacy
g) make	(someone) with assault

2 Complete the following sentences with expressions from 1. You will need to change the tenses of the expressions in some cases.

a) All I did was ask him to smile for the camera, and he _________ .
b) His aggressive behavior is unacceptable. He should be _________ .
c) I asked her why she was upset, but she told me to _________ .
d) It really _________ when people don't stop at red lights.
e) Are you _________ annoy me? You know I hate it when you smoke in the house.
f) David graduated from high school at seventeen and never went to college, and now he's a millionaire. I should have _________ .
g) I regret asking my mother to stay. I feel that my _________ .

Discussion

Discuss the following:

a) Celebrity gossip and scandal are boring.
b) Movie and rock stars are paid too much.
c) Tabloid-type newspapers and magazines should be banned.
d) Information available over the Internet should be controlled.
e) The private lives of politicians and royalty should never be discussed by the press.
f) Highly paid movie stars are public property.

LANGUAGE TOOLBOX

To interrupt
Sorry to interrupt, but…

To stop interruption
If you'd just let me finish,…

To return to the subject
Yes, but as I was saying,…

Close-up

Irregular verbs

1 Test your knowledge of irregular verbs. The irregular verbs below have been divided into five groups.

1	2	3	4	5
swim	break	let	grow	bring
drink	speak	set	fly	fight
ring	choose	cost	throw	catch

Why are they divided in this way? When you know the answer, add these words to the appropriate groups.

steal   hit   know   begin   teach

How many more verbs can you add to each group? Look at the list of irregular verbs on page 147.

2 Test your partner's knowledge of irregular verbs.

For example:
Student A: *Eat…?*
Student B: *Ate, eaten. Drink…?*
Student A: *Drank, drunk. Go…?*

A Letter from Rio

1 Read this letter from Sandra to her friend Joe. Complete the letter with appropriate words. If you need help, look at the words in the box below. There is one word for each blank. They are not in the correct order.

Anyway	news	but
great	apparently	feel
applied	hear	what
doing	Apart	happy
lots	part	heard soon
forward	embarrassing	
sorry	By the way	

July 14

Dear Joe,

It was great to (1) ______ from you. I'm (2) ______ I haven't written sooner, (3) ______ my mother hasn't been very well, so I've been taking care of her. She's a lot better now.

I was so (4) ______ to hear about your promotion. You deserve it—you've worked so hard at that job. (5) That's ______ ! I wish you were still living in Rio so we could go out and celebrate.

Actually, I have some good (6) ______ too—I got a new job! You know I was fed up with my old job. Well, one day I was just looking through the ads in my local newspaper when I saw a job for an English school principal. As you know, I've been looking for a job where I could use my English. So I (7) ______ for the job and got it. I'm really enjoying it, and I've already learned (8) ______ of new things. I have to answer the phone (sometimes in English!), send out information about the school, and deal with any problems the students have. And the best (9) ______ is that I'm getting more money!

(10) ______ , have you (11) ______ about Anna and Giorgio? They called off the wedding. I have no idea why, but (12) ______ Giorgio went back to Italy, and Anna's refusing to talk to anybody about it, even her old friends. I (13) ______ sorry for her parents—they've already sent out all the invitations, and now they have to tell everybody that the wedding's canceled. How (14) ______ ! I wonder if she's given him back that gorgeous ring! (15) ______ , I guess it's better that they broke up now rather than after the wedding!

(16) ______ from that, everything's fine here in Rio. It's getting hot and I'm looking (17) ______ to going on vacation next month. Don't forget that you're always welcome to come and stay—we'd love to see you.

Anyway, I have to go now. Write (18) ______ and tell me how you're (19) ______ .

Lots of love,
Sandra

P.S. Guess (20) ______ ! I finally passed my driving test.

2 Work with a partner. Explain the relationships between Sandra, Joe, Anna, and Giorgio.

3 Answer each of the following questions with one or more of the above names.

a) Who lives in Rio?
b) Who used to live in Rio?
c) Whose mother has been sick?
d) Who's been promoted at work?
e) Who got a new job?
f) Who called off their wedding?
g) Who went back to Italy?
h) Whose parents have sent out wedding invitations?
i) Who's going on vacation in August?
j) Who passed his/her driving test?

4 Joe answered Sandra's letter. Use the expressions below to write his reply.

Dear Sandra,
It was great...
I'm sorry...
I was so happy...
Thank you for the invitation to come and stay, but actually, I've already made vacation plans. I'm going...
By the way, Giorgio called me. Apparently,...
Apart from that,...
Anyway,...
Write soon.
Lots of love,
Joe
P.S. Guess what!

7 *Party*

1 Think of a festival you know or have heard about. How much do you know about it?

a) What is the name of the festival?
b) When does it take place?
c) How long does it last?
d) What do you know about its history?
e) How do people celebrate?
f) How does the festival end?

2 Read this article about a big Spanish festival and find answers to the questions in 1.

SPAIN'S THIRD LARGEST CITY SEES WINTER OFF WITH A BANG

It's March, and I'm in Valencia, Spain's third largest city, with my new friend, José. It's 1 A.M. All around us, fireworks are going off, and the streets are full of noisy revelers. "Welcome to Las Fallas," José grins. "Here you're going to see how Valencians party!"

Seven hours later, I understood what he meant.

Las Fallas (the bonfire) explodes over Valencia every March from the 12th to the 19th. It takes all of the previous year to get organized, and everybody joins in the preparations. The city buzzes with a festive vibe all week, but, like all good parties, it is at night when people really get down to some serious celebrating.

The tradition of Las Fallas began in the 18th century. At that time, craftsmen used special candles to light up the dark nights while they were working. At the end of winter, they celebrated by burning all their waste material in a ceremony that brought together people from all the neighboring communities. Before burning the waste material, they made it into lifelike statues and then dressed them up to look like well-known but unpopular local characters.

Nowadays the statues, some of them over 100 feet tall, are made of cardboard and represent different aspects of modern Spanish society. The whole previous year is spent fund-raising, planning, and constructing the monuments, some of which are worth over $200,000. But they all go up in flames with the maximum amount of fire and noise before the end of the festival.

The Valencians like their guests to enjoy themselves, but after an hour's sleep, I am woken up by the sound of firecrackers and a brass band parading beneath my window. Valencia by day may be sleepier than Valencia by night, but during Las Fallas there's always something going on. From the outskirts of the city, 200,000 girls and boys, wearing traditional dress, march into the center of town, bringing flowers to decorate the statue of the Blessed Virgin.

The festival reaches its climax on March 19, a public holiday and St. Joseph's Day. This is the night when the cardboard statues are burned. As midnight approaches, a feeling of anticipation rises up from the streets and hangs over the city. Firecrackers go off every second or two, and midnight passes in a shower of explosions. The last statue burns down and ends Las Fallas. It is a sad moment, but the Valencians don't have time to mourn the end of this year's festival. After all, they're too busy planning for the next one.

(Adapted from *The Independent*, Sunday, February 8, 1998)

Glastonbury 1998

Phrasal verbs

1 Complete each sentence below with the correct ending from the box. All the sentences include phrasal verbs from the article on page 58.

a) Don't sit around by yourself—join…
b) Half the town burned…
c) Even if I don't have an alarm clock, I always wake…
d) It was a beautiful night with a full moon that lit…
e) My cousin was injured when a firecracker went…
f) We'll all miss you. The whole family's going to come to see you…
g) We've wasted enough time. Let's get…
h) What's going…
i) You can't wear jeans to your brother's wedding—everybody will be dressing…

> off at the airport. up the whole sky. up for the occasion. up at six in the morning. on here? It's way past your bedtime. off in his hand and burned him. in the fun. down to some serious work. down in a fire in 1948.

2 Match the phrasal verbs in 1 with the meanings below.

a) destroy completely by fire
b) wear special clothes
c) explode
d) participate in an activity
e) happen
f) illuminate
g) say good-bye before a trip
h) stop sleeping
i) begin seriously or enthusiastically

3 Complete these paragraphs with the same phrasal verbs. You may need to change the verb tenses to make them fit the sentences.

A

…They bribed a security guard to leave the briefcase in the house. But at about three in the morning, the congresswoman (1) ______ ______. She couldn't get back to sleep, so she went out for a walk. When the bomb (2) ______ ______, she was in an all-night diner two miles away. The explosion was huge. It (3) ______ ______ the whole sky, and the house was (4) ______ ______.

B

John's leaving for a year in Brazil next week, so we're having a party to (5)______ him ______. It's going to be informal—you don't need to (6)______ ______ or anything. Just come as you are and (7)______ ______ ______ some serious dancing. We're going to play some party games, but if you don't want to (8)______ ______, that's O.K. There'll be lots of other things (9)______ ______.

4 *Dictionary:* Work in teams of three. Team A: Look at page 139.
Team B: Look at page 143.

Pronunciation

1 The words in the box are from the article on page 58. They contain seven vowel sounds in English. Work with a partner. Match the underlined sounds to the phonetic symbols.

> around band busy candle city different festival
> full fund good guest holiday modern public

2 27 Listen and check.

3 Add more examples of your own for each sound.

Close-up

Future forms

1 28 Zoë and Sandy share an apartment. Zoë comes home one evening to find Sandy miserable. Listen to their conversation and find out why Sandy's unhappy.

2 Look at tapescript 28 and find three different structures that refer to the future.

3 Which form is used:

a) at the moment of making a decision?
b) to talk about your intentions—what you've decided you want to do?
c) to talk about fixed plans?

4 Read the conversations below to find out how the evening continued for Sandy and choose the most appropriate verb forms.

Zoë and Sandy

(Phone rings.)

Becky: Hello.
Sandy: Hi, Becky, it's Sandy.
Becky: Hiya.
Sandy: Becky, **will you do / are you doing** anything tonight?
Becky: Yes. **I'll meet / I'm meeting** Alex and Suzy in about half an hour.
Sandy: Where **will you go / are you going?**
Becky: To the movies. Would you like to come with us?
Sandy: Yes, I'd love to. Where **will you meet / are you meeting?**
Becky: At their house, but we could meet you in front of the theater on George Street eight-thirty.
Sandy: O.K., thanks. See you later. (Puts the phone down and calls out to Zoë.) **I'll go / I'm going** to the movies with Becky.
Zoë: Good idea.
Sandy: And next time I see David, **I'm telling / I'm going to tell** him to get lost.
Zoë: Hmm. **I'll believe / I'm believing** that when I see it.

(Phone rings.)

Zoë: Hello.
David: Is Sandy there, please?
Zoë: Yes, hold on a minute—**I'll get / I'm going to get** her for you. (Whispers.) It's David.
Sandy: (Coldly.) Oh, hello, David.
David: Look, I'm really sorry I didn't call earlier, but I had to work late.
Sandy: Oh, that's all right—I forgot you were going to call anyway.
David: Listen, I'm really sorry, but I can't see you tonight. **I'll have / I'm having** dinner with my parents.
Sandy: It doesn't matter—**I'll go / I'm going** to the movies anyway.
David: Oh, O.K. Well, **I'll call / I'm going to call** you.
Sandy: When? I mean, all right. Bye.
David: Bye.

(Sandy puts the phone down.)

Zoë: You didn't tell him to get lost.
Sandy: Well, he apologized—and **he'll have / he's having** dinner with his parents. Anyway, I have to go. See you later.

(Later, in front of the theater.)

Sandy: Hi, Alex. Hi, Becky. Where's Suzy?
Becky: Oh, she changed her mind at the last minute. David called her and asked her to go out to dinner at that new Japanese restaurant.
Sandy: What?! Now **I'm definitely telling / I'm definitely going to tell** him to get lost!

5 29 Listen and check your answers.

Language Reference p. 61

6 Work with a partner and complete each reply. Use *will ('ll), (be) going to,* or the present continuous.

a) There's no food in the house.
Don't worry…
b) Can we meet for dinner on Tuesday?
I'd love to, but…
c) Have you decided where to go for your vacation?
Yes, we decided last week. We…
d) Are you ready to order?
Yes, I think…
e) Does Jack know we've changed the time of the meeting?
That's a good question.
f) The car needs some work.
Yes, I know…
g) About your trip to New York, do you know there's a taxi strike there next week?
Yes, Annie told me about it…
h) Is there an agenda for the conference yet?
No, but…
i) Your hair's getting long.
Yes, I know…

Invitations

1 Read tapescripts 28 and 29 again and find:

a) two ways to ask somebody if he/she is free to go out
b) two ways to invite somebody to do something
c) two ways of refusing an invitation
d) the excuse David gives Sandy for not going out with her.

2 Use language from the tapescripts to write a dialogue based on the plan below.

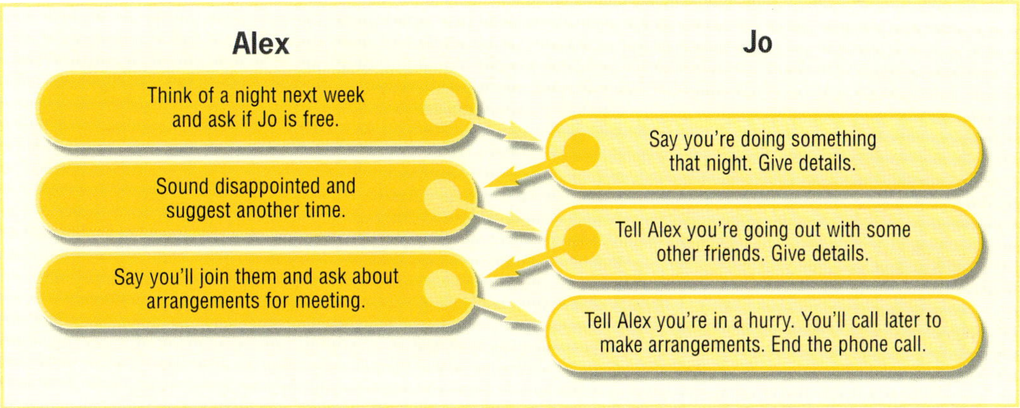

3 Practice the dialogue. Take turns being Alex and Jo.

4 Work with a partner.

Student A: You want to meet B and go somewhere.
Student B: You don't want to go anywhere with A. Make excuses.

Language Reference: Future forms

The present continuous and the structures *will ('ll)* and *(be) going to* are three common ways to talk about the future. Each one tells us something different about what happened before the moment of speaking.

Will ('ll)

Form: *will ('ll)* + simple form of the verb
Use: to state a new decision; to make promises and offers.
*It's cold in here. **I'll turn on** the heat.*
*Don't worry. **I'll call** you tomorrow.*
***I'll help** you carry your suitcase.*

(be) going to

Form: *be* + *going* + infinitive
Use: to talk about your intentions.
*After college **I'm going to travel** for a year.*
*Next time I see him, **I'm going to tell** him what I think.*

Present continuous

Form: *be* + present participle (*-ing* form)
Use: to show that you are talking about your future plans, for example, appointments and organized events.
***I'm playing** tennis with Judy on Saturday.*
*We**'re having** a party on Friday night. Would you like to come?*
For other uses of these structures, see Unit 9.

Look at these three examples of different answers to the question:

Do you have any plans for the weekend?

1 Decision

*No, I don't. I think **I'll call** Jane and see if she's free.*

2 Intention

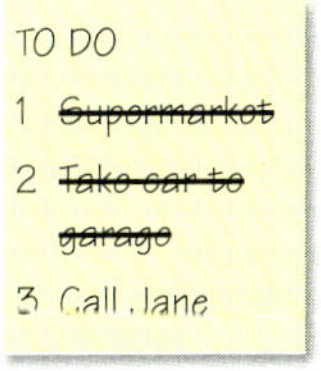

*Not yet. **I'm going to call** Jane and see if she's free.*

3 Plan

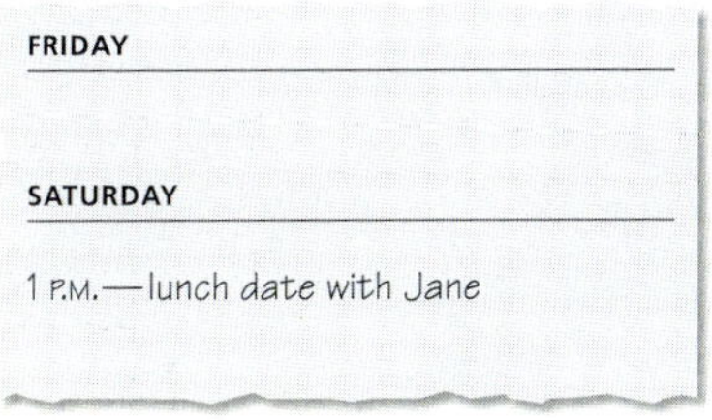

*Yes. **I'm having** lunch with Jane on Saturday.*

Parties

1 What kind of parties are these?

- housewarming
- graduation
- costume
- 18th birthday
- surprise
- Halloween

Masked Ball, Venice

2 What other types of party can you think of?

Allison, George, and Rachel

3 Work with a partner. What do you think makes a good party? Write a list and agree on the three most important "ingredients."

4 30 Listen to Allison, George, and Rachel talking about the ingredients of a good party. Compare their ideas with yours.

5 Complete the questionnaire below. Then turn to page 142 and compare your score with a partner.

Are You a Party Animal or a Party Pooper?

1 You've been invited to a party, but you're working the next morning. Do you…

a) think "you only live once" and go and have a good time?
b) go to the party but leave at ten o'clock?
c) send your apologies and spend the night at home?

2 It's your birthday. Do you…

a) have a quiet family get-together, blow your candles out, and go to bed early?
b) hope that nobody has remembered, because you don't want to get older anyway?
c) have a big party and invite everybody you know?

3 You've been invited to a party by somebody you don't know very well. Do you…

a) go to the party and hope you'll meet lots of new people?
b) refuse the invitation because it's too scary?
c) go to the party but take a friend with you to make sure you'll have someone to talk to?

4 You arrive at a party and realize that the only person you know is the host. Do you…

a) panic and hide in the bathroom?
b) go and introduce yourself to anybody who looks interesting?
c) end up talking to the most boring person there because nobody else wants to talk to him/her?

5 Your favorite song comes on, but nobody else is dancing. Do you…

a) wait until a few other people are dancing and then join them?
b) stay where you are becasue you prefer to dance to your favorite record in the privacy of your own home?
c) start dancing by yourself?

6 Somebody suggests playing party games. Do you…

a) suddenly remember a previous engagement?
b) feel embarrassed, but join in anyway?
c) suggest your favorite game and organize it?

Vocabulary

1 Complete as many of these sentences as you can from memory, using one word in each blank. Compare your sentences with a partner. Then look back at the questionnaire to check your answers.

a) My philosophy is "you only ______ once, so ______ sure you ______ a good time."
b) When I want to ______ an invitation, I sometimes say that I have a ______ engagement, even if it's not true.
c) I'm not very good at going up to strangers and ______ myself.
d) Even when I'm not looking forward to going out, I usually end ______ enjoying myself.
e) From time to time, I really enjoy an evening at home by ______ .

2 Which of the sentences are true for you? Discuss with a partner.

Let's Party!

Anecdote

1 Think of a good party you've been to or one that was a disaster. You are going to tell your partner about it. Choose from the list the things you want to talk about. Think about what you will say and what language you will need.

- ☐ Whose party was it?
- ☐ What was the occasion?
- ☐ Did you take a gift for the host?
- ☐ Who did you go with?
- ☐ Where was the party?
- ☐ Were there any decorations?
- ☐ Were there a lot of people there?
- ☐ Did you know most of the people there?
- ☐ What kind of food and drink did you have?
- ☐ What was the music like?
- ☐ Did you dance?
- ☐ Did you meet anybody nice there?
- ☐ What time did it finish?
- ☐ Did you stay until the end?

2 Tell your partner about the party.

3 Work in groups. You are going to take part in a contest to organize the best party. Decide on the following:

- budget
- date and time
- who to invite
- place
- clothes
- decorations
- entertainment (music, games, etc.)
- food and drink

4 Tell the rest of the class about your party. Try to convince your classmates to come.

It's My Party…

1 Look at the picture. What do you think the song is about?

2 31 Listen to the song and see if you guessed correctly. Identify the following three people in the picture:

- the hostess
- Johnny
- Judy

What is the relationship between them?

3 Listen to the song again and read the lyrics. In each line of the three verses there is an extra word. Find the word and cross it out.

Chorus

It's my party, and I'll cry if I want to,
Cry if I want to, cry if I want to.
You would cry too if it happened to you.

Verse 1

Nobody really knows where my Johnny has gone,
But Judy left at the same time.
Why was he still holding her hand,
When he's supposed to be all mine?

Chorus

Verse 2

Play all of my records, keep dancing all night,
But just leave me alone for a while,
'Til Johnny's back dancing with me,
I've got no more reason to smile.

Chorus

Verse 3

Judy and Johnny just walked in thru the door,
Like a queen walking with her king.
Oh, what a birthday party surprise,
Judy's wearing his gold ring.

Chorus

It's My Party was recorded by Lesley Gore in 1963.

It's My Party

It's My Party, Lesley Gore's first single in 1963, became a number one hit within weeks. Although she recorded several top 40 hits during the 60s, it was her only number one song.

Special Occasions

Writing **1** Match the letters of invitation to the replies.

1

Dear…
Thanks for the invitation to dinner. I'd love to come. I haven't seen Brett and Allison in ages, and your friend sounds really interesting. I'll bring some wine.
Look forward to seeing you on Saturday.

Love

2

Dear…
It was great to hear from you. Sorry it's taken me a while to reply, but I've been up to my eyes in work recently. I'm happy to hear that you're having such a good time at college and that you've made lots of new friends. David sounds nice. Three weeks? That must be a record for you!!
I'm writing to ask you what you're doing the last weekend in May. I was wondering if you'd like to come and spend a few days at the shore. How about bringing David with you? (Can he cook?!) Please try to come.
I'm really looking forward to seeing you.
Write soon and let me know.

Lots of love xxx

3

Dear…
Thank you for the kind invitation to your anniversary party. Unfortunately, I won't be able to make it, I'll be in Italy on vacation.
I hope the party goes well.
Best wishes for a happy anniversary on the 4th.
Love x

P.S. Give my love to Uncle Ken.

4

Dear…
Thank you for inviting me for the weekend, but I have exams the following week, so I won't be able to make it. I'd love to come another time, though. Maybe after my exams. I'll call you and we'll set a date.
Wish me luck on my exams.
Love

5

Dear…
I hope you're well and that you're enjoying your new job. I'm writing to you because we would like you to join us for a small party to celebrate our 30th wedding anniversary on September 4 at the Ferncourt Hotel.
I hope you can come. Please give us a call to let us know.

Love

6

Dear…
This is just a short note to ask you if you could come to dinner next Saturday. I'm sorry it's such short notice, but an old friend of mine called me yesterday to say she's coming for the weekend, and I'd love you to meet her. I think I've talked to you about her. Her name's Janet and she works for a movie company in California. I'm going to ask Brett and Allison too. I hope you can make it.

Love

2 Complete the following expressions so that they make sense. Then look back at the letters on the previous page to compare.

a) We would like you to join us for a small party to ...
b) This is just a short note to ask you if you could ...
c) I hope you ...
d) How about ...
e) Thank you for the kind invitation to your anniversary party. Unfortunately...
f) I'm really looking forward ...
g) Thanks for the invitation to dinner. I'd love ...
h) Please try to ...
i) I was wondering if you'd like ...
j) Thank you for inviting me for the weekend, but ...

3 Label each sentence in 2 as follows:

I for an invitation
A for accepting an invitation
R for refusing an invitation

Underline the sentences that you consider to be the most formal. Compare your choice with a partner.

4 Work with a partner. Write a letter of invitation to another pair of students in the class. Include the date, the time, and the place.

Exchange your letters and write a reply accepting the invitation if you are free or refusing it if you are not.

5 Match the greeting cards to the messages below. What is the occasion for each of these greetings?

a) Congratulations. I hope you'll be very happy together.
b) Congratulations. When's the big day?
c) We're thinking of you and your family at this sad time.
d) Congratulations. Hope she has her mother's looks and her father's talent for golf.
e) Get well soon.
f) We had a great time. Don't forget to let me have that recipe.
g) Many happy returns! Don't worry, you're only as old as you feel!
h) Good luck. When's the housewarming party?
i) All the best. We'll miss your smile around the office.
j) Congratulations! You finally did it.

8 Review 1

Test Yourself

Here are some questions about Units 1–7 of *Inside Out*. Find the grammar mistakes in the questions and correct them.

Can you answer the questions? Look back over Units 1–7.

Once in a Blue Moon

Adverbs of frequency

LANGUAGE TOOLBOX

hardly ever often
every six months
occasionally
from time to time
twice a month
every morning
once in a blue moon
never always
every other week
on Mondays
now and then
rarely generally
usually

1 Write questions with *How often do you …?*

a) *How often do you go to the movies?*

b) ______________________

c) ______________________

d) ______________________

e) ______________________

f) ______________________

2 Ask other students the questions in 1. Who in the class does each activity the most and the least often?

Friends

Listening

1 32 Each of the people below is friends with one of the others. Listen and write down any key words (places, events, times, etc.). Decide who is friends with whom.

1 Sue ____________

2 Juan ____________

3 Elisa ____________

4 Enrico ____________

5 Cindy ____________

6 Jim ____________

2 Do you have a friend that you met in an unusual way or in an unusual place?

Feel Like Going Out?

Future forms

1 Choose the most appropriate form. In some cases there is more than one possibility.

Tomoko: Hi, Marie. (1) **Are you doing / Do you do / Will you do** anything tonight?
Marie: Yeah, I (2) **'ll see / 'm going to see / 'm seeing** a movie with Peter and Berta. Do you feel like coming with us?
Tomoko: What (3) **are you going to see / are you seeing / will you see**?
Marie: We're not sure yet. We (4) **meet / 'll meet / 're meeting** at six thirty, and then maybe we (5) **'re trying / 're going to try / 'll try** that new Indian restaurant before we go to the theater.
Tomoko: Yeah, I (6) **'m coming / 'll come / 'm going to come** along if you're sure it's O.K.
Marie: Of course. We (7) **meet/'ll meet/'re meeting** outside school. Six thirty.
Tomoko: I (8) **give / 'll give / 'm going to give** you a ride if you like. (9) **I'll call / I going to call / I'm calling** you before I leave my house.
Marie: Great. I (10) **'m seeing / 'm going to see / 'll see** you later then.
Tomoko: Bye.

2 Work with a partner and improvise a similar conversation.

Sound and vision

Pronunciation

1 Look at the ten vowel sounds and the three vowel sounds with the letter *r*. Then say the word for each picture on page 140 and match the vowel sound to one of the vowel sounds below. For example, *bird* is /ər/.

/i/	/ɪ/	/ʊ/	/u/	/ɛ/	/ə/	/ɔ/	/æ/	/ʌ/	/ɑ/	/ər/	/ɔr/	/ɑr/
see	big	look	blue	egg	among	bought	cat	cup	box	word	more	start

2 Think of three more words for each sound.

Keep in Touch

Tense review **1** Put each verb in parentheses into the most appropriate tense.

New York
May 15

Dear Vera,

Just a quick note (in English!!!) to say that I (1) __________ (have) a fantastic time here in New York. I (2) __________ (be) here for over two weeks now! The English literature course (3) __________ (be) really good, and my English (4) __________ (get) better every day. I (5) __________ (meet) lots of interesting people, and I (6) __________ (become) very friendly with some of them.

Guess what! (7) __________ (you/remember) Miguel, who we (8) __________ (meet) in Oaxaca last year? Well, his brother (9) __________ (study) here. Can you believe he's actually in my class? Anyhow, he (10) __________ (tell) me that Miguel (11) __________ (come) here next month. He (12) __________ (spend) a few days here in New York on his way to Toronto. I (13) __________ (hope) he (14) __________ (remember) me!

So, how's life for you? (15) __________ (you/miss) me? I (16) __________ (be) kind of homesick at first, and I really (17) __________ (want) to see you, but I (18) __________ (feel) fine now. (19) __________ (you/see) Marcella recently? She (20) __________ (study) so hard for her exam when I last (21) __________ (see) her. The exam (22) __________ (be) next week, isn't it? (23) __________ (tell) her that I (24) __________ (think) of her.

Well, I (25) __________ (have) a class in five minutes, so I (26) __________ (finish) now. I (27) __________ (write) again soon.

Take care and lots of love,

Maria xxxx

2 Write a short letter to a friend, telling him/her your news.

Do You Know New York?

Sentence stress **1** 33 Which do you think are the most strongly stressed words in this dialogue?

Val: Where do you live?
Tony: In New York.
Val: Oh, really? Whereabouts?
Tony: Do you know New York?
Val: Pretty well. I have a friend there.
Tony: Oh, good. Uhm, I'm right near the Empire State Building.
Val: Nice! Which street?
Tony: Park Avenue. Do you know it?
Val: I think so. It's the next street after Lexington, right?
Tony: Yeah, that's right.
Val: Yeah, my friend lives on Lexington and Thirty-Sixth Street.

Listen and check. Then work with a partner and practice the dialogue.

2 Write your own similar dialogue and practice it.

Did You Know...?

Passive Can you rearrange the information to make ten facts?
For example: Thirty-five billion bananas are harvested in Brazil every year.

a)	Thirty-five billion bananas	use in the U.S.	every year.
b)	One thousand four hundred sq. mi. of the world's forest	rule by the House of Windsor	every day.
c)	The World Cup	invent	in 1928.
d)	Six thousand five hundred gallons of gas	next see	in 2002.
e)	Three hundred babies	eat in Japan	every year.
f)	Sliced bread	harvest in Brazil	since 1910.
g)	Great Britain	destroy	every week.
h)	Halley's comet	hold in Japan and South Korea	in 2061.
i)	Twenty people in India	born in the world	every minute.
j)	Thirteen thousand tons of fish	kill by falling coconuts	every second.

People and Places

Relative clauses

1 Complete these questions with the missing words: *who*, *whose*, *that*, *which*, and *where*. Can you name:

a) the city __that__ was the birthplace of Marco Polo?
b) the pacifist ________ led India to independence?
c) the city ________ gave us the Beatles?
d) the French scientist ________ won the Nobel Prize in 1911?
e) the cosmonaut ________ was the first person in space?
f) the country ________ soccer legend Pele played for?
g) the singer ________ first number one song was *Like a Virgin*?
h) the city ________ the prophet Mohammed was born?
i) the mountain ________ is home to the Greek gods?
j) the city ________ John F. Kennedy was assassinated?
k) the only British monarch ________ ruled for over sixty years?
l) the explorer ________ was the first to reach the South Pole?
m) the country ________ Alexander the Great was born?

2 Work in small groups. The answers to the questions in 1 can be found in the box. There are more answers than questions. The group that answers the most questions correctly is the winner.

Amundsen Argentina Armstrong Brazil Curie Dallas Egypt Elizabeth Gagarin Gandhi Lennon Liverpool London Macedonia Madonna Mecca New York Olympus Pasteur Polo Rome Turkey Venice Victoria

3 For the answers that you didn't use, write similar questions, using "Can you name...?"

Far, Far Away

Adjectives

1 Choose the correct alternative in bold in the text on the right.

2 Complete Anna's postcard to her friend with adjectives in an appropriate form.

India captures the imagination. Colorful, **exciting/excited,** at times **exasperated/exasperating**, but never, ever dull. To some it is the most **fascinated/fascinating** place on earth, and you are sure to be **captivated/captivating** from the moment you arrive. India's **amazed/amazing** diversity provides something for everyone. From the Himalayas, where you are dwarfed by some of the **most high/highest** mountains in the world, to the magical deserts and **charmed/charming** palaces of Rajasthan; from the **most busy/busiest** streets imaginable, where simply taking a stroll can leave you absolutely **tired/exhausted**, to the hedonism of the palm-fringed beaches of Goa, where you'll feel a hundred percent **relaxed/relaxing.** India is much more than a place you visit. India is an assault on the senses. A place you will never forget.

Hi Lynn,
I'm having an absolutely (1) ________ time in Goa. The weather is (2) ________ , the hotel is (3) ________ , and the food is really (4) ________ . I've been here only a few days, and already I feel really (5) _______ . It's very similar to where we were last year, but this place is much (6) ________ and not as (7) ________ . The local sights around here are all pretty (8) _______ , and all in all, I'd say the place is absolutely (9) ________ . It's probably the (10) ________ place I've ever been to. I've met lots of people—most of them are (11) ________ , but a few are (12) ________ . In fact, I met someone yesterday who's absolutely (13) ________ . Wait until you see the pictures! See you in a couple of weeks. Miss you!
Anna xxxx

Lynn Bradley
19 Barnes Road
Teaneck, NJ 07666
USA

3 Think of a vacation you've taken or a place you've visited. Imagine you're there now. Write a postcard to a friend.

A Letter to a Friend

General review

Here is Vera's reply to Maria's letter on page 69. Find and correct the mistakes. There are at least 20 mistakes.

Pôrto Alegre,
May 23

Dear Maria,
Thanks for your letter last week. It's great to hear that you have a good time in New York and I'm glad the school and the course are good.

So, when Miguel is coming to New York? Maybe I visit you at the same time! And what is Miguel's brother like? Is he looking like him? Write soon and tell me all about it.

Life here is fine, although we all miss you lots. We especially have missed you last weekend. Susanna was having a party for her birthday. Everybody were there, and I spent most of the night dancing.

Remember the people which last month we met at the Superhead concert? Well, Susanna was invited them to the party, and we all got along really well. We had an absolutely good time. Stefan and me really hit it off! In fact, I'll see him again tomorrow. He calls me the day after the party to ask me out. I'm so exciting! I'll write soon and let you know how it's all going.

Marcella she say hello to you. Her exam has been yesterday. I don't speak to her since then, but I'm sure she did fine.

Me, Mom, Dad, and Thomas are passing next week a few days with my grandparents in São Paulo. As you know, we go usually there a year two times. I generally enjoy it, but I'm glad always when it's time to come home. And this year it'll be more harder than ever to be away!!!
Write again soon, and have fun!

Love,

Vera xxxxxxx

9 Soaps

1 Combine these words and partial words to form at least ten more family words.

mother	brother	nephew	second	-in-law	oldest
ex-	step	single	sister	child	older
father	son	cousin	half	parent	younger
daughter	aunt	husband	niece	first	youngest
uncle	grand	great-	wife	only	middle

2 Use as many of the words as you can to describe yourself.

3 Draw a diagram to illustrate some of your own family relationships.

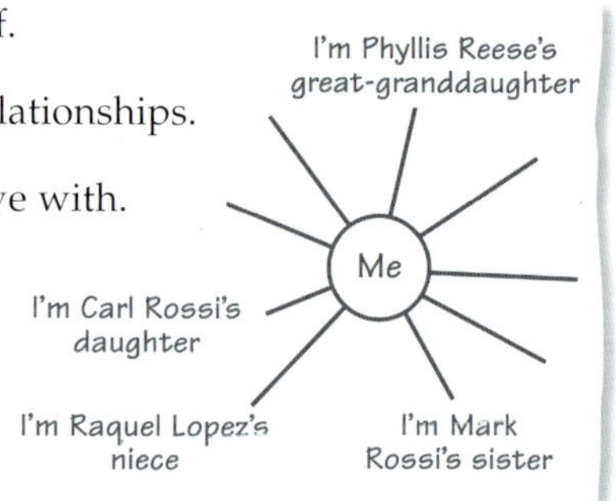

4
- Put (parentheses) around the family members you live with.
- Underline the relatives that live the closest to you.
- ~~Cross out~~ the relatives you see the least.
- Circle the relative you saw the most recently.
- Put an asterisk (*) next to the oldest relative and two asterisks (* *) next to the youngest.
- Check (✓) the relative you get along the best with.

5 Work with a partner. Compare your diagrams. Take turns talking about some of the relatives you have identified. What are they like? What kind of lives do they lead?

Pacific Heights

1 Read *Who's Who in Pacific Heights*. Match the characters in **BOLD** to their pictures in the family tree on page 73. Write the names of the characters above the pictures.

Who's Who in *Pacific Heights*

The series is set in Pacific Heights, California. **MAX DALTON** and **PHIL TURNER**, his son-in-law, run a large cosmetics corporation, DCC, which has been in the family for over 150 years. Max became the president of Dalton Cosmetics Corporation five years ago when his father died and soon afterward hired Phil as his junior partner. Together, they have transformed DCC from a small family business into a successful multinational company. They are in the process of negotiating a very important deal with a French distributor. The pressures of work are beginning to affect the health of 60-year-old Max.

Max's second wife, **SARAH**, is a dynamic woman in her early fifties who runs her own business. She has always been an attractive woman and is the only member of the family with red hair. She insists that it is natural.

Max has two daughters by his first marriage. There's a big age gap between them: **PENNY** is in her late thirties, and **LOU** is just 21. Lou has always wished that she were a boy (and looks like one with her long slim legs and short spiky hair). She's the baby of the family, and Penny tends to mother her. Lou has never gotten over the death of her mother, and she has a difficult relationship with Sarah. The two girls take after their mother with their blonde hair and blue eyes.

In addition to a daughter named Amy, Sarah has two sons from a previous marriage. Dave, 28, and his 27-year-old brother, **DANIEL**, look alike with their brown hair and dark brown eyes, but Daniel is more outgoing than his older brother. Dave works as a sales manager for a computer company and is married to Clare. Daniel works as a sound engineer for a recording company and recently got engaged to Annick, whose father runs the French distribution company that is about to sign an important contract with DCC. Daniel met the beautiful young Frenchwoman soon after his ex-girlfriend, Katy, left him for John, Daniel's best friend. At the time, Daniel was heartbroken.

Katy and Annick are both in their mid twenties, but apart from that, they are very different. Annick is classically beautiful with her long thick dark hair and fine Mediterranean features, while Katy is attractive in a less conventional way: She has long blonde hair with red and brown streaks, sparkling blue eyes, and a flirtatious smile. Annick works for her father's company; Katy works as a set designer for a movie company.

EDITH, Max's mother, holds the whole family together. At the age of 78, she is still very active, and everybody confides in her when they have a problem.

TV Gazette

Pacific Heights: Scenes 2–4

1 How much can you remember about the characters in *Pacific Heights*? Complete these sentences.

a) ________ is engaged to ________ .

b) ________ is married to ________ .

c) ________ broke ________ 's heart.

d) ________ is ________ 's business partner.

e) ________ has a difficult relationship with ________ .

f) ________ confides in ________ .

g) ________ recently broke up with ________ .

2 Read the background information about the characters in *Pacific Heights* Scenes 2–4 and fill in the blanks with the names of the characters. There may be more than one answer.

a) ________ is married to ________ .

b) ________ is ________ girlfriend.

c) ________ and ________ are identical twins.

d) ________'s wife is older than him.

e) ________ and ________ are involved with an animal rights group.

3 Think about your own friends and family. Can you complete any of the sentences in 1 and 2 with people you know personally? Tell your partner about them.

Who's Who in *Pacific Heights* Scenes 2–4

Phil Turner is an ambitious man in his early forties, and he is hoping to take over as Managing Director of DCC when Max Dalton retires. Max has a good working relationship with Phil but is secretly jealous of his son-in-law's youthful energy and athletic good looks.

Phil and Penny have three children who have all inherited their father's dark hair and their mother's blue eyes—a stunning combination. Ella and Mara are identical twins, and only their closest friends can tell them apart. Although they're only 16, they're very independent. Their 19-year-old brother, Charlie, is a champion surfer whose good looks have made him extremely popular with women. One of Ella and Mara's friends, Becky, is his present girlfriend, but what Becky doesn't know is that Charlie is also having an affair with Clare, Dave's wife. Clare, who is a therapist, has always liked younger men. Dave is 28, five years younger than Clare. As a sales manager for an international company, Dave often travels abroad on business.

At the age of 24, Amy is Sarah's youngest child. She lives with her boyfriend, 26-year-old Mark, and they have a three-year-old son, Jack. They are both part-time students, so they share the household chores and childcare. They also belong to an animal rights group whose latest campaign involves a demonstration against tests carried out on animals at DCC.

TV Gazette

Dave and Clare

Charlie

Ella and Mara

Listening **1** 35 Look at the drawings from the director's storyboard. Listen to scenes 2–4 and put the pictures in order.

A

Scene ____________
Mark and Amy talk about the demonstration.

B

Scene ____________
Ella and Mara talk to their parents, Phil and Penny.

C

Scene ____________
Conversation between Ella and Mara.

2 Answer these questions:

a) Where's Charlie's surfboard?
b) What's Ella and Mara's problem?
c) What's Becky's problem?
d) What's Amy's problem?

Vocabulary **1** Complete each of these expressions from Scenes 2–4 with the correct word.

a) What have you been up **to / around / down**?
b) It's **around / beneath / up** to you.
c) I see what you **mean / say / feel**.
d) I must have **made / done / said** a mistake.
e) I've told you once, and I'll tell you **instead / again / last**.
f) She'll get **under / over / up** it.
g) It serves him **wrong / left / right**.
h) Do you have any **belief / opinion / idea** what they do to them?

2 Match the expressions in 1 to these sentences.

1 I realize now that I was wrong.
2 I understand.
3 What have you been doing?
4 Do you know what happens?
5 You should have listened to me before.
6 It's your decision.
7 It's his own fault.
8 She'll recover.

3 Listen to Scenes 2–4 again and put the expressions in 1 in the order in which you hear them.

4 Complete the summary of Scenes 2–4.

Ella and Mara told their parents _________ , but Penny and Phil told them _________ .

Meanwhile, Charlie arranged to go and spend the weekend with Clare while Dave was away in Mexico. He told his parents _________ .

Mara told Ella _________ .

Amy said _________ . Mark told her _________ .

Pacific Heights: The Next Episode

1 Work in groups. Predict what will happen in the next episode of *Pacific Heights*, based on the following information:

WATCH THE NEXT EPISODE OF

Pacific Heights

and find out what happens when:

- Max catches up with Daniel.
- The animal rights demonstration turns to violence.
- Clare and Charlie try to have a secret weekend together and end up entertaining half the family.
- Will Ella and Mara still want to travel when a new guy arrives at school?
  Will Daniel go ahead with his wedding plans?
  Will the family find out that Amy is involved with the animal rights group?

IT'S ALL IN THE NEXT EPISODE OF *Pacific Heights*

TV Gazette

2 Write a similar TV preview to the one above for the episode *after* next.

3 Read what other groups have written and compare your predictions. Which version do you like the best?

Close-up

will for prediction

Language Reference p. 81

1 *2020 Vision*. In a recent report, the following predictions were made about British family life:

- In the year 2020, the divorce rate will be over 50%.
- In the year 2020, one in three people will be living alone.
- By the year 2020, the traditional nuclear family will have become a minority.

a) In your opinion, are these predictions negative or positive?
b) Are they valid predictions for your own country?
c) If these predictions come true, what will the consequences be?

LANGUAGE TOOLBOX

This time next year, …
The next time you see me, …
Sometime soon, …
By the time I'm (forty), …
In (five) years, …

2 What are the names of the underlined structures in the three predictions above?

3 Work with a partner. Match the three symbols on the time line to the three structures.

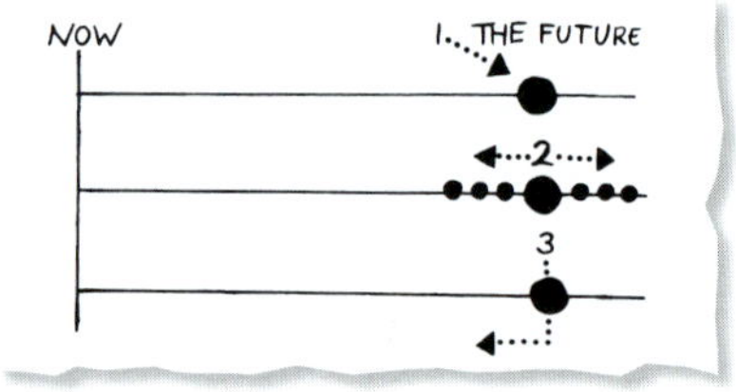

4 Talk to your partner about your own future.

will + continuous and _will_ + perfect

1 Tania O'Donnel is an art dealer. She lives in Laguna Beach, California. This is what she will be doing tomorrow.

Look at the times and the things Tania has to do and complete each of these sentences, using *will be (doing)* or *will have (done)*.

a) Six o'clock: She __________ (take) a shower.
b) Seven o'clock: She __________ (take) a shower, and she __________ (eat) breakfast.
c) Eight o'clock: She __________ (drive) to Los Angeles.
d) Nine thirty: She __________ (visit) the new de Kooning exhibit.
e) Eleven thirty: She __________ (leave) the de Kooning exhibit, and she __________ (talk) to Roland Hoff.
f) Twelve thirty: She __________ (finish) her meeting with Roland Hoff, and she __________ (have) lunch with Dani.
g) Two o'clock: She __________ (have) lunch, and she __________ (meet) her accountant.
h) Five thirty: She __________ (drive) back to Laguna Beach.

6 A.M.	shower
7 A.M.	breakfast
8 A.M.	drive to Los Angeles
9 A.M.	new de Kooning exhibit
10 A.M.	
11 A.M.	Roland Hoff (a new painter)
12 noon	lunch with Dani
1 P.M.	accountant
2 P.M.	
3 P.M.	
4 P.M.	
5 P.M.	drive back to Laguna Beach
6 P.M.	

2 Write similar sentences about what you will be doing tomorrow.

3 Write three predictions: one about yourself, one about your partner, and one about your country.

Language Reference: *will* for the future

will ('ll)/won't + verb

Will as a future form has several important uses.

1. For prediction
   In the year 2020, the divorce rate ***will be*** *over 50%.*
2. For promises and offers
   Don't worry, ***I'll help*** *you.*
3. For refusals
   It's no use asking. I ***won't tell*** *you anything.*
4. For requests
   Will *you* ***marry*** *me?*

You will find more information about future forms in Unit 7.

You'll be hearing from my lawyer.

will + continuous and perfect forms

1. Continuous
   will + be + -ing
   In the year 2020, one in three people ***will be living*** *alone.*
   This time next week, ***we'll be lying*** *on the beach in Cancún.*

   We can use this structure for an action around a time in the future. The action starts before and finishes after a specific point.

   For example, imagine today is Tuesday. Next Tuesday you're going on vacation: you're going to the beach. It's not important to know exactly when you'll go to the beach or exactly when you'll return to the hotel.

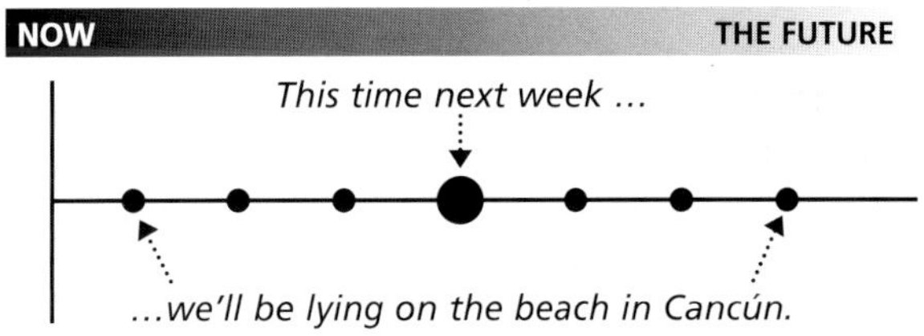

2. Perfect
   will + have + past participle
   By the year 2020, the traditional nuclear family ***will have become*** *a minority.*
   I'll have finished *the report by three, so we can meet after that.*

   We can use this structure to describe a future event from the point of view of a later time.

   For example, imagine you have to finish a report. You don't know exactly when you'll finish it, but you're sure it'll be before three o'clock.

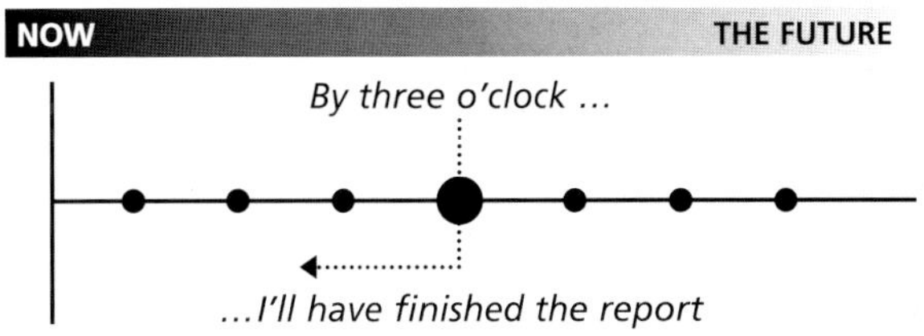

   We can use the preposition *by*, meaning *not later than*, with this structure.

10 *Time*

Time

The earth is about 4,700 million years old. If the time scale is reduced so that the earth is one year old, humans would have appeared at 8:35 P.M. on December 31.

1 Look at these three sayings about time:

捷 足 先 登 jié zú xiān dēng The one who is first to act achieves success. Chinese	**Время – лучший врач** Time is the best doctor. Russian	***Chili chonse chili ndi nthawi*** There is a time for everything. Chichewa language, Malawi

How many sayings about time can you think of in your own language? Choose three and translate them into English.

2 What do these English sayings mean to you? Are they similar to any in your own language? Which ones do you like best?

- Never put off until tomorrow what you can do today.
- Better late than never.
- There's no time like the present.
- Tomorrow never comes.
- Today is the tomorrow we worried about yesterday.
- Time heals all wounds.
- Time is money.
- Time flies when you're having fun.

Punctuality

Discuss the following in small groups:

a) How punctual are you? Do you usually arrive late, early, or on time? Think about some of these events:

- a first date
- an English lesson
- a job interview
- a wedding
- a movie
- a soccer game
- a rock concert
- a family dinner

b) What about your friends and relatives? Are you typical of people in your country?

Listening **1** Read the questionnaire below and check off your answers. Then compare with a partner.

QUESTIONNAIRE

1 You have to attend a meeting that is scheduled to start at nine o'clock. Do you arrive...

a) exactly on time? ☐
b) ten minutes early? ☐
c) up to ten minutes late? ☐

2 You've arranged to meet a friend in the shopping mall. How long do you wait if your friend is late?

a) Five minutes. ☐
b) Fifteen minutes. ☐
c) Half an hour or more. ☐

3 You're at home working on an important piece of work that has to be finished for tomorrow when a friend stops by unexpectedly. Do you...

a) invite the friend in and hope he/she won't stay too long? ☐
b) invite the friend in but tell him/her that you don't have much time to spare? ☐
c) tell the friend you're busy and you'll call him/her when you have more time? ☐

4 You have to do a job that's difficult or unpleasant. Do you...

a) accept that you have to do it and do it immediately so that you can forget about it? ☐
b) put it off to another day? ☐
c) leave it until the last minute because you need to feel the adrenaline rush produced by stress? ☐

5 In your opinion, a hardworking person works...

a) eight hours a day. ☐
b) eight to ten hours a day. ☐
c) twelve or more hours a day. ☐

Now, write one hundred times, "I must not waste my time."

2 36 Listen to the radio show with Roberta Wilson, a time-management consultant, and Paul Roesch, the interviewer, discussing the same questions. Take notes on what they say about each one. Do you agree with them?

3 Work with a partner. Write down at least three activities you think are a waste of time.

Pronunciation

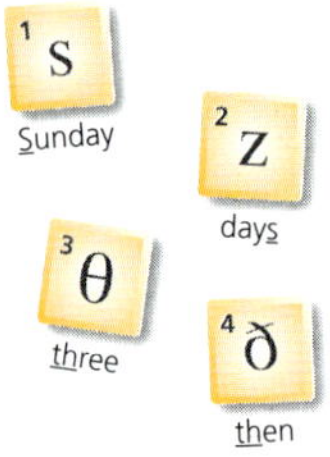

1 Work with a partner. Say the words in the box. Then match the underlined sounds to the phonetic symbols on the left.

thirty	there	month	second
Thursday	Tuesday	weather	Wednesday
Saturday	weeks	first	third
hours	weekends	that	these

For example:
/θ/ thirty

2 37 Listen and check.

Dates

1 Choose five dates that are important to you. Then dictate them to your partner. Say why you chose them.

2 38 Listen to Julie talking about dates that are important to her. Write down the dates as you hear them and take notes on why they are important to Julie. Compare with a partner.

Prepositions

1 Test your prepositions. Complete these sentences with *on*, *in*, or *at*.

a) My mother was born _____ the 1950s.
b) I work best _____ night.
c) We always have a big family meal _____ New Year's Eve.
d) I spend at least two weeks at the beach _____ the summer.
e) I start work every morning _____ 9 A.M.
f) I always try to get home from work _____ time to read my children a bedtime story.
g) I never take a nap _____ the afternoon.
h) I would like to have lived _____ the Middle Ages.
i) My birthday is _____ March. In fact, it's _____ March 6.
j) I started learning English _____ 1995.
k) Nothing special happens in my family _____ Christmastime.
l) My boss never starts meetings _____ time. She's usually at least ten minutes late.
m) I usually get depressed _____ Monday mornings.
n) I spend a lot of time with my friends _____ the weekends.
o) I'm busy _____ the moment.

2 Are the sentences in 1 true or false for you? Turn them into questions and ask your partner. Find out as much as you can.

For example:

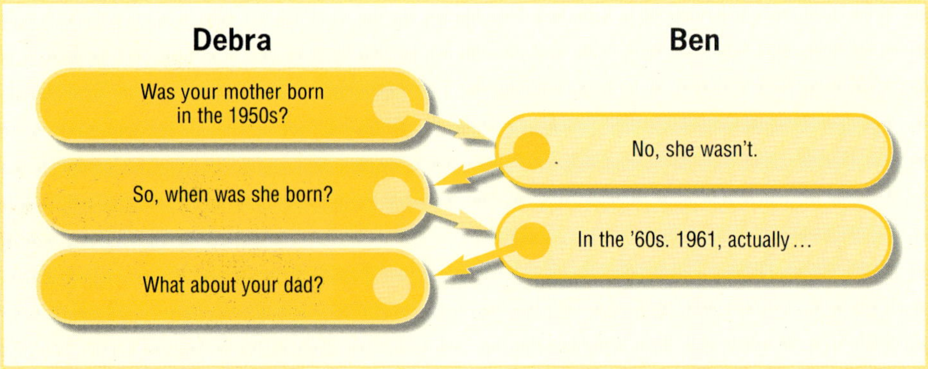

Time expressions

1 Look at the monthly calendar and follow the instructions.

DECEMBER

M	T	W	T	F	S	S
–	–	1	2	3	4	5
6	7	8	9	10	11	12
13	14	15 Today	16	17	18	19
20	21	22	23	24	25	26
27	28	29	30	31	–	–

a) ~~Cross out:~~

Christmas Day
New Year's Eve
Christmas Eve

b) Imagine today is the 15th.

Underline:	Circle:	Put in (parentheses):
the day before yesterday	tomorrow	in four days
the weekend before last	this Saturday	in two weeks
the day after tomorrow	a week from today	all last week
next Monday	a week from tomorrow	two weeks ago

Which dates are still free?

2 Use expressions in 1b to tell your partner about some of the things you've done recently and your future plans.

For example:
The weekend before last, I went walking in the mountains with some friends.

3 Use the words in the box to describe the times shown.

about	just before	just past	just after	almost	around	-ish

4 Work with a partner. Use the expressions in 3 to tell your partner about at least six things you have done so far today and what time you did each of them.

Things to Do...

Look at the "things to do" lists below.

- Are you the kind of person who makes lists?
- Are these the kinds of lists you make?
- How many "things to do" do you have on your list now?

1 Read the article on page 87 and match the four people mentioned to their lists.

TIME-SAVING TIPS: LISTS

Making lists is relaxing. It makes you feel important—all those things to do. It dictates the shape of the immediate future, it calms you down (it's O.K., it's on a list somewhere), and it makes you feel good when you cross something off (list-making is standard practice in therapy for depression). It might even help you to get things done, too.

There are two types of people when it comes to making lists. Type A makes orderly lists, prioritizes, and calmly sets to work on them. Type B waits until panic sets in, grabs the nearest envelope and scribbles all over it, sighs with relief, and promptly loses it.

The more you have to do, the more you need a list, and few people with high-powered jobs get by without them.

Barbara Vanilli, chief executive of a large chain of supermarkets, says, "Before I go to bed, I have to write down everything that's going to stop me from sleeping. I feel I won't forget anything I've written down, so my lists are a great comfort."

Women always think they're better at lists than men. Men tend to have Tasks that they organize into Action Plans, whereas women just have lists of Things to Do. Jacqueline Maddocks, head of Maddocks Publishers, says, "My male co-workers make lists only for work, whereas I have to make lists for work and for home too. It's essential to write things down. If you're constantly thinking, 'I must remember this,' it blocks your mind."

James Oliver, a psychologist, has created his own "time-management matrix." He writes a list of things to do and then organizes the items into categories: things that have to be done right away, other things that it would be good to do today, things that are important but don't have to be done immediately, and things that are less urgent but that he doesn't want to forget. "Using categories to organize the world is the way the human mind works," he says. "After that, you should put things into hierarchies of importance." But he warns against the danger of Excessive List Syndrome. "If people get obsessed with making lists, it doesn't work. They have too many categories and lose their capacity to prioritize."

It's all a question of what works best for you, whether it's a neat notebook, a forest of scraps of paper, or the back of your hand. Having tried all these, student Kate Rollins relies on a computerized list, that she prints out each morning and scribbles on during the day. "My electronic organizer has changed my life," she says. "Up to now, I've always relied on my good memory, but now that I'm working and studying, I just have too much to keep in my head."

So what are you waiting for? No, you're not too busy to make today the first day of your upgraded time-managed life. In fact, there's no better time than the present to get an upper hand on time and begin to take increased control of your work and life. So, get out your pencil and paper and make a list. ■

(*Weekend Telegraph*, Saturday, December 13, 1997.)

2 Talk about the article from memory, using these prompts:

- good things about making lists
- type A / type B
- before bed
- women / men
- matrix
- categories
- excessive list syndrome
- electronic organizer
- what are you waiting for?

Combinations

1 Complete as many of these sentences as you can from memory to make combinations. Then look back at the article to check.

a) What do you plan to do in the ________ future? (line 5)

b) Is it ________ practice to wear dressy clothes in your company or school? (lines 8-9)

c) Do you know many people with ________ jobs? (line 21)

d) Is Bill Gates still ________ executive of Microsoft? (line 22)

e) Do you have a / an ________ organizer? (line 68)

2 Work with a partner. Ask each other the questions from 1.

3 Which of these words can form combinations with the underlined nouns from 1? Check them in your dictionary and write some new sentences.

low-paid	distant	senior	personal	normal

List any more combinations related to work or time that you know.

Close-up

must* and *should

1 Look at James Oliver's time-management matrix and match the following sentence beginnings to the squares on the matrix.

a) I *have to* do it today,…
b) I *should* do it today,…
c) I *have to* do it soon,…
d) I *should* do it soon,…

	URGENT	NOT URGENT
IMPORTANT	I	II
NOT IMPORTANT	III	IV

2 Complete each of the sentences in 1 with an appropriate ending.

1 …but if I run out of time, I can leave it until first thing tomorrow.
2 …so I'll see if I have time next week.
3 …or there'll be trouble tomorrow.
4 …so I'll do it next week.

3 Write your own "things to do" list according to the matrix above. Use it to talk to your partner about your priorities for today/this week/this month.

Language Reference p. 90

4 Work with a partner. Match the following headings to the four sets of verbs and phrases in the chart below: permission; no obligation; obligation; prohibition.

A ________ have to must is/are supposed to	**C** ________ don't have to
B ________ can't isn't/aren't allowed to isn't/aren't supposed to	**D** ________ can is/are allowed to

5 Think about the place where you work or study. Are there many rules and regulations? What are they?

Office Cultures

1 Look at the people in their different workplaces.

- Are the clothes the people are wearing formal or casual?
- How do they compare to workplaces you know?
- What kinds of companies do you think they are? Why?

2 39 Listen to the people in the pictures talking about their companies. Did you guess correctly?

3 Listen again and correct the information below if necessary.

OFFICE 1
- Working hours are flexible.
- Women aren't allowed to wear slacks.
- You can smoke in the cafeteria.
- You're allowed to eat lunch at your desk.

OFFICE 2
- You can't smoke in the office unless you're working late.
- You have to go to the café downstairs if you want something to eat.
- You aren't supposed to have a break every two hours.
- You can wear jeans.

OFFICE 3
- You don't have to dress up.
- You're supposed to start work at eight o'clock.
- You can't smoke in the building.
- If you want coffee, you have to go to the cafeteria next door.

4 Would you like to work in any of these offices?

Language Reference: Obligation, prohibition, and permission

Must, should, and *can* are *modal auxiliaries*. All modals have certain special characteristics; for example:

1 They are used to modify the meaning of another verb.
2 They take the simple form of the verb.
*That's a terrible cough. You **should** see the doctor.*
3 They do not add an *s* in the third person.
*He's putting on a lot of weight. He **should** go on a diet.*
4 You cannot use them with another auxiliary—even in questions and negatives.
***Can** you go? You **shouldn't** do that.*

Have to is similar to a modal auxiliary in its meaning but not in its form.

1 It includes *to*.
*I **have to** go to the dentist.*
2 It takes *s* in the third person in the simple present.
*She's a diabetic, so she **has to** take insulin.*
3 Questions and negatives are formed with *do* in the simple present and *did* in the simple past.
*This is a very informal office. You **don't have to** wear a tie.*

Modals are used to express a great range of meanings. The differences between them are sometimes subtle.

must and *have to*

The difference between *must* and *have to* is not great.

Must is used to talk about personal obligations. It is usually used only in writing and in formal speech.
*I'm gaining weight. I **must** go on a diet.*
*I **must** call my mother. I haven't seen her in ages.*

We usually use *have to* instead of *must* to express obligation.
*Everybody **has to** pay taxes.*
*I **have to** take an English mid-term next week.*

mustn't and *don't have to*

Mustn't and *don't have to* are very different from each other.

Mustn't is used for prohibition. It is usually used only in writing and in formal speech. We usually use *can't* instead of *mustn't*. (See below.)
*You **mustn't** smoke in a gas station.*
*You **mustn't** tell anyone the password.*

When you use *don't have to,* it means there is no obligation, negative or positive.
*Teachers **don't have to** wear ties.*
*You **don't have to** leave yet. There's an all-night bus.*

can/can't

Can't is usually used instead of *mustn't*.
*You **can't** smoke in a gas station.*

Can tells you that an action is possible and/or permitted.
*You **can** leave now if you want to.*

must and *should*

Must is a simple, strong obligation. *Should* is weaker: a less important obligation, or one that is not respected.

*I **should** go to see the doctor, but I have too many other things I have to do.*
*I **should** study for the test, but I'm going out with some friends instead.*

It can also be used for recommendations.
*You **should** stop smoking. You're killing yourself.*

Other expressions

There are many other expressions that are related to permission and obligation.

Be allowed to is similar to *can*.
*You **are allowed** to go home early on Friday if we've finished all our work.*

Supposed to is sometimes similar to *should*. It can imply that people do not follow the rules all the time.
*I'm **supposed to** wear a suit to work, but I sometimes wear jeans and a T-shirt.*

To Whom It May Concern

1 Choose two correct ways to start a business letter from Column A.

A	B
Dear Mr. Peter,	Lots of love,
Dear Mr. Peter Maggs,	Yours,
Dear Mr. Maggs,	Best wishes,
Dear Mr. or Mrs.,	Your friend,
Dear Sir or Madam,	Sincerely,

Match the ways of starting a business letter with appropriate endings from Column B.

Do you know any other ways of starting or ending business letters?

2 Here are some examples of phrases often used in business letters. Complete the sentences with the words in the box.

apply	unfortunately	hearing	response	complain
May 16	confirm	enclose	grateful	pleased

a) Thank you for your letter dated ___________ , which I received this morning.

b) I would be ___________ if you could send me some information about summer courses at your school.

c) I ___________ my résumé for your attention.

d) ___________ , I am not available on the date you suggest in your letter.

e) I would be ___________ to come for an interview at any time convenient to you.

f) I am writing to ___________ about the damage caused by your company when they delivered a sofa to my home last week.

g) We look forward to ___________ from you as soon as possible.

h) We would be grateful if you could ___________ your reservation in writing.

i) I am writing in ___________ to your advertisement in *The Washington Post*.

j) I would like to ___________ for the position of IT assistant in your school.

3 Match each of the sentences in 2 to one of the functions below. There are two sentences for function c.

a) asking for information
b) applying for a job
c) beginning a letter
d) closing a letter
e) giving bad news
f) giving good news
g) complaining
h) saying that you are sending something with the letter
i) asking for confirmation

4 Anthony Clifford is interested in applying for the position of flight attendant. Read his letter and decide whether you think he would be considered a suitable candidate. Why/Why not?

WORLDWIDE *AIRLINES*

FLIGHT ATTENDANTS

Worldwide Airlines is currently seeking friendly, service-oriented people who take pride in their performance and appearance.
Applicants must be over 20 years of age and have at least two years of work experience.

- Physical requirements:
  able to lift, push, and pull heavy articles as required.
  Minimum height 5′4″, maximum height 6′4″.
- Languages: able to read, write, speak, and understand English. Other languages an advantage.

Interested candidates can write to the following address for an application form and additional information:
Worldwide Airlines Inc.,
PO Box 2983, Chicago, IL 60601 USA.

```
                              1566b 49th East Street
                              Santa Barbara, CA
Worldwide Airlines Inc.
PO Box 2983
Chicago, IL
USA                           February 5, 2002

Dear Mr. or Mrs.,

Application for the position of flight attendant

I saw your advertisement in the Los Angeles Times
and I want to be a flight attendant.
I am 21 years old, and I have just graduated from
college. I have put my résumé with this letter so
that you can see what I've done, and I'd love to
come for an interview anytime you like.
How about sending me an application form and some
more information about the job?
I can't wait to hear from you!

Lots of love,

Tony
```

5 Improve Anthony's letter by using some of the phrases in 1 and 2 above.

6 Look at a corrected version of the letter on page 141 and compare it to your own version.

11 *Journey*

1 Read this excerpt from a book called *The Beach,* by Alex Garland. Why did the author decide to travel?

split up (line 1): end a relationship; break up
show up (line 5): arrive
lose (your) head (line 7): go crazy
emotionally blackmail (line 8): use emotions to manipulate someone
take precedence over (line 13): become more important than

A few years ago I was going through the process of splitting up with my first serious girlfriend. She went away to Greece for the summer, and when she came back, she'd had a holiday romance with some Belgian guy. As if that wasn't enough, it seemed that the guy in question was going to show up in London some time over the next few weeks. After three hellish days and nights, I realised that I was dangerously close to losing my head. I biked over to my dad's flat and emotionally blackmailed him into lending me enough cash to leave the country.

On that trip I learnt something very important. Escape through travel works. Almost from the moment I boarded my flight, life in England became meaningless. Seat-belt signs lit up, problems switched off. Broken armrests took precedence over broken hearts. By the time the plane was airborne, I'd forgotten England even existed.

The Beach

The Beach is the first novel by British author Alex Garland.

It was made into a movie starring Leonardo DiCaprio.

2 Work with a partner. Have you ever traveled for any of these reasons? Tell your partner.

- to escape boredom
- to try to mend a broken heart
- to broaden your experience of the world
- to learn languages
- to get a tan
- to live out your dreams
- to take a break from your career
- to visit historical sites or travel along a historical route
- to raise money for charity

Can you think of any other reasons to travel?

3 Where have members of your class been? Ask other students in the class and make a list of countries, regions, and famous cities. Try to find a place for every letter of the alphabet. You can include regions and cities in your own country.

4 Describe where five of the places in your list are, using the expressions below. Say where the place you live is. Find as many ways to describe it as you can.

It's in	the north of / southwest the northern / southwestern part of	(Florida). (Brazil).
It's	on the coast in the mountains in (Lombardy)	to the north of (Los Angeles). not far from (Denver). between (Milan) and (Brescia).

Conrad's Around-the-World Trip

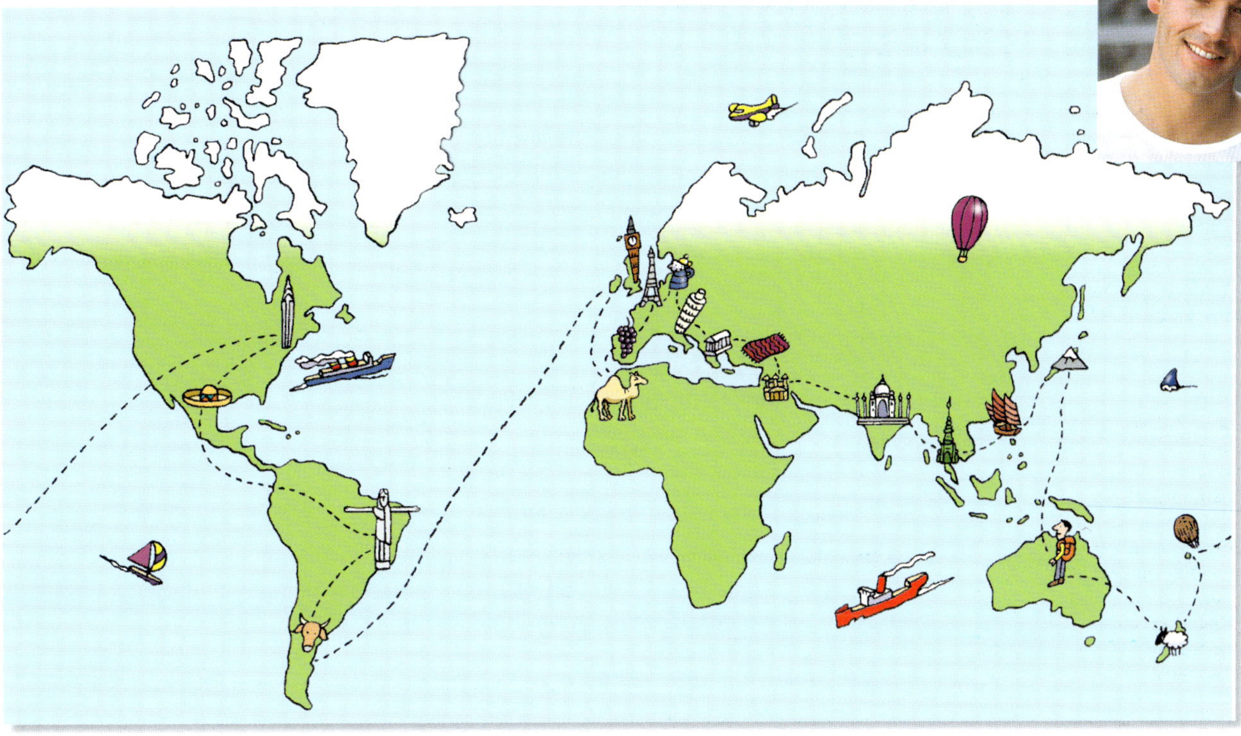

1 Look at the pictures taken by Conrad on his around-the-world trip. Could any of them have been taken in your country? Where?

2 40 Listen to Conrad showing his vacation pictures to a friend. He tries to get the friend to guess where the places are. Which two pictures do they talk about?

3 Where do you think the remaining four pictures were taken? Discuss with your partner. Write down any places where a picture definitely couldn't have been taken.

Check on page 140.

1

2

3

4

5

6

Close-up

Speculating and deducing

1 Listen to the conversation between Conrad and his friend again. Complete these sentences with the guesses the friend makes:

First picture	Second picture
It must be _________ .	It must be _________ .
I guess it could be _________ .	It can't be _________ .
It's probably _________ .	Maybe it's _________ .

2 Put the five expressions in 1 into three categories.

a) I'm absolutely sure
b) I'm almost sure
c) I'm not really sure

3 Add these expressions to the three categories in 2:

It might be... It may be... Maybe it's...

4 Discuss these questions with your partner:

a) Which of the expressions in 1 and 3 contain a *modal auxiliary*?
b) Look at the example below and complete the sentences, using one of the words in the box for each blank. Discuss your choices with a partner.

must	mustn't	can	can't

There's someone at the door.
It __________ be Carmen; she's working late tonight.
It __________ be John: he always comes home around this time.

Language Reference p. 94

5 Move the second sentence of each item (a–h) to the end of a different first sentence so that each item makes sense. Don't change any of the words.

a) They can't be broke. You must be kidding.
b) You've been driving all day. You must be delighted.
c) That hotel must be doing well. There's never anybody in it.
d) I must be getting old. I've heard so much about you.
e) A new car on my salary?! They go skiing every year.
f) The new restaurant can't be very good. It always has the "No Vacancies" sign up.
g) You must be Sarah's husband. I can't remember anything about last night.
h) Congratulations on your engagement. You must be absolutely exhausted.

Language Reference: Speculating and deducing

There are many ways to say how certain or uncertain we are about something. Here are some of them:

Modal auxiliary + infinitive

*It **must be**...*
*It **may be**... / It **could be**... / It **might be**...*
*It **may not be**... / It **might not be**...*
*It **can't be**...*

Other phrases

*It's **definitely**...*
*It's **probably**...*
***I think** it's...*
***Maybe** it's... / **Perhaps** it's...*
***I don't think** it's...*
*It **probably isn't**...*
*It **definitely isn't**...*

Notes:
In this context, the opposite of *must* is *can't*.
*The keys **can't be** in my coat, because I wasn't wearing it. They **must be** in your bag.*
It must be means "I'm sure it is"; *it can't be* means "I'm sure it isn't."

There is no important difference between *may, could,* and *might* in this context.

Wish You Were Here

1 These are three postcards Conrad wrote from places in the pictures on page 93. Complete them with the words below. Use each word only once.

fascinating	sandy	peaks	jams	breathtaking	overlooking	touristy
spicy	friendly	gorgeous	palm	clear	breaking	paradise

Dear Brad,
This is a (1) ________ city, but you can't imagine the traffic (2) ________ and the noise. I'll never complain about the traffic at home again—or the food! The food's really (3) ________ here. It's a really (4) ________ place, but the people are very (5) ________ . I met a (6) ________ Australian woman who invited me to Sydney.
Conrad

Brad Goodwin
14 South Street
Boston, MA
02215
USA

Dear Paul,
I'm writing to you from my hotel (7) ________ the lake. The view is (8) ________ . In the distance, I can see snowy mountain (9) ________, and down by the hotel pool, I can see a free lunch buffet—I have to go!
Conrad

Paul Kelly
417 Walnut Ave.
Los Angeles, CA
90069
USA

2 Which places do you think he sent the postcards from?

3 Write postcards from two of the other places Conrad visited.

Dear John,
Yes, I'm in (10) ________ !
(11) ________ beaches stretch as far as the eye can see, and the water is (12) ________ and warm. The only sound is the wind in the (13) ________ trees and the waves (14) ________ on the shore. I'm never coming home.
Conrad

John Pizzigallo
40 Ryan Drive
Boston, MA
02215
USA

Anecdote

4 41 We asked the three people in the picture to imagine they could spend a dream weekend anywhere in the world. Listen to their answers to the following questions. Each time there is a pause, guess where the person would like to go.

- ☐ Who would your ideal companion be?
- ☐ How would you get around?
- ☐ What would you wear?
- ☐ What would you buy?
- ☐ What would you eat and drink?
- ☐ What essential items would you take with you?
- ☐ Who would you most like to meet there?
- ☐ What sights would you want to see?
- ☐ Who would you send a postcard to?
- ☐ What would spoil your perfect weekend?

Liz, Rick, and Cristina

5 Imagine your own dream weekend. You are going to tell a partner about it. Choose from the list in 4 the things you want to talk about. Think about what you will say and the language you will need.

6 Tell your partner about your dream weekend. Would you make good traveling companions?

Close-up

***would* for unreal situations**

1 Look at these four questions. Underline the auxiliaries.

a) What did you do?
b) What are you doing?
c) What will you do?
d) What would you do?

2 Add the following endings to the four questions in 1.

...when you finish college
...yesterday
...if you won the lottery
...right now

Language Reference p. 96

3 Which sentences refer to real situations?

4 Imagine you opened the door of the classroom and found you were in...

- Siberia
- Hawaii
- Scotland
- the Kalahari desert
- Cairo
- the Amazon rainforest

Work with a partner. Choose one place and discuss what it would be like.

- What would it look like? What sounds and smells would there be? What would the buildings be like?
- What would the weather be like?
- What would the people look like? What would they be wearing?
- What would you eat and drink?
- What would you be able to do? What wouldn't you be able to do?
- Would you have a good time?

Language Reference: *would* for unreal conditionals

would (not) + infinitive

The contracted forms are *'d* and *wouldn't*.
*I'**d wear** a hat on the beach.*
*I **wouldn't go** to the Sahara without sunblock.*
***Would** you **travel** alone to Thailand, or **would** you **go** with friends?*

Would is the past tense of *will*, but this does not really explain how you use it.

Imaginary or improbable situations

One of its main uses is to show that we are talking or writing about a situation that is *imaginary* or *improbable*. For example, imagine you opened the door of the classroom and found yourself in Iceland:

- *It **would** be cold.*
- *Everybody **would** be wearing warm clothes.*
- *You'**d** be able to visit hot springs.*
- *Most people **would** speak English well.*

Unreal conditionals

Would is often found in *unreal conditional sentences.*
*If I had the money, I'**d buy** a new car.*

You will find more about conditional sentences in Units 13, 14, and 15.

Note: You will find more information on *would* for past habits in Unit 5.

Coast to Coast

1 Read this account of Nick Campbell's motorcycle trip across the U.S. What problems did he have?

NICK CAMPBELL sat at the side of the road and wondered what to do next. He looked at the secondhand Harley Davidson he'd bought from a backstreet garage back home in Miami at the beginning of his trip six weeks before.

For years he had dreamed of crossing the United States from east to west by motorcycle and he'd finally decided that it was now or never. He'd given up his job, sold his car, and set off for the trip of his dreams. He'd been lucky, or so he thought, to find this old Harley Davidson and had bought it for a very reasonable price—it had cost him just $600. But three miles from Atlanta, he had run out of luck. The motorcycle had broken down.

He pushed the bike into town and found a garage. The young mechanic told him to leave the bike overnight and come back the next day. The following morning, to his surprise, the man asked if the bike was for sale. "No way," he replied. He paid his bill and hit the road.

When he got to Kansas, the old machine ran out of steam again. This time Nick thought about selling it and buying something more reliable, but he decided to keep going. When the bike was working well, he loved it.

However, in Denver, Colorado, the bike broke down yet again, so he decided to take it to a garage and put it up for sale. The mechanic told him to come back in the morning.

The next day, to his amazement, the man offered him $2,000. Realizing the man must be a little crazy, but clearly not short on cash, Nick asked for $3,000. The man agreed, and they signed the papers. Then the mechanic started laughing. In fact, it was several minutes before he could speak, and when he could he said, "That's the worst deal you'll ever make, boy." He…

(Adapted from *The Independent on Sunday*, February 22, 1998)

2 Discuss the following in small groups.

a) How much did Nick pay for the bike?
b) How much did he sell it for?
c) How much money did he make from the sale?
d) Guess why the mechanic said, "That's the worst deal you'll ever make, boy."

3 Now read the real ending to the story on page 142. Do you think the mechanic was fair? How do you think Nick felt?

Anecdote

4 Think back to a trip you have taken. You are going to tell a partner about it. Choose from the list the things you want to talk about. Think about what you will say and what language you will need.

- ☐ Where was the trip from, and where was it to?
- ☐ What form of transportation did you use?
- ☐ Who did you go with?
- ☐ How much time did you spend preparing for it?
- ☐ What did you take with you?
- ☐ What was the weather like?
- ☐ How long did it take you?
- ☐ How many times did you stop along the way? What for?
- ☐ Did anything unusual or unexpected happen?
- ☐ Would you go on the same trip again? Why/Why not?

5 Tell your partner about the trip. Give as much detail as possible.

Close-up

Past perfect

1 Where was Nick Campbell at the beginning of the story?

2 What happened in Miami, Atlanta, Kansas, and Denver?

3 Discuss the following with a partner:

a) Which events are described using:
- the past perfect
- the simple past.

b) How is the past perfect formed?

c) Which of these three explanations best describes how we use the past perfect?
- to look back at a past event
- to look back at a past event from another point in the past
- to look back at a past event from another, more recent, point in the past.

4 Complete each of the following sentences, using the past perfect:

a) Michael was looking forward to the trip to Moscow because…
b) He was late leaving his house because…
c) That morning the traffic was very slow from his house to the airport because…
d) At check-in he had to accept an aisle seat because…
e) He bought three new ties in the duty-free shop because…
f) The departure was delayed because…
g) The connecting flight in Copenhagen was canceled because…

5 Work with a partner. Write a similar set of sentences. Make sure each sentence uses the past perfect.

For example:
Vicky was looking forward to her dinner with Roy because…

Language Reference: Past perfect

We can use the past perfect to show clearly that one past event happened before another past event.

For example:
(1) *I lent her $5.* (2) *She forgot about it.*
➜ *She forgot that I **had lent** her $5.*

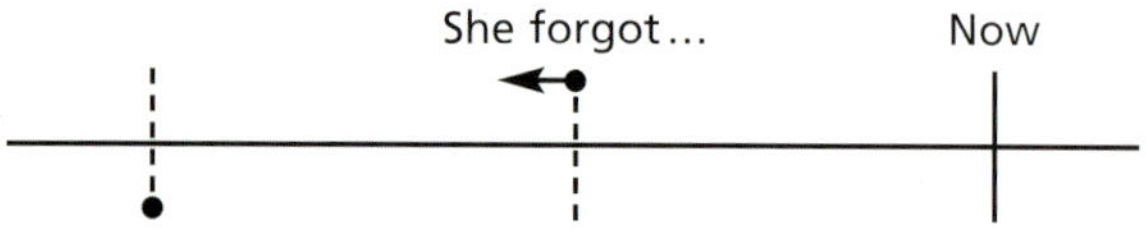

The contracted forms *I'd, he'd,* etc., and *hadn't* are used in speech and informal writing. The contraction of *had* is the same as the contraction of *would ('d)*, but the context always makes it clear which one is intended.

Conjunctions

Conjunctions such as *after, when, by the time,* and *because* are often used to combine a simple past clause with a past perfect one.

*The movie **had started when** I arrived.*
By the time the plane was airborne, ***I'd forgotten*** England even existed.
*He had a flat **because** he **hadn't checked** his tires.*
***After** we'**d signed** the contract, we opened a bottle of champagne.*

Tell Us a Story

1 Read this true story and explain the significance of the following words and phrases:

a) microwave b) safety lock c) Swiss army knife d) Indian Ocean.

A photographer named John was flying first class from London to Nairobi in Kenya when one of the co-pilots came out of the cockpit to make some coffee in the microwave. He couldn't get the machine to work, so he asked his fellow pilot to help him. As the other pilot left the cockpit, he let the heavy metal door close behind him. The pilot started an urgent, whispered discussion with his colleague. The two pilots had locked themselves out of their cockpit and, as they told the photographer (who promised not to tell the other passengers), the door was fitted with a safety lock. This meant that not even the pilots could open it from outside the cockpit. John remembered that he had put his Swiss army knife in his hand luggage. However, he couldn't remember where he had put his hand luggage and spent five minutes opening and closing overhead lockers until he found it. John and the pilots attacked the door with the knife, the lock started to come loose, and when they broke into the cockpit, the plane was cruising eastward over the Indian Ocean.

(Adapted from *Focus*, January 1999)

2 Work in teams. Add adverbs from the three boxes below to the story. Add as many as you can.

A adverbs of attitude
unbelievably naturally unfortunately sadly fortunately curiously

B adverbs of manner
carelessly unexpectedly

C adverbs of time
immediately a few months ago gradually eventually
after a while finally several weeks later in the end

3 Discuss the following with your partner.

a) Do you think pilots often make this kind of mistake?
b) What do you think is the safest way to travel?
c) Do you prefer to travel by air, by road, by rail, or by sea? Why?

4 Work in groups and write a story.

a) Choose one of the story "skeletons" on the right or invent one of your own.
b) Discuss each sentence and add as many details as you can think of.

For example:
Who were the people? What were they like? Where did they go on vacation?

c) Write the story and include the following:
- at least two adverbs of *attitude* from box A
- at least one adverb of *manner* from box B
- at least three adverbs of *time* from box C
- at least three *past perfect* sentences from box D below.

D past perfect sentences
They hadn't gone far when the car broke down.
She had never met anybody like him before.
By the time the police arrived, everybody had calmed down.
It was the most breathtaking view they had ever seen.
He had never felt like this before.
When they looked behind them, they saw the damage they had done.

STORY SKELETON 1
A man went abroad on vacation.
He met a woman and they fell in love.
He asked her to marry him.
The man went home.

STORY SKELETON 2
Three friends went on vacation in a car.
They camped.
Things went wrong.
They got home safely.

5 Read one another's stories and vote for the best one.

12 Basics

1 Work with a partner. Read through the statements below and guess whether each one is true or false for your partner.

Your partner:

- has eaten at a restaurant in the last week.
- follows a healthy diet.
- drinks a lot of coffee.
- always has wine with meals.
- is a good cook.
- eats a big breakfast.
- often eats fast food.
- usually eats lunch alone.

2 Ask your partner questions to find out whether you were correct. How many did you guess right? Did you find out anything surprising?

First Date

1 What kinds of things can go wrong on a first date?

2 42 Listen to the first part of the conversation. How do you think the two people feel?

3 43 Listen to the next part of the conversation and find out what went wrong.

4 Listen to the whole conversation again and complete each sentence with an appropriate quantifier.

a) Would you like ________ wine?
b) Two glasses of red wine, please, and could we have ________ crackers, too?
c) I didn't know you were a vegetarian. I don't think there are ________ vegetarian dishes on the menu.
d) Yes, there are. Look, there are ________ of things.
e) And could we have ________ bread and water, please?
f) Oh no, did it get on your skirt?
Just ________ . It's O.K.
g) Excuse me, waiter! Can you bring more napkins? I spilled ________ wine.
h) It's O.K., honestly. Hardly ________ of it got on my skirt. Just a drop.

Close-up

Quantity

1 Put the quantifiers from 4 on page 100 into these three categories:

countable nouns	noncountable	both countable and noncountable
a few	a little	some

2 Now add these quantifiers to the categories in 1.

a lot of   not much   several   very few   not many   a couple of   very little

3 In each of the following sentences, there are two words that are possible and one that isn't. ~~Cross out~~ the incorrect word in each sentence.

a) There wasn't **much/~~some~~/any** salt in her soup.
b) There was **some/a piece of/a few** ham in her vegetarian salad.
c) **A few/Several/A little** of his French fries were burned.
d) There were **hardly any/little/not many** desserts they liked on the menu.
e) There were only **a couple of/a little/a few** flavors of ice cream to choose from.
f) There were **no/very few/any** taxis outside when they left the restaurant.
g) He had never had **some/any/so many** problems in this restaurant before.
h) They had **anything/hardly anything/nothing** in common.

Countable and noncountable nouns

1 Test your knowledge of countable and noncountable nouns. Classify these words:

car   cell phone   computer   job   meat   love   travel   pasta   music   refrigerator
passport   washing machine   money   humor   rice   tobacco   oxygen

2 Choose words from 1 to complete the sentences below. Compare with a partner.

I could live without...   I couldn't live without...
I could live without a...   I couldn't live without a...

3 Complete these grammar rules and give examples.

a) You can use numbers (one, two, three, etc.) only with ________ nouns.
b) ________ nouns have a singular and a plural form.
c) ________ nouns only have one form (usually—but not always—singular).

4 Decide whether the following nouns are countable, noncountable, or both (countable / noncountable). There are three of each type.

bread   soda   food   glass   sandwich   lamb   pea   oyster   salt

5 Complete these sentences with three of the countable/noncountable nouns from 4. Use each noun twice, once as countable and once as noncountable.

a) The ________ are in the cupboard over the sink.
b) ________ is popular all over the world.
c) In the spring, there are ________ in all the fields around my uncle's farm.
d) Would you like another piece of ________ ?
e) I'm thirsty—I think I'll have a ________ .
f) ________ is one of the hardest materials there is.

6 Is each of the following nouns countable or noncountable?

people   news   jeans   scissors

Language Reference p. 102

7 Choose the correct words, plural or singular, in these sentences.

a) I believe that most people **is/are** basically good.
b) The news **was/were** on when I got home.
c) **Those/That** jeans really **look/looks** good on you.
d) If you're looking for the scissors, **they're/it's** in the kitchen.

Language Reference: Countable and noncountable nouns

Nouns are *countable* (C), *noncountable* (N), or both (C/N).

Countable nouns

Countable nouns have a singular and a plural form, and you can use numbers with them.

one idea → two ideas
one table → two tables
one man → two men

You can use *definite* and *indefinite* articles with them: ***the** idea, **the** ideas, **an** idea.*

Noncountable nouns

Noncountable nouns have only one form. Most of the time, this is singular.

***Knowledge is** power.* (Popular saying)
***Beauty is** truth.* (John Keats)
*When **hunger knocks** at the door, **love flies** out the window.* (Proverb)
***Food comes** first—morals later.* (Bertolt Brecht)

You cannot use noncountable nouns with numbers, and you can rarely use them with the indefinite article.

A few noncountable nouns only have a plural form.
*These **clothes are** too small for me.*
*My **pants need** to be ironed.*
*My **jeans are** ripped.*
Other plural noncountable nouns include *shorts, sunglasses,* and *scissors.*

Nouns that are both countable and noncountable

Many nouns have more than one meaning. They can be countable with one meaning and noncountable with another.
***Glass** is a useful material.* (N) (glass as a material)
*Can I have **a clean glass**?* (C) (an individual object)

Partitives

Partitives are ways of counting noncountable nouns.
***an item of** clothing*
***a piece of** information*
***a carton of** milk*
Sometimes the partitive can be left out.
*Can I have **a coffee**?* (= a cup of coffee)
*Would you like **a soda**?* (= a glass, can, or bottle of soda)

Oddities

There are some oddities. Two of the most important are:
1 people (C) – singular form/grammatically plural:
People are strange.
2 news (N) – plural form/grammatically singular:
*Hurry up; **the news is** on.*

Quantifiers

Quantifiers are ways of talking about quantity other than by using exact numbers. You can use some with countable nouns, some with noncountable nouns, and some with both.

Quantifiers for countable nouns include *a few* and *many:*
a few tables
How many men?

Quantifiers for noncountable nouns include *a little* and *much.*
***A little learning** is a dang'rous thing.* (Alexander Pope)
How much money?

You can use *a lot* and *some* with both countable and noncountable nouns.
a lot of/some ice cream
a lot of/some French fries

Eating Out

1 Match each of these waiter/waitress questions with an appropriate response.

a) Who's the fish?	Yes, thanks.
b) And to drink?	Over here.
c) Do you have a reservation?	Non, please.
d) Is everything O.K.?	No, that's everything.
e) Anything else?	Just some oil and vinegar, please.
f) Smoking or nonsmoking?	A bottle of the house red, please.
g) Would you like dressing on that?	Yes, under "Clinton."

2 What would you say? Choose the appropriate word.

a) You're at the bar and you want to buy somebody a drink…
"What can I **drink/get/pay** you?"
b) The waiter is taking the orders and you don't want an appetizer…
"**Anything/Nothing/No** appetizer for me, thanks."
c) Somebody is offering you some more wine and you don't want very much…
"Just a **little/piece/small**, thanks."
d) The waiter is offering you food and you don't want any more…
"I'm **all right/very well/not interested**, thanks."
e) There's a phone call for you just as the food arrives. You want your friends to start eating…
"Don't **expect/wait for/stop** me."

3 Read this conversation in a restaurant. What do you notice about it?

Waiter: Did you call?
Man: Yes. There are two of us. The name is Jones.
Waiter: Go and sit over there by the window.
...
Waiter: Haven't you decided yet?
Woman: No, we're not ready. Go away and get us some drinks.
Waiter: What do you want?
Woman: Two iced teas.
Waiter: You got it.
...
Woman: Hey! Come here.
Waiter: What do you want?
Woman: Give me a side salad and the chicken.
Waiter: O.K. And you?
Man: Don't give me an appetizer. I just want the grilled salmon steak.
Waiter: What do you want with it?
Man: A side salad. Oh, and get us some house red and mineral water.
Waiter: All right.
...
Waiter: What did you think of the food?
Man: It was O.K.
Waiter: Do you want coffee now?
Woman: Yes, two. Black. And bring me the check.
Waiter: Yeah, O.K.

4 Work in groups of three. Imagine the conversation is taking place in an expensive restaurant. In groups of three:

a) Rewrite the conversation with more appropriate language.
b) Insert your own section where something terrible/funny/embarrassing happens.
c) Practice the conversation.
d) Perform your revised version for the rest of the class.

Anecdote

5 Think back to a restaurant where you have spent an enjoyable (or unpleasant!) evening. You are going to tell a partner about it. Choose from the list the things you want to talk about. Think about what you will say and what language you will need.

- ☐ Where was the restaurant?
- ☐ What was it like?
- ☐ Was it full or empty when you walked in?
- ☐ And when you left?
- ☐ What sort of people were eating there?
- ☐ Was it noisy or quiet?
- ☐ Who were you with?
- ☐ What did you have to eat?
- ☐ What did you have to drink?
- ☐ Did you have to wait a long time for your food?
- ☐ Was the waiter or waitress helpful?
- ☐ Did you have a dessert?
- ☐ Did you enjoy your meal?
- ☐ Were there any problems?
- ☐ How long did you spend in the restaurant?
- ☐ Was the meal expensive?
- ☐ Who paid?
- ☐ Did you leave a good tip?

6 Tell your partner about the restaurant. Give as much detail as possible.

What's for Dinner?

1 Look at the picture. How many items of food can you name?

2 Look at the following items of fresh food. Look up any words you don't know in your dictionary. Explain the use of the colors.

bacon bass beans cauliflower celery cod cucumbers figs
garlic eggplant grapefruit leeks lettuce limes lobster melons
mushrooms mussels olives onions oranges peaches peppers
plums raspberries salmon sardines sausage shrimp spinach
strawberries tomatoes trout tuna turkey veal zucchini

Underline the stressed syllable in each of the words with more than one syllable.

3 Ask questions to find out what kinds of food your partner likes.

4 Work in small groups. Choose one of the following situations and plan an appropriate meal. The meal should consist of at least three courses.

a) For a friend of yours and her new boyfriend. The boyfriend is a vegetarian.
b) For a romantic evening.
c) For a hot summer day.
d) For a friend who's on a diet.
e) For a child's sixth birthday party.

When you have finished, read your menu aloud to the rest of the class and ask your classmates to guess which situation you chose.

Incredible Edibles

1 Here are some words to describe the taste or texture of things you eat:

crunchy	spicy	tasty	crisp	salty
bland	sweet	bitter	chewy	greasy
creamy				

Use your dictionary if necessary and use the words in the box above to describe the taste or textures of the different kinds of food below.

> raw carrots salted peanuts
> plain white rice caramel chocolate sauce
> seafood milk chocolate cheap steak
> curry pizza fresh bread apples
> your mother's cooking water anchovies
> strong coffee fried eggs

2 These are some of the more unusual things people eat around the world. What do you imagine they taste like?

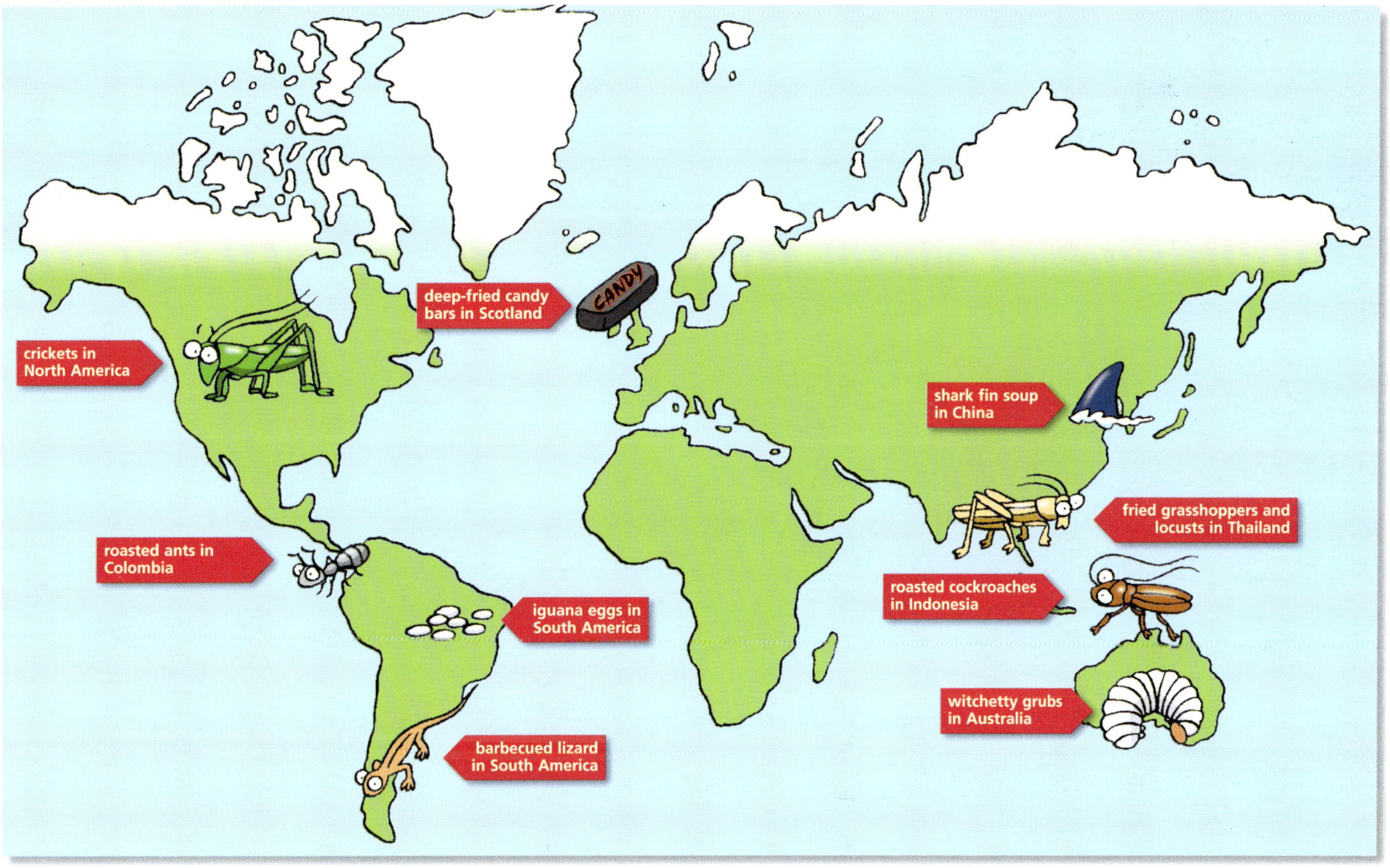

3 44 Listen to an interview with somebody who has eaten lots of strange things around the world. Write down the words that are used to describe the taste of each dish.

4 Would you consider eating any of the dishes mentioned? What is the strangest thing you have ever eaten? Tell the rest of the class.

Bedtime

1 A survey of people's sleep habits was conducted, based on the questions below. Answer the questions and then compare your answers with a partner.

1 On average, do you think you get enough sleep?

a Yes
b No
c Don't know

2 Do you need to be mentally alert for your job?

a Yes
b No
c Don't know

3 How many hours do you usually sleep on weeknights?

a Less than 5 hours
b 5 to 6 hours
c 6 to 7 hours
d 7 to 8 hours
e more than 8 hours

4 On average, how much sleep do you get on weekend nights?

a Less than 5 hours
b 5 to 6 hours
c 6 to 7 hours
d 7 to 8 hours
e more than 8 hours

5 When you're sleeping, what do you think your brain is doing?

a Resting
b Working
c Don't know

2 Find expressions in the sleep survey report on page 107 that match the figures below.

For example:
33% – one in three

a) 5–15% (line 14)
b) 33% (line 21)
c) 60–80% (line 27)
d) 51–60% (line 30)
e) 80–99% (lines 34 and 52)
f) 40–49% (line 46)

3 What facts do the figures relate to?

SLEEP SURVEY REPORT

According to recent medical research, sleeping more than nine hours or less than six hours a night can shorten your life expectancy. Those who are likely to live longest are people who regularly get between seven and eight hours a night.

A survey of 1,000 adults conducted by the Better Sleep Council (BSC) found that few people understand the important role sleep plays in normal daily brain functions, and many people actually reduce their brain power by getting too little sleep.

One in three adults admit that they do not get enough sleep, and lack of sleep is leaving millions of people without the energy to work as hard as they should.

Although a large number of people say that they need to be mentally alert in their work, over half of the people interviewed say that they sleep just under seven hours a night during the week.

On the other hand, most of the people interviewed say that they sleep more than seven hours a night on weekends. This suggests that a significant number of people try to catch up on their sleep on weekends instead of getting enough sleep during the week, when they need it most.

According to this survey, nearly half of the population believes that the brain rests when the body sleeps. In fact, the opposite is true. Sleep allows the brain to go to work, filing and storing the day's events. "Most people incorrectly think the brain is resting or recuperating during sleep. Actually, some parts of the brain are more active when you're asleep," confirms Dr. Mark Mahowald, director of the Minnesota Regional Sleep Disorders Center. "Your brain is like a cluttered desktop at the end of the day. At night, when you're asleep and no more information can be put on the desk, or in your brain, your brain can then file away the information." ●

Report writing

1 Work with a partner. Write five questions to ask people about their sleep habits, using the words and expressions in the box.

dream	have nightmares	talk in your sleep	snore	sleepwalk
sleep on your back, on your side, or on your front	take a nap	alarm clock		
feel sleepy	suffer from insomnia	yawn	fall asleep while traveling	
fall asleep in front of the television	early bird	night owl	go without sleep	
in a double bed	sleep late on weekends			

2 Now ask other students in the class all five questions and write down their answers.

3 Write sentences reporting the results of your survey. Use expressions from the Language Toolbox to help you.

LANGUAGE TOOLBOX

According to recent medical research/a recent survey, …
A new survey of … conducted by … found that …
On the other hand, …
This suggests that a significant number …
In fact, …
Actually, …

13 Communication

1 45 Listen and complete these useful numbers and addresses.

a) Associated Press Web site: www. _________ org
b) CNN Web site: _________ .cnn _________
c) MTV Web site: www _________
d) ESPN sports results: _________ espn _________ .com
e) Yahoo travel: http: _________ /yahoo _________
f) Amtrak reservations: _________ USA _________
g) AccuWeather Web site: www _________
h) White House switchboard: _________ 456 _________

Practice saying the numbers and addresses as fast as you can.

2 How many phone/fax numbers or e-mail/Web site addresses do you know by heart? Take a few minutes to write some of them down. Think of your family, friends, work, etc.

Dictate some of these numbers or addresses to your partner. Then ask each other questions to find out as much as you can about them.

Whose ...?	Who ...?	What ...?	Where ...?	How often ...?	When ... last time ...?

Hello ... This is the police. If you are being attacked from behind by a mad ax-murderer, press one ...

After the Beep ...

1 Look at this picture of Richard. Imagine what he's like.

- How old is he?
- Is he married?
- girlfriend?
- interests?
- friends?
- job?

2 46 Listen and take notes on the six messages on Richard's answering machine. What clues do you hear about his work, friends, and lifestyle?

Telephone language

1 Richard made two calls after picking up his messages. Read the conversations and complete them with the expressions in the box. One of the expressions in each set of three is wrong. Choose the most appropriate expression from the other two.

a) Hello./Good morning./Speak!
b) Is (...) there?/I'd like to speak to (...) please./Is there (...)?
c) Are you (...)?/Is this (...)?/Who's calling, please?
d) Hold on, please. I'll transfer your call./Hang on. I'll get her./One instant.
e) I am (...)./It's me./This is (...).
f) What are you doing later?/What do you do later?/
Are you available later on today?
g) I'll look forward to seeing you tomorrow./To tomorrow./See you tomorrow.

Phone conversation 1

Jane:	a) Hello.
Richard:	Oh, hi. b) ________
Jane:	c) ________
Richard:	Yes, hello, Jane. How are you?
Jane:	Fine, thanks. d) ________
	...
Maggie:	Hello.
Richard:	Hi! e) ________
Maggie:	So you got my message. I thought you'd forgotten about me.
Richard:	Don't be silly. Of course I haven't forgotten you. I've just been busy, that's all.
Maggie:	Busy playing computer games, probably.
Richard:	No, not all the time. Anyway, how are you?
Maggie:	Not too bad. A little tired. Too much work, as usual. Which reminds me—have you heard anything from the travel agent?
Richard:	Oh, yes. They have the tickets.
Maggie:	Great! Oh, I really need this vacation.
Richard:	Listen, I can't talk now, but f) ________
Maggie:	I have to work tonight, but I thought we could go to a movie tomorrow.
Richard:	O.K., I'll come by at about seven.
Maggie:	g) ________
Richard:	Bye.

Phone conversation 2

Receptionist:	a) Good morning. Southwestern Bank. Can I help you?
Richard:	Yes, b) ________
Receptionist:	c) ________
Richard:	My name's Richard Swainston.
Receptionist:	O.K., d) ________
	...
	Oh, Mr. Swainston, I'm afraid she's on the other line. Would you like to hold?
Richard:	Yes, thank you.
	...
Alison:	Alison Moore.
Richard:	Oh, hello. e) ________
Alison:	Oh, yes. Mr. Swainston. Thank you for getting back to me so promptly. There seems to be a problem with your account.
Richard:	Really? What kind of problem?
Alison:	Well, you're over your limit by more than $800. You really need to come to the bank to take care of it. f) ________
Richard:	Actually, no, I'm kind of tied up today. Would tomorrow be convenient for you?
Alison:	Yes, that's fine. Ten thirty?
Richard:	Yes, ten thirty's fine for me.
Alison:	Well, thank you for calling. g) ________
Richard:	Good-bye.

2 47 Listen to the telephone conversations and check.

Just hang on a sec, please.

3 Work with a partner. Refer to the answering machine messages on page 108. Write down and practice the following telephone conversations:

- Richard calls his friend Jeff and arranges to meet him tonight.
- Richard calls Smith Insurance and arranges a meeting with Ian Watson.

4 48 After his meeting with Alison Moore at the bank, Richard did what any independent young person would do. He called his mother. Listen to the conversation once and decide whether each of the following sentences is true or false:

a) When Richard calls his mother, she tells him that she's lonely because her husband's out playing golf.
b) Richard has had money problems before.
c) Mrs. Swainston thinks that Richard is careful with his money.
d) Richard's sister had an expensive wedding.
e) Richard asks his mother to give him some money so that he can get married.
f) Mrs. Swainston is unhappy with the way Richard manages his money.
g) Mrs. Swainston agrees to lend him $800, but only if he promises to get married.
h) Richard often calls his mother just to chat.

5 What does this phone call tell us about the relationship between Richard and his mother? Do you ever have similar conversations with your parents?

Close-up

Real conditionals

1 Look at tapescript 48. Listen again and complete these sentences.

a) Well, of course it is. What do you expect if _________ ?
b) Look, Mom, if you can just help me out this time, _________ .
c) I'll do it this time, but this really is the last time. If you get yourself into trouble again, _________ .

2 Think of different ways Mrs. Swainston might have completed this sentence:

Oh, Richard, have you gotten yourself into debt again? Because if you have,

a) don't…
b) I'm not going to…
c) you can…
d) I won't…
e) …

Bye, dear. Don't forget to write—or call us at 555-6934, or fax us at 555-7824, or e-mail us at proudparents@smithers.com, or visit our Web site at www.smithers.com…

3 Here are some sentences said by a parent. Match clauses from Column A with clauses from Column B and add *if* to make realistic sentences.

For example:
Take a front-door key if you're going to stay out late.

A		B	
a)	take a front-door key	1	I'll give them all away
b)	you're going to listen to that awful music	2	you can leave the table
c)	you don't put your toys away	3	you can't play computer games
d)	you hurt yourself	4	you're going to stay out late
e)	you'll be late for school	5	you're good
f)	you've finished your dinner	6	don't come crying to me
g)	you haven't finished your homework	7	keep it short
h)	you're going to be silly	8	shut your bedroom door
i)	I might buy you ice cream	9	I'm not playing
j)	you're going to call your friend	10	you don't hurry up

What age (0–18) do you think the child would be for the parent to say each of these things?

4 Choose five of the sentences from 3 and change *if* to *unless*. What other changes do you have to make?

5 Are you superstitious? Explain any superstitions that exist in your country.

For example:
If you knock wood, it protects you against bad luck.

6 Look at the following sayings. Work in groups and decide what you think each saying means. Write sentences explaining the sayings, using *if*. Do you have an equivalent saying in your language?

a) Easy come, easy go.
b) You snooze, you lose.
c) No pain, no gain.
d) It's no use crying over spilled milk.
e) When the cat's away, the mice will play.
f) Many hands make light work.
g) An apple a day keeps the doctor away.
h) Strike while the iron is hot.
i) Too many cooks spoil the broth.
j) Absence makes the heart grow fonder.

Language Reference: Real conditionals

Real conditionals talk about real or possible situations, usually in the present or the future. They generally have two clauses: an *if clause* and a *main clause.*

If you're going to stay out late,	*take a front-door key.*
If you don't put your toys away,	*I'll give them all away.*

The *if* clause

In most real conditionals, we use the present in the *if* clause, even when we are talking about the future.

Simple present
*If you **arrive** early, wait for me in the lobby.*

Present continuous
*If you**'re going** to Rio for your vacation, I can recommend a great hotel.*

Present perfect
*If you **haven't finished** by ten, you'll miss the train.*

We don't always have to use the simple present, present continuous, or present perfect. Look at the first example in this Language Reference section. It uses *going to*.

We can also use *can* and *can't:*
*If you **can't finish** the exercise, ask the teacher for help.*

Occasionally we can use the past tense, but only to talk about something we know or believe really happened:
*If it **rained,** we took the bus to school.*
*If you **didn't call** me, who did?*

There are alternatives to *if. Unless* is the most important one. It means *if + not.*
There is no important difference between ***Unless** you agree...* and ***If** you **don't** agree...*

The main clause

In the main clause, the most common structure is the simple present. Some modal auxiliaries (especially *will, can, must,* and *may*) are also common, and so is the imperative.

If he finds out the truth,...
- *...it**'s** all over for you and me.*
- *...we**'ll** be in big trouble.*
- *...you **can forget** about our trip to Jamaica.*
- *...**deny** everything!*

The *if* clause and the main clause can often go in either order.
If I feel like going out, I'll give you a call.
I'll give you a call if I feel like going out.
Use a comma after the *if* clause in the first type of sentence.

You will find information about unreal conditionals in Units 14 and 15.

If you have studied the conditional with *if* + simple present + *will* or with *if* + simple present + simple present, you already know a lot about this type of sentence. These are common examples of real conditionals.

1 A **stereotype** is a fixed general image or set of characteristics that a lot of people believe represent a particular type of person or thing. *Accents can reinforce a negative stereotype.*

2 If people **are stereotyped** as something, others form a fixed general idea or image of them, so that it is assumed that they will behave in a particular way. *You are likely to find many people who have stereotyped ideas about women.*

(Collins Cobuild English Dictionary)

Stereotypes

1 According to a newspaper article, these are some of the things you'll never hear men say:

- Let's ask that woman for directions.
- Hi, Mom. I just called to chat.
- Where's the toilet cleaner?

And these are some of the things you'll never hear women say:

- Would you please stop sending me flowers? It's embarrassing.
- Do you think I'd look better if I put on a few pounds?
- I've just killed that enormous spider in the bathroom.

Do you agree?

2 Which category do you think the newspaper article put the following statements in?

a) Of course I'd love to have dinner with your sister. The only thing on TV tonight is football. b) Should I check the tire pressure when I go to the gas station? c) Let's turn off the TV I want to talk about our relationship. d) Thanks so much for ironing my shirt. e) Don't worry; I'll clean that up. f) Do you think I look fat in these pants? g) I saw this gorgeous suit in that new shop in town. The jacket's really stylish, and it wasn't expensive. h) You drive, honey. You're a much better driver than I am. i) Look, I'm sick of talking about our relationship, O.K.? j) But I just don't need another pair of shoes.	**Answers according to the newspaper article:** Things you'll never hear a man say: a, c, e, f, g, h Things you'll never hear a woman say: b, d, i, j

3 What kinds of stereotypes of men and women could you make from the comments in 1 and 2? If you are a woman, complete the sentences in Column A. If you are a man, complete the sentences in Column B.

A	B
Men are...	Women are...
Men like...	Women like...
Men never...	Women never...
Men are good at...	Women are good at...
Men aren't very good at...	Women aren't very good at...
The best thing about being a man is...	The best thing about being a woman is...
The worst thing about being a man is...	The worst thing about being a woman is...

Compare your sentences.

4 Complete these expressions, using one verb for all the expressions in Column A and one verb for all the expressions in Column B.

A	B
...the shopping	...the beds
...the cooking	...dinner when there are guests
...the dishes	...the important decisions
...the odd jobs around the house	...an effort to keep in touch with family and friends
...most of the driving	...arrangements for baby-sitters
...laundry	...family appointments to see doctors, dentists, or teachers
...the ironing	...the biggest mess in the kitchen
...the family taxes	...the most noise
...the cleaning	...their mind up the quickest
...the vacuuming	...the longest phone calls

5 Think about your own family. Who makes/does the things in 4?

For example:
My mother does the shopping and cooking, but we take turns doing the dishes.
We make all the important decisions together.

6 Discuss the following questions:

- What things have changed in your lifetime for the family?/ for women?/for men?
- Do you think women should have the same rights as men?
- Do you think women have the same rights as men in your country?
- Do you think women are in a better position now than women of your grandmother's generation were?
- Do you think women are happier now than women of your grandmother's generation were?

ASPIRATION AND REALITY – % of women who think they:

country	should have all the same rights as men	do have the same rights as men	are in a better position than grandmother's generation	are happier than grandmother's generation
Australia	77	25	95	38
Belgium	70	12	90	41
Britain	73	9	93	42
Canada	70	8	93	33
Germany	70	7	94	29
Japan	21	0	96	82
Mexico*	81	18	69	53
Netherlands	80	20	92	25
South Africa*	63	23	77	54
Switzerland	39	14	92	27
United States	62	8	93	28

Source Angus Reid/*The Economist* poll

*Urban sample only

Compare your answers to the results of the poll carried out by *The Economist*, based on interviews with more than 3,000 women.

What Do Men and Women Really Think?

1 Work with a partner of the opposite sex if possible. Answer the questionnaire for yourself, and then guess the answers for your partner.

survey

One thousand men and women between the ages of 18 and 35 were interviewed for a survey to find out the differences between what men and women really think. This is the survey.

1 After a first date, how soon would you want him or her to call you?
a) The next day.
b) Within three days.
c) Within two weeks.
d) Anytime.

2 When you say "I'll give you a call," do you mean:
a) I'll call you tomorrow?
b) I'll contact you when I feel like seeing you again?
c) Don't call me?

3 If he or she didn't arrive on time for a first date, how long would you wait?
a) Five minutes.
b) Fifteen minutes.
c) Half an hour.
d) No limit.

4 Do you think it's O.K. for men to:
a) use beauty products?
b) still live at home when they are over 30?
c) stay at home and look after the children while their partners go out to work?

5 How would you feel if your partner forgot your birthday?
a) Upset.
b) Angry.
c) You wouldn't care—it's only a birthday.

6 Which of the following items would you like to receive as a present?
a) Flowers.
b) Computer games.
c) Clothes.
d) A cell phone.

7 Which of the following statements do you agree with?
a) Men should hold doors open for women.
b) Men and women are equal, so it's insulting to women if men hold doors open for them.
c) Men and women are equal, but women still like having doors held open for them.

8 Have you ever done any of the following to attract a member of the opposite sex?
a) Bought new clothes.
b) Changed your hair.
c) Dieted.
d) Lied about your age.

9 Should the wives/husbands of public figures stand by their partners?
a) Yes.
b) No.

10 Do you think marriage is the ideal romantic relationship?
a) Yes.
b) No.

2 Here is a summary of some of the more interesting results of the survey. Fill in each blank with *men* or *women*.

survey HIGHLIGHTS

ON CALLING The majority of both men and women want to be called within three days. However, 35% of (1) ________ said they would expect to be called the next day, while only 19% of (2) ________ gave this answer.

ON DATES On average, (3) ________ are prepared to wait for their date longer than (4) ________ . Eighteen percent of (5) ________ said that they would wait for only five minutes, whereas 67% of (6) ________ would be prepared to wait half an hour or more.

ON CHILDCARE (7) ________ are far more in favor of men staying at home to take care of the children than (8) ________ . While 65% of (9) ________ said it was fine, only 30% of (10) ________ agreed. The majority of (11) ________ do not feel that it is appropriate for the man to stay at home with the children.

ON BIRTHDAYS The results of the survey suggest that (12) ________ attach greater importance to birthdays than (13) ________ : 29% said they would be angry and upset if their partner forgot their birthday.

ON ATTRACTION Three out of four (14) ________ have bought new clothes to attract a member of the opposite sex, compared to only one in five (15) ________ . Similarly, while just under half of the (16) ________ interviewed have changed their hair or gone on a diet, only one in ten (17) ________ admitted to doing the same. However, a significant number of both men and women admitted lying about their age, with the important difference that (18) ________ tended to say they were older while (19) ________ were more likely to knock a few years off their age.

ON MARRIAGE The results of the survey show that (20) ________ are more in favor of marriage than (21) ________ . Sixty-one percent of (22) ________ didn't think much of this institution, whereas four out of five (23) ________ interviewed gave a resounding thumbs-up to marriage as the ideal romantic relationship.

ANSWERS ON PAGE 141.

3 Would the results of the survey have been different in your country?

Report writing

Work in groups and complete the following tasks:

1 Write a multiple-choice questionnaire to find out about people's attitudes to one of the following:

- cell phones
- computers
- housework
- marriage

2 Complete the questionnaire in class and combine the results.

3 Write a report to summarize your findings. Use expressions from the survey highlights above.

14 Style

1 Match the verbs below to the noun phrases from the box to describe the kinds of things people do before they leave the house in the morning.

have get make do read put turn take

a shower	coffee	homework	the radio on	dressed	breakfast
make-up on	the children ready		the dishes	the bed	the TV on
the paper	a cup of tea				

2 Think about your own morning routine from the time you get out of bed to the time you leave the house.

- What do you do? What order do you do things in?
- How long does each activity usually take you?

Compare routines with a partner. What are the differences?

3 Read about these two morning routines. Choose the most appropriate verbs.

PERSON 1

My alarm goes off early, and it takes me ten minutes to eat my breakfast, have two cups of coffee, take a shower, and pack my briefcase and thirty minutes to (1) **get dressed / wear**. I start thinking about what I'm going to (2) **get dressed / wear** while I have my breakfast. After a shower, I (3) **put on / wear** my underwear, and then I look in my closet and choose a pair of pants. If they still (4) **fit / look** me, I put them on. If they feel a little tight around the waist, I (5) **try them on / take them off** and spend a few minutes feeling guilty about all those chocolates I had last night. Then I choose a looser pair of pants and think about a shirt that (6) **goes with / fits** it. I usually (7) **have on / try on** two or three shirts before I find one that (8) **looks / wears** right and (9) **feels / fits** comfortable. Finding a pair of socks usually takes about five minutes— I can find two dozen socks, but none that (10) **look / match**. By then, I'm late.

PERSON 2

I get up as late as I possibly can and jump in and out of the shower. I (1) **put on/fit** the pants I (2) **had on/got dressed** the day before and take a shirt out of the closet—it doesn't matter which one, as long as it's ironed. I find a jacket that (3) **fits/goes with** the pants, look down and check that my socks (4) **match/feel,** and that's it. Nearly all my clothes are either green or brown because I've been told that they are the only colors that (5) **suit/match** me. So I never really have to worry about what I (6) **look like/go with**. The important thing is to make sure I have enough time to enjoy my favorite drink of the day: that first cup of coffee . . .

Do you think each of these is a description of a man or a woman? Do the descriptions fit anybody you know?

4 On a piece of paper, write a short account of how you get ready in the morning. Don't write your name on it. When you've finished, fold the piece of paper and give it to your teacher. Then take another student's piece of paper and guess who it belongs to.

5 Work with a partner. Describe how you would get ready for some of the following:

- a job interview
- a first date
- an evening at the theater
- Saturday night out with your friends
- a wedding
- a long flight
- a day on the beach
- a Sunday-afternoon stroll around town

Suits You

1 Which of the sentences below describes your style best? Compare with a partner.

- Comfortable. I like baggy pants, loose-fitting shirts, and sneakers.
- Up-to-date but original.
- I have to look nice for work, but I wear casual clothes on the weekends.
- I've been wearing the same clothes for ten years. I have no idea what's in fashion, and I don't care.
- The only way I could possibly describe my style is scruffy. I wear jeans, sweatshirts, and sneakers, and I never look neat.
- My style would be different if I had more money. I'd buy designer labels, especially Gucci and Versace. I love dressing up in glamorous outfits.
- Something else:

2 49 You are going to listen to some people talking about their favorite clothes. Number the pictures below in the order in which you hear about them. Not all of the clothes are mentioned.

3 Which of the items do you think is the ugliest? Which ones do you like?

Close-up

Adjective order

1 Put the words in each group into the correct order to describe clothes.

For example:
a turtleneck sweater white—*a white turtleneck sweater*

a) T-shirt an short-sleeved old
b) green a cardigan plain
c) beautiful scarf a cashmere
d) sweater a v-neck striped
e) silk flowery vest a

Make five new combinations of adjectives and nouns.

Language Reference p. 119

2 a) Put the adjectives in the box into these five categories: age; material; pattern/color; opinion; style.

old	striped	beautiful	wool	leather	secondhand	horrible	plaid
short-sleeved	new	full-length	terrific	plain	designer	silk	red

b) In most languages, when we use two or three adjectives to describe a noun, there are rules about the order of the adjectives.

Put the categories in the correct order for English. Is it the same in your language?

3 Write down different combinations of clothing under the following headings:
I have this in my closet; I wouldn't be caught dead in this.

For example:

I have this in my closet:	I wouldn't be caught dead in this!
baggy black corduroy pants	a secondhand nylon shirt
a plaid suit	green leather skirt

Work with a partner. Take turns reading one of your items aloud, but don't say which heading you wrote it under. Your partner has to guess which heading each item belongs to.

Anecdote

4 Think of a favorite clothing item or accessory that you have bought. You are going to tell your partner about it. Choose from the list the things you want to talk about. Think about what you will say and the language you will need.

- ☐ What is it?
- ☐ What does it look like?
- ☐ What does it feel like?
- ☐ How long have you had it?
- ☐ What store did you buy it in?
- ☐ Who was with you when you bought it?
- ☐ Was it very expensive?
- ☐ Do you think it was worth the money?
- ☐ How often do you wear/use it?
- ☐ Do you have any special memories associated with it?
- ☐ Have you ever lent it to someone?
- ☐ How would you feel if you lost it?
- ☐ What do you like best about it?

5 Tell your partner about the item of clothing or accessory.

Idioms

1 Write down the names of some clothes that have:

a) zippers
b) buttons
c) hems
d) cuffs
e) buckles
f) sleeves
g) heels.

2 Test your knowledge of idioms. Choose the correct word in each expression below and say what you think the expression means.

a) Keep your shirt **on/up/off;** you're so impatient!
b) I'm sorry, I didn't mean to offend you. It was just an **up-/off-/around-** the-cuff remark.
c) If you want to pass that exam, you'll have to buckle **over/down/around** to work very soon.
d) It's so obvious when Claire's in love—she wears her heart **under/by/on** her sleeve.
e) We're saving up to go on vacation, so we'll have to **tighten/loosen/forget** our belts for a while.
f) I haven't seen Bill and Wendy together in a while—do you think she finally **wore/gave/missed** him the boot?
g) Mike gets hot **under/around/in** the collar easily; he should learn to control his temper.
h) I've run out of ideas—let's ask John. He usually has something **beside/between/up** his sleeve.

3 Match the expressions in 2 to these definitions:

1 to behave in a way that makes your feelings obvious
2 to spend less money
3 to get angry
4 to have an idea or a plan
5 to say something without thinking about it first
6 to get rid of somebody
7 to start working seriously
8 to remain calm and have patience

4 Think of something that happened to you recently. Use one of the expressions in 2 and tell your partner about it.

Language Reference: Adjective order

In most languages, when two or three adjectives are used to describe a noun, there are rules about the order of the adjectives. In English, this is the order:

		ADJECTIVES			
Opinion →	Age →	Pattern and color →	Material →	Style →	**NOUN**
horrible,	secondhand,	striped,	cotton,	short-sleeved	shirt.
terrific,	old,	leopard-print,	fake fur,	full-length	coat.
beautiful,	new,	blue,	silk,	designer	suit.

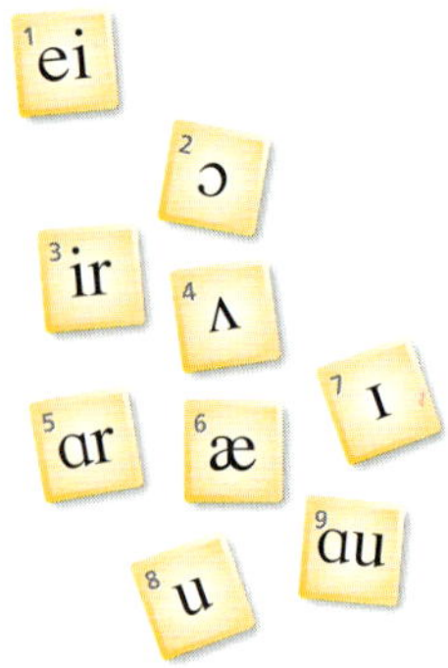

First Impressions

1 Match words and phrases from Column A and Column B, according to the sounds of the underlined letters.

A		B	
a)	overweight	1	a pierced nose
b)	broad shoulders	2	smart
c)	a beard	3	a thick neck
d)	stubble	4	eyebrows
e)	a scar	5	a relaxed style
f)	baggy pants	6	bald
g)	slim build	7	scruffy
h)	suit	8	a shaved head
i)	a wide mouth	9	high-heeled boots

2 Which of these adjectives can you use with *hair, eyes,* or *skin*?

blue	deep-set	brown	clear	fair	pale	dark	tanned

3 Work with a partner. Use the words in 1 and 2 to describe the people below.

4 If you met the people in the picture in 3 for the first time, what would be the first thing you would notice about each of them?

5 Can you tell anything about a person from a first impression? Are your first impressions usually right?

6 Read the description below and match it to one of the people in 3.

Say you're a girl. Say you're a girl and you're at a party, or at the supermarket, or in a nightclub. Say you're a girl and you're at a party, or at the supermarket, or in a nightclub, and I come up to you.

Say you've never set eyes on me before.

Some things you'll know immediately. You'll see that I'm just under six feet tall and of average build. If we shake hands, you'll notice that my grip is strong and my fingernails clean. You'll see that I have brown eyes that match my brown hair. And you'll see that I have a scar across the center of my left eyebrow. You'll guess that I'm somewhere between twenty-five and thirty years old.

You'll ask me what I do for a living, and I'll tell you that I'm an artist, which is true, and that I make a living from it, which isn't. I won't tell you that I work in a small art gallery in Venice Beach three days a week to make ends meet. You'll look at my clothes, which will probably be my friend's clothes, and wrongly assume that I'm rich. Since I won't mention a girlfriend, you'll probably assume correctly that I'm single. I won't ask you if you have a boyfriend, but I will check your finger to see if you're engaged or married.

From *Come Together*, by Josie Lloyd and Emlyn Rees

Come Together

Come Together was written by a couple. Each of them wrote alternate chapters of the book. It tells the story of the same relationship from the point of view of the man and the woman.

7 Complete the description below for one of the other people in 3.

> Say we meet at a party, and we've never met before. You'll see that I'm ________ tall and of ________ build. You'll see that I have ________ hair and ________ eyes. You'll guess that I'm somewhere between ________ and ________ years old.
>
> You'll look at my clothes and assume that my style is ________ . If we speak, I'll tell you that I ________ , which is true, and that I ________ , which isn't.

8 Read your description to a partner and ask him/her to guess which person you've described.

9 Write a description of yourself or another student in the class.

Ugly

Jon Bon Jovi

Jon Bon Jovi was born John Francis Bongiovi Jr. on March 2, 1962. His first band was Atlantic City Expressway. He made his breakthrough with the song *Runaway*.

1 50 Listen to the song.

a) Is it a romantic song?
b) Who is the singer talking to?
c) What does he think of her?
d) What does she think of herself?

2 Look at the lyrics of the first two verses of the song. The lines have been cut apart. In Column A the lines are in the correct order, but in Column B they are mixed up. Listen again and match the two parts of each line.

A	B
If you're ugly,	you really are to me
In your eyes	a camera sometimes
If you could see yourself	as beautiful as you
You'd wish you were	for you to see
And I wish I was	I'm ugly too!
So I could take your picture	with my mind
Put it in a frame	like others do
How beautiful	the sky's a different blue

Close-up

I wish

1 Look at the lyrics in 2. What structure is used after *I wish*?

2 Make *I wish* sentences for the following situations.

For example:
I'm poor. → *I wish I had more money.*

a) I live in a tiny house in the suburbs.
b) I have a boring job.
c) My car's 15 years old.
d) My wife doesn't understand me.
e) My children never listen to a word I say.
f) I never have time to do the things I like.
g) I hardly ever see my friends.

3 What wishes do you have about your own life? Write down a few and then tell your partner about them.

I wish I were …
weren't so …
had … / didn't have …
lived …
could …

Interview with Jon Bon Jovi

1 What do you know about Jon Bon Jovi?

2 In the interview below, he answers some of the following questions:

a) If you could be anywhere in the world right now, where would you like to be?
b) What do you do in your spare time?
c) Who would you most like to have lunch with?
d) What makes you angry?
e) What would surprise people most about you?
f) If your best friend were about to marry someone you thought was totally unsuitable for him, would you give an honest opinion?
g) What scares you?
h) If an old flame invited you to dinner, would you go?
i) If you could change anything, what would it be?
j) What's the best thing about your work?

Match a question to each of his answers.

Q&A JONBONJOVI

1 ______________________ ?

My mother. At the peak of Bon Jovi's early success, the group went through a period of real extravagance. We hired private planes, chartered the biggest yachts in the world, took all our friends on vacation to exotic islands, bought each other Ferraris and gave our parents expensive presents. But Mom would always much rather I went over for Sunday dinner instead of buying her another gift.

2 ______________________ ?

Being a rock 'n' roll star is not as romantic as people think. It's actually a very strenuous job—especially when you're on the road 240 days a year. Songwriting, creating something that you can have forever, is what gives me the greatest thrill.

3 ______________________ ?

People who come to interview me and only want to talk about my hairstyle.

4 ______________________ ?

I'd spend more time with my wife, Dorothea, and my kids, Stephanie and James. I take them with me whenever possible. They all came to live with me in London for three months while I was filming the thriller *The Leading Man*, but I still don't see enough of them.

5 ______________________ ?

I used to worry about living up to the success of the last record, especially after *Slippery When Wet* sold 14 million copies. But these days, I'm much more relaxed, and personal artistic satisfaction means more than commercial success.

6 ______________________ ?

That I'm not out on the town every night. When I was in London filming, I would drive to work at 6 A.M. and see people coming out of the clubs and feel thankful that I'd had a good night's sleep. I'm all for going out for a night at a bar every once in a while, but you can't do it every night.

(Adapted from *Candice*, October 1997)

3 Work in small groups and discuss your own answers to the questions in 2 above.

Close-up

Unreal conditionals

1 Look at the interview with Jon Bon Jovi again. Which tense does the interviewer use after the word *if*? Why?

2 51 Listen and read the dialogues below. What is the relationship between the people in each dialogue?

A

Anna: If you're looking for a new skirt, there's a sale at DKNY.
Dan: Is there? Well, come on. If we don't leave now, it'll be closed when we get there.

B

Mark: If I pass the exam, can I have a new pair of Doc Martens? And a CD? And…
Laura: If you spent less time thinking about clothes and music and more time on your schoolwork, I'd be a lot happier.

C

Paul: This is really nice. If I had the money, I'd always wear Hugo Boss suits.
Chris: If you like it, why don't you buy it? You look great in it.

D

Sue: O.K. Who's been wearing my Calvin Klein jacket?
Julia: Well, don't look at me.
Sue: Well, if it wasn't you, who was it?
Julia: Well, I don't know. Anyway, what do you expect if you leave your things all around the house?
Sue: That has nothing to do with it. If you're going to borrow things, you should ask. Look at this stain.

3 Underline the *conditional* sentences.

Language Reference p. 125

4 Work with a partner. Discuss these questions with reference to the examples in the conversations.

a) How many clauses are there in each conditional sentence in the conversations?
b) In each case, is the speaker talking about a situation that he/she sees as *real* or *unreal*?
c) What verb tenses are used in the *if* clauses? What happens to the verb tense in the *if* clause in the *unreal* conditionals?
d) How is this similar to *I wish* (page 122)?
e) What happens in the main clause in the unreal conditionals?

5 Write at least five sentences about yourself and talk about them with a partner.

a) If I had more money/time,…
b) If I could speak English/Chinese,…
c) If I were younger/older,…
d) If I could sing/dance/play a musical instrument/drive,…
e) If…

If I were married to you, I'd divorce you!

Language Reference: *I wish* and unreal conditionals

I wish

I wish is one of the ways of talking about *unreal* situations. After *I wish,* the tense backshifts.

FACT	*WISH*
***I'm** a teacher*	*but I **wish** I **weren't/wasn't** a teacher. I **wish** I **were/was** a doctor.* *
*I **live** in New York*	*but I **wish** I **didn't live** in New York. I **wish** I **lived** in Paris.*
***I'm studying** English*	*but I **wish** I **weren't/wasn't studying** English. I **wish** I **were/was studying** Chinese.*

* *Was* is sometimes used instead of *were* in informal speech.

Unreal conditionals

If for unreal conditionals follows the same rule as *I wish.*
***If** I **were/was** a doctor…*
***If** I **lived** in Paris…*
***If** I **were/was studying** Chinese…*

In the second clause of the sentence, we generally use *would*. We can also use *might* or *maybe* + *would* for possible results.
*If I were/was a doctor, **I'd** be able to help people more, and **I'd** make more money.*
*If I lived in Paris, **I'd** visit the Louvre every day, and **I'd** have croissants and coffee for breakfast at a sidewalk café.*
*If I were/was studying Chinese, **I'd** have fewer problems with grammar. And I **might** be able to study in China for a year.*

There is more information about *I wish* and conditionals in units 13 and 15 and about *would* in unit 11.

> If you have studied the structure *if* + past + *would* + verb, you already know a lot about this type of sentence.

15 *Age*

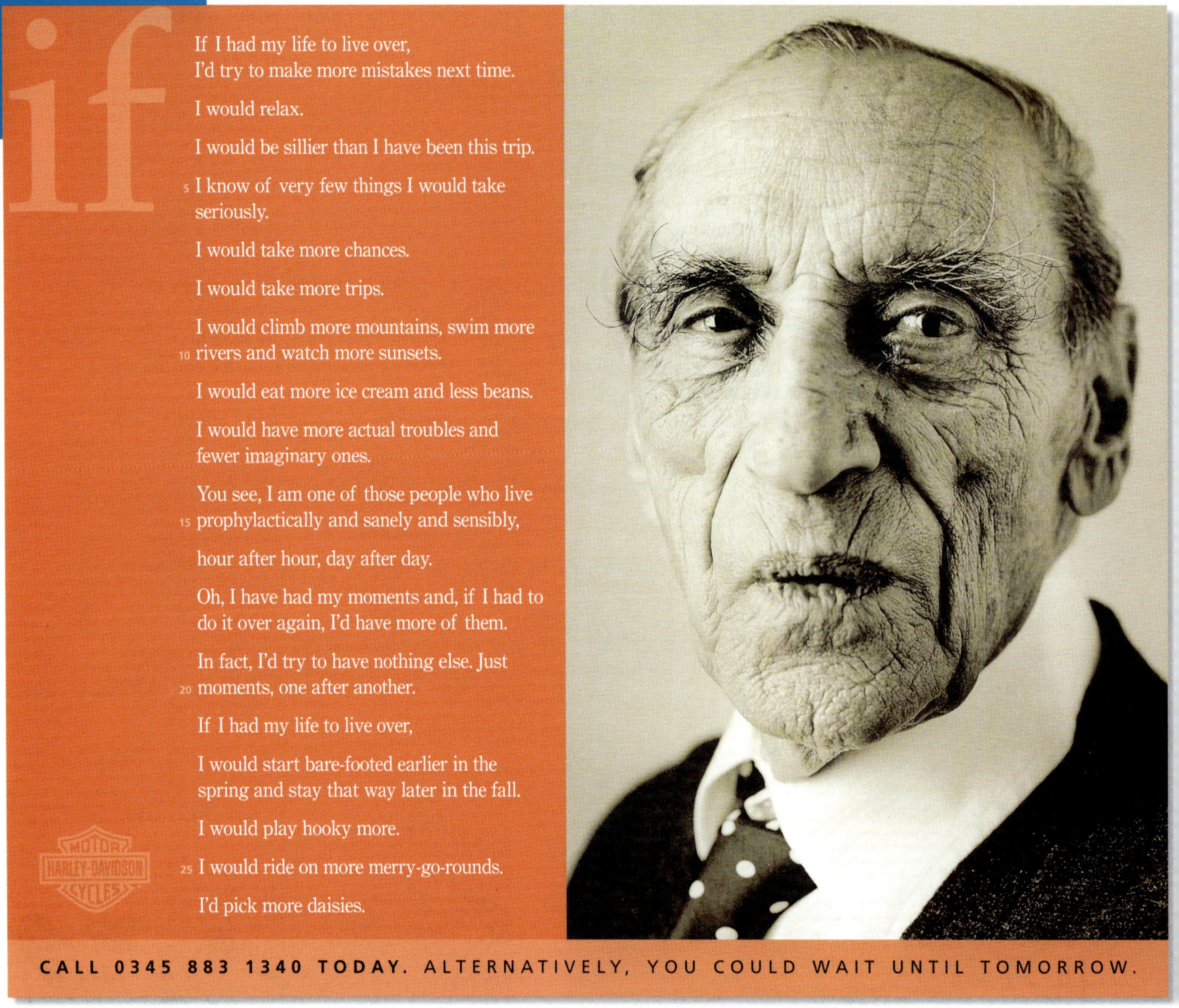

prophylactically (line 15): very carefully
sanely (line 15): in a normal or reasonable way
barefooted (line 22): without shoes
play hooky (line 24): stay out of school without permission
daisy (line 26): small wildflower with white petals

1 Work in groups. Invent an identity for the man in the advertisement.

- What's his name?
- How old is he?
- Where does he live?
- What's his family background?
- What has he done in his life?
- Is he happy?

Work with students from other groups. Compare descriptions.

2 Read the poem and decide whether it fits the character you have invented. How does the man in the poem feel about his life?

3 Why did Harley-Davidson choose this poem to advertise its motorcycles? What kind of person is the advertisement aimed at?

Wishes

1 The poem you just read is about an old man looking back over his life. Think about your future. Make a list of five or more things you'd like to do in the future and why you can't do them now.

For example:

What I'd like ...		**Why it's impossible ...**	
I'd like to	*buy a new leather jacket,...*	but	*I can't find one I like.*
I'd like to	*travel around the world,...*	but	*I have to finish school.*

2 Rewrite your list, using conditional sentences.

For example:
If I could find a jacket I liked, I'd buy it.
If I didn't have to finish school, I'd travel around the world.

3 Work with a partner. Compare your sentences.

4 Look back at the poem. Complete these sentences for the man. Use the words in the box.

sensible	seriously	adventurous	anxious	fun	risks	enjoy

a) I wish I'd been more...
b) I wish I'd been less...
c) I wish I'd taken more...
d) If only I'd had more...
e) I wish I hadn't been so...
f) I wish I hadn't taken life so...
g) If only I'd done more of the things I...

Close-up

I wish* and *if only

1 Work with a partner. Look at the sentences in 4 above.

a) What verb form follows *I wish*... and *If only*... in these particular sentences?
b) Are the sentences about situations in the past, the present, or the future?
c) Are they about things that really happened?
d) Look at the sentences below and find the verbs.

Language Reference p. 128

Facts	*Wishes*
I studied math, literature, and business at school.	I wish I'd studied Italian. If only I'd known what was going to happen.
Now I'm studying economics at Syracuse.	I wish I were/was studying Italian literature.
	I wish I lived in Rome.
Sadly, it's all over with Gina.	If only she hadn't broken up with me.
She went back to Rome last week.	I wish I'd gone with her.

What happens to the verbs when you change from a fact to a wish?

2 The people in these pictures regret decisions they have made or things they have done. What do you think each person regrets? Write sentences beginning *I wish…* or *If only…* for each picture.

A
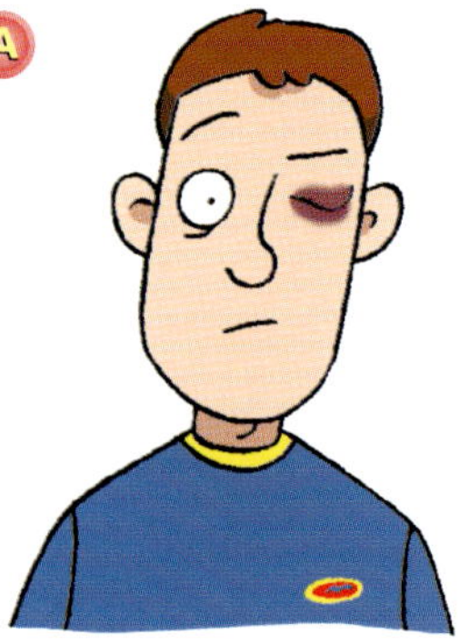

B

C
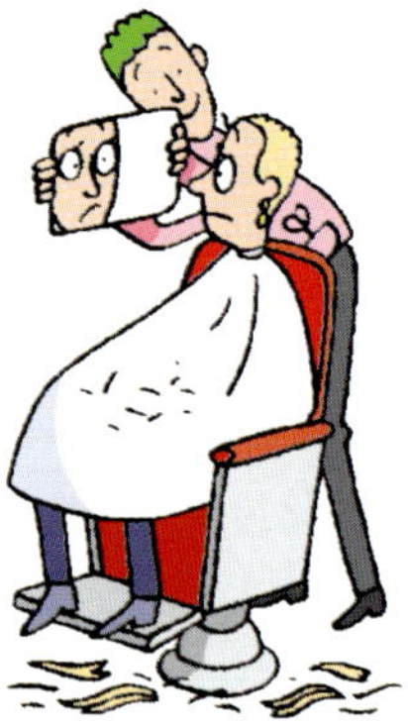

D

E

F

G

H

3 Write at least two wishes for the person in each of these situations.

a) I have to play tennis with Jack on Saturday. The thing is, not only is he horrible at tennis, he's also a pain in the neck. And now Nico has asked me if I want to play with him. *I wish…*

b) I went to see *The Texas Chainsaw Massacre* with Carmen last week, and she's had nightmares about it all week. *I wish…*

c) Ten years ago, when I was 16, I quit school and went to work in my dad's business. Now the business has gone bankrupt, and I'm out of work. *If only…*

d) I started smoking when I was a teenager. I'm up to two packs a day now and I'm desperate to stop, but I just can't. *If only…*

e) We got married when we were both 18. We were in love, and we thought it would last forever. But as we've gotten older, we've drifted apart, and now we fight all the time. *I wish…*

4 Have you made any bad decisions in your life so far? Tell your partner about them.

Language Reference: *I wish* and *if only*

Wish and *if only* are two ways of talking about *unreal* situations. We can use them to express regrets about the present or past.

In *unreal* situations, the tense usually backshifts. For example:

1 Present changes to past

*I **live** in Lincoln.* → *I wish I **lived** in Rome.*

*I'**m going** to the movies with Pete on Saturday.* → *I wish I **were/was going** to the movies with Miguel.*

*I **can't** stop smoking.* → *If only I **could** stop smoking.*

2 Past changes to past perfect

*I **studied** economics.* → *I wish I'**d studied** Italian literature.*

*I **went** to Florida for my vacation.* → *I wish I'**d gone** to Spain.*

*I **started** smoking when I was a teenager.* → *If only I **hadn't started** smoking.*

See also the Language Reference section about *I wish* in Unit 14.

Act Your Age

1 Do you think there is a maximum or minimum age limit for:

- getting married
- having children
- learning a new language
- traveling around the world
- worrying about how you look
- leaving home
- starting a new career
- dancing to pop music in public
- learning to ski
- riding a motorcycle
- wearing jeans

Discuss your answers with a partner. Are there any other activities you think have age limits?

2 Read the article and decide which statements are true for the writer.

a) I wish I'd never met him.
b) I should have been honest about my age.
c) If I'd told him my age at the beginning, he might have left me.
d) I shouldn't have told him about my disastrous existence.
e) If I were a man, the age difference wouldn't be a problem.
f) It's all his fault; if I hadn't met him, I wouldn't have turned into an ageist and a liar.

Ageism

Ageism is prejudice against older people—for example through refusing them employment. It is a fairly new word, following the examples of racism and sexism.

Ageism Turned Her into a Liar

For most of my life, age has seemed unimportant. My friends of both sexes have been younger, older, or the same age. When I was in my early thirties, I had a very enjoyable and fulfilling relationship with a man of 23. One of the most attractive men I know is in his mid fifties.

THE FIRST time I experienced a problem with age was on my fortieth birthday. Much to my surprise, it was a deeply traumatic event. Forty seemed to be so much older than 39. I used to like it when people told me I looked young for my age, but then I realized that they were just telling me how old I was. Anyway, I slowly got over the shock and tried to convince myself that life begins at 40…

I met him playing badminton. He was impressed with my exciting lifestyle—lots of traveling and some writing. I found him fun, kind, amusing, and very attractive. He's 31 and looks about 19. He has no idea how old I am.

All my life I've been totally honest. I return extra change to astonished shopkeepers, I've never traveled without a ticket, and in job interviews I always come out with all the reasons I should not be employed.

Early on in the relationship, I told him the truth about my disastrous existence—my divorce, my financial difficulties, the relationship that destroyed my faith in men. I even admitted that I dye my hair. The sky did not fall in, and he didn't run screaming from the house. I did tell him I'm older than he is, but something stopped me from coming clean about my actual age.

And now I'm in trouble—serious trouble. Silence has made the problem much greater. If I had told him before, it wouldn't have become such a big issue. If I had been brave enough to admit that I was 11 years older than him, I wouldn't be in this crazy situation now. I lie about jobs, years abroad, and education; he wonders how I've managed to fit so much living into my life; I conveniently can't remember the music of my teenage years.

The other day, I even hid my passport under a pile of papers. I'm worried about organizing a get-together with my friends in case one of them says something like, "Doesn't she look good for her age?"

The longer I remain silent, the more likely he is to find out, and I'm frightened. For once in a very long time I've found someone who makes me happy, and I don't want to lose it.

I know that if I were a man, I would never have gotten into this mess. Eleven years' difference is nothing for a man. But it's the other way around and the world judges older women harshly, and I'm afraid he would do the same.

I have become an ageist and a liar, and I have no one to blame but myself.

3 The following is a summary of the article. Put the lines of the summary in the correct order.

( ) over the shock and tried
(1) She has always had friends
( ) traumatic event. But she got
( ) to convince herself that life begins
( ) but herself for the situation she's in.
(2) of all ages. In fact, one of the most attractive
( ) clean about her age. Silence has made the problem
( ) at 40. She met him playing badminton but didn't come
( ) women so harshly. But she knows that she has no one to blame
( ) much greater, and now she thinks that the longer she remains silent,
( ) men she knows is in his mid fifties. Her fortieth birthday was a deeply
( ) the more likely he is to find out. She thinks it's unfair that society judges older

4 What would you do if you were the writer?

5 Write the conversation they have when she tells him the truth. Begin like this:

Him: You look worried. What's on your mind?
Her: Well, there *is* something I've been meaning to tell you.

6 52 Listen to the conversation. Did you imagine a similar situation?

7 Work in small groups and discuss these questions:

a) How old are your youngest and oldest friends?
b) Do you know any couples who have big age differences?
c) What would you do now if you were the writer?
d) Have you ever lied about your age?
e) Can you think of any situations in which you would lie about your age?
f) What ages do you think are turning points in life?

Close-up

Unreal conditionals

1 Here are some comments the woman makes about her difficult situation. Match them to the time sequences in the box.

a) If I had told him before, it wouldn't have become such a big issue.
b) If I had been brave enough to admit that I was 11 years older than him, I wouldn't be in this crazy situation now.
c) I know that if I were a man, I would never have gotten into this mess.

time sequences		
present situation	➔	past result
past situation	➔	past result
past situation	➔	present result

2 Write conditional sentences according to the cues. Think carefully about the verb tenses.

For example:
You arrived early. I wasn't ready. ➔ *If you hadn't arrived early, I would have been ready.*

a) I ate too much last night. I'm not feeling very well.
b) He went to college. He got a good job.
c) She has a fast car. She got here in under two hours.
d) You had only a sandwich for lunch. You're hungry now.
e) I didn't see you. I didn't say hello.
f) There was a power outage. I lost two important computer documents.
g) You didn't ask anyone for directions. We're lost.
h) He loves her a lot. He forgave her.

Unreal! The Conditional Game

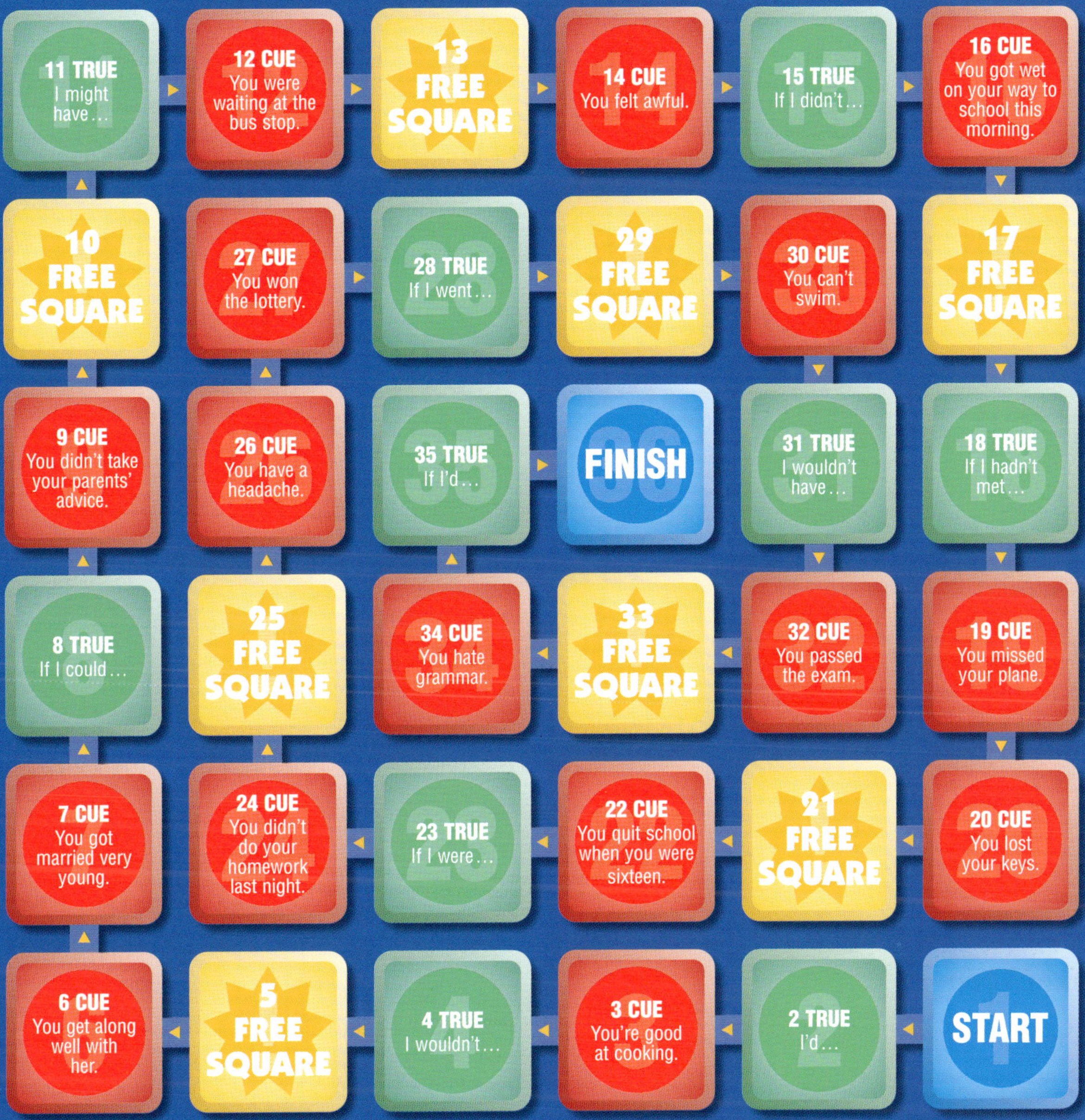

RULES OF THE GAME

Play the game in small groups.
You will need a die and counters.

1 Place your counters on the square marked START and throw the die.
2 The first player to throw a six starts the game.
3 The first player throws the die again and moves his/her counter along the board according to the number on the dice.
4 Players then take turns, moving clockwise around the board. If a player lands on a "CUE" square, he/she has to use the words on it to make a conditional sentence. For example:

3 CUE You're broke.

If I weren't broke, I would have paid for your lunch.
or
If I hadn't bought a new car, I wouldn't be broke now.

If a player lands on a "TRUE" square, he/she has to use the words on it as the beginning of a sentence that is true for him/her.
If a player lands on a "FREE SQUARE," he/she doesn't have to do anything.

What Would You Have Done?

1 Read these stories and discuss what you would have done.

A I was in the supermarket yesterday and I saw this elderly woman shuffling up and down the aisles. She didn't have a shopping cart and was putting items right into her huge purse. Anyway, I didn't think any more about it and continued doing my shopping, and when I went to the check-out line, to pay, there she was in front of me. I watched her put one can of cat food on the counter and pay for it, and then she walked out with her purse full of stolen items.

B Something awful happened to me last week. I'd invited six people over for dinner, and you know how I hate cooking. Anyway, I spent all afternoon preparing the meal, and actually I was pretty happy with how it turned out. I even managed to get all the vegetables ready at the same time as the meat. So, the vegetables were on the table, and I just had to get the chicken out of the oven. I lifted it out and, I don't know how it happened, but I dropped it on the kitchen floor, and before I could pick it up, the cat had licked it. She regretted it afterward, because she burned her tongue.

C My friend put me in a really difficult position the other day. She'd bought this dress for a special office party, and I don't know why, but she had to ask me what I thought of it. I mean, she wouldn't have bought it if she hadn't liked it, would she? And she paid a fortune for it. Anyway, she put it on, and I immediately thought, "No, orange is not your color." Not only that, but some people just don't have the legs for short skirts. To be honest, she looked ridiculous.

D On my last birthday, my husband gave me only an envelope. I was really excited. I thought it was going to be tickets for a trip to Egypt. He knew that it was my lifelong dream to see the pyramids. Anyway, when I opened the envelope, there was a check inside for $15,000 and a little note saying, "Happy birthday honey. This is for a face-lift."

E I had a very strange experience the other day. I was in Atlanta for a meeting, and it was lunchtime. It was a beautiful day, so I bought a sandwich and went for a walk. I was just on my way back to the office when I noticed a scruffy, bearded man asking for money on the street. I recognized him immediately. It was someone I went to college with, this incredible baseball player. He'd always been a rebel, but he was really smart. We'd been very good friends, but I lost touch with him when we graduated.

2 53 Listen and find out what the people did. Do you think they each did the right thing?

Language Reference: Unreal conditionals

The *if* clause

If the situation is unreal (imaginary or very improbable), we show this by backshifting the verb.

real	unreal
I'm an economist.	***If I weren't/wasn't** an economist, ...* ***If I were/was** a musician, ...* ***If I had** a different job, ...*
real past	unreal past
I studied economics at college.	*If I **hadn't studied** economics, ...* *If **I'd studied** music, ...* *If I **hadn't gone** to college, ...*

Remember that we sometimes use *was/wasn't* instead of *were/weren't* in informal speech.

The main clause

The main clause usually uses *would* or *might*.

***If I were/was** a musician,...*
*...I think **I'd be** happier.*
*...**I'd probably earn** less money than I do.*
*...I **might become** famous.*

For the past, use *would have* or *might have*.

***If I'd studied** music, ...*
*I **would have chosen** the violin as my instrument.*
*I **might have gotten** a job with the Boston Symphony.*

You can usually reverse the order of the two clauses:
I probably would have chosen the violin as my instrument if I'd studied music.

Notes: Sometimes the *if* clause is in the past and the main clause is in the present, or vice versa.

past + present
***If I'd become** a musician, ...*
*I **would make** less money.*

present + past
***If I didn't make** so much money, ...*
*I **wouldn't have been able** to buy my Porsche or my apartment in New York.*
See also Units 11, 13, 14, and 15.

If you have studied the structure *if* + past perfect + *would* + simple form of the verb, you already know a lot about this type of sentence.

Sweet Sixteen

1 Work in small groups and discuss the following questions:

- Do you think that the age you are is a good age to be?
- What do you think is the best age to be? Why?
- Have you ever wished you were older or younger?

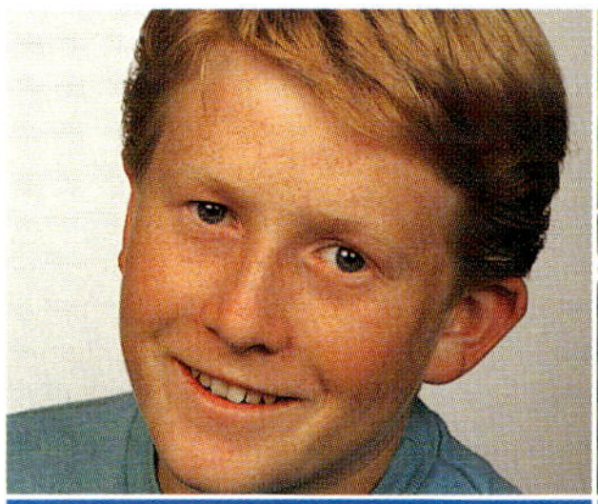
Fred (12)

Jerry (16)

Yvette (21)

Carla (mid thirties)

2 54 These four people were asked the same questions. Listen to the interviews and take notes on their answers.

3 Match the person to the question he / she was asked.

a) Do you mind if I ask you how old you are?
b) How old are you now?
c) You just had an important birthday, right?
d) How old are you?

Which is the most polite form?

Delicate questions

When you want to ask about something delicate, indirect questions are often more polite than direct questions.

For example:

Direct question	*Indirect question*
How old are you?	Do you mind if I ask (you) how old you are?
Do you have a girlfriend?	Do you mind if I ask (you) if / whether you have a girlfriend?

Instead of *Do you mind* + present, you can use *Would you mind* + past as a more formal alternative.

Taboo /təbu/
taboos. If there is a **taboo** on a subject or activity, it is a social custom to avoid doing that activity or talking about that subject, because people find them embarrassing or offensive. *The topic of addiction remains something of a taboo.* Also an adjective. *Cancer is a taboo subject, and people are frightened or embarrassed to talk openly about it.*

(Collins Cobuild English Dictionary)

1 Make indirect questions from the cues.

Do you mind if I ask you …

a) where / buy / your / shirt?
b) why / study / English?
c) get / here / on / time?
d) where / go / after / class?
e) enjoy / this / class?
f) what / do / this / tonight?

Now ask your partner the questions.

2 Work with a partner. In your country, which of these questions do you not ask somebody you don't know very well?

a) What perfume are you wearing?
b) How much do you make?
c) Where did you buy your shoes?
d) How much do you weigh?
e) Who did you vote for in the last election?
f) Are you married?
g) Is that your natural hair color?
h) How much did your house cost?

3 Can you think of any other "taboo" questions? Add them to the list.

4 Work with a partner. Change the direct questions in 2 into indirect questions using *Do you mind if I ask you … ?*

5 Take turns asking and answering the questions. Give a true answer or politely refuse to answer.

LANGUAGE TOOLBOX

No, I don't mind.
No, not at all.
I'd rather not say.
I'd rather not answer that.
Yes, I do mind, actually.

16

Review 2

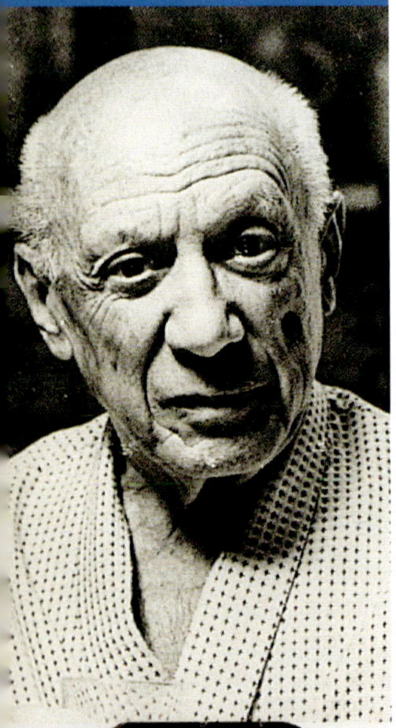
Pablo Picasso

Who Said What?

1 Here are some quotes by well-known people. Match the quote to the person.

a) "The Beatles are more popular than Jesus Christ."
b) "In the future, everyone will be famous for fifteen minutes."
c) "Rock 'n' roll has no future."
d) "Painting a picture is either easy or impossible."
e) "England is a nation of shopkeepers."
f) "Words are the most powerful drug used by mankind."
g) "I love Mickey Mouse more than any woman I've ever known."
h) "I've never hated a man enough to give diamonds back."
i) "There's no such thing as a bad Picasso."
j) "I don't want to belong to any club that will accept me as a member."
k) "I never think about the future."
l) "There is no sin except stupidity."

Walt Disney	Salvador Dali	Groucho Marx	Pablo Picasso	Oscar Wilde
Zsa Zsa Gabor	Albert Einstein	Rudyard Kipling	Napoleon Bonaparte	
Andy Warhol	Frank Sinatra	John Lennon		

Check your answers on page 140.

Groucho Marx

2 Report the quotes in 1.

For example:
John Lennon once said the Beatles were more popular than Jesus Christ.

3 If you could be famous for 15 minutes, as the quote in 1 suggests, what would you like it to be for? Think of three things.

For example:
I'd like to score the winning run in a World Series game.

I wish ...

1 Read these three wishes. Then add one of your own.

I wish there were more hours in the day.
(Sue)

I wish I'd climbed Mount Fuji when I was in Japan.
(Vaughan)

I wish I could play the piano.
(Jon)

Zsa Zsa Gabor

2 Collect your classmates' wishes and write them down.

3 What are the most common wishes in your class? What are the most unusual wishes?

Wish tree

A tradition in Japan is to write a wish on a piece of paper and then tie it to a tree.

In Your Dreams

Conditionals

1 Work in small groups and discuss these questions.

If you …

a) could be anywhere in the world for the next 24 hours, where would you go?
b) were on a five-year space mission and could take one of your possessions, what would it be?
c) could have the answer to any one question, what would you want to know?
d) could change one thing about your country, what would it be?
e) could relive one week of your life, which week would it be?
f) could have one day with someone from history, who would it be?
g) won $1 million in the lottery next week, what would you do with the money?
h) could change your sex for one year, what would you do during that time?
i) could be transported into the future, when and where would you like to go to?
j) could be any animal, what would you be?

2 Report three interesting things from your discussions to the class.

The Real You

Conditionals

1 Complete the questionnaire below.

DISCOVER THE REAL YOU!

SECTION 1	SECTION 2	SECTION 3	SECTION 4
1 If you are with a group of people, do you generally … a) like to have the whole group as your audience? b) talk with one person at a time?	**1** Would you say you usually get along better with … a) reliable, stable people? b) unpredictable, spontaneous people?	**1** Would you be happier if you were known as … a) a person who is always reasonable? b) a person who is always compassionate?	**1** If you go somewhere for the day, do you usually … a) plan what you will do and when you'll do it? b) just go?
2 Do you tend to have … a) casual friendships with a lot of people? b) close friendships with a few people?	**2** If you were a teacher, would you rather teach … a) fact-based courses? b) courses involving theory?	**2** What is more important, someone's … a) rights? b) feelings?	**2** When you have a special job to do, do you … a) organize it carefully before you start? b) find out what is necessary as you go along?
3 If there is some gossip about one of your friends, will you usually be … a) one of the first to hear about it? b) one of the last to find out what's going on?	**3** If you could choose, would you prefer to be … a) practical and good at fixing things? b) creative and artistic?	**3** Would you say you more often let … a) your head rule your heart? b) your heart rule your head?	**3** If you had been asked last Saturday morning what you were going to do that day, would you have … a) known pretty well? b) had no idea?
4 Would you say you … a) can be enthusiastic about most things if necessary? b) can be enthusiastic only about things of particular importance to you?	**4** Would you say you are … a) conventional? b) original?	**4** Given the choice, would you rather work for someone who is … a) always fair? b) always kind?	**4** Do you generally do things at the last minute? a) sometimes b) often
5 If you could choose, would you rather things around you were … a) busy? b) quiet?	**5** Which of these words do you prefer? a) certainty b) possibility	**5** Which of these words do you prefer? a) determined b) devoted	**5** Would you say the routine parts of your day are … a) restful? b) boring?

2 Work with a partner. Exchange questionnaires and turn to page 142 to find out what it means. Is the description an accurate summary of your partner?

I Predict…

will **1** Here are some predictions about the future made by some students. Put the verb in parentheses into an appropriate future form. Then write four predictions of your own.

Giuseppe Italy
In two years, (1) I'll be living (live) in the same country as I am now.

Mayumi Japan
I (5) ________ (forget) how to speak English 20 years from now.

Maria Mexico
I (2) ________ (get married) by the time I'm 30.

Joe U.S.
By the end of the year, I (6) ________ (travel) to a new country.

Renato Brazil
In five years, I (3) ________ (speak) English every day.

Björn Sweden
I (7) ________ (be) a millionaire ten years from now.

Ulrike Germany
By this time next week, I (4) ________ probably (fall) in love again!

Jean Canada
Before I die, I (8) ________ (visit) the moon!

2 Interview a classmate to find out whether each statement in 1 is true or false for him / her. Take a class survey.

For example:
Eight people in our class think they'll be living in the same country as they are now in two years.

The World of Languages

Questions **1** Work with a partner and discuss the following questions:

a) When was language first written down?
b) When was the first alphabet developed?
c) How many languages are there in the world?
d) Which are the five most spoken languages in the world?
e) How many words are there in English?
f) Which are the most common words in English?
g) Which languages do the words *ketchup* and *shampoo* originally come from?
h) Which country has 13 languages on its bank notes?

2 55 You are going to hear Kim Thomas, a professor of linguistics, being interviewed. Listen and check your answers to the questions in 1.

3 Listen again. Write five more questions about the interview. Ask some classmates your questions.

For example:
Who were the first people to write down their language?

Doing the Right Thing

Modals **1** Work with a partner and take the following quiz.

How would you cope around the world? Are the following statements TRUE or FALSE?

1 You shouldn't tip in India. ● T ● F
2 In England, you don't have to carry ID with you. ● T ● F
3 In Holland, friends are supposed to kiss each other four times when saying hello and good-bye. ● T ● F
4 You should never give a clock as a gift in China. ● T ● F
5 In Japan, you can't vote until you are 19. ● T ● F
6 You can drive as fast as you want in Germany. ● T ● F
7 In England, people are expected to take turns buying drinks in a pub. ● T ● F
8 In Zimbabwe, you can pay fines with flowers. ● T ● F
9 In Spain, children under 16 aren't allowed into bars. ● T ● F
10 You are expected to take some cheese with you when you are invited to dinner in France. ● T ● F
11 In Japan, you shouldn't blow your nose in public. ● T ● F
12 When giving flowers in Germany, you should give an even number. ● T ● F
13 You have to show up to vote in Australia. ● T ● F
14 In most states in the U.S., you can drive a car when you're 15. ● T ● F
15 You must eat with your left hand in Sudan. ● T ● F
16 In Sweden, you aren't allowed to smoke until you are 16. ● T ● F
17 In England, you must never turn your back on a picture of the Queen. ● T ● F
18 You don't have to wear a motorcycle helmet in Italy. ● T ● F
19 In Finland, you can't buy alcohol in a supermarket. ● T ● F
20 In Saudi Arabia, it's normal for stores to close for about 15 minutes four times a day. ● T ● F

Check your answers on page 142.

2 Can you think of any rules in your country? What would a visitor need to know?

Greetings from Vietnam

General review Read the letter to Marcella. Choose the best alternative. In some cases, both alternatives are possible.

Dear Marcella,

Well, we're finally here in Vietnam, and we (1) **have / 're having** an absolutely (2) **good / wonderful** time. We're now in a (3) **beautiful small / small beautiful** market town in the mountains in the northernmost part of the country. The town is at the end of a steep valley, and there are the most (4) **amazing / amazed** terraces as far as the eye can see. Miguel (5) **said me / said** he thought they (6) **were / are** the most spectacular views he (7) **had / has** ever seen. I've taken so (8) **much / many** pictures since we (9) **are / 've been** here. I think I (10) **'ve / 'd** taken only about a dozen before we (11) **arrived / had arrived** here in Sapa. We (12) **go / 've taken** a long walk every day so far. In the evenings, we're pretty (13) **exhausting / exhausted,** so we just have dinner—Vietnamese food is (14) **very / absolutely** incredible.

Yesterday, Stefan had his hair cut by the woman (15) **which / who** owns the hotel (16) **that / where** we're staying. He says he (17) **likes / liked** it, but he (18) **shouldn't / can't** have looked in a mirror! It looks awful!

We think we might (19) **to stay / stay** here for a (20) **few / little** more days before heading back south. With a little luck, this time next week, we'll (21) **have left / be leaving** the mountains behind us and we'll (22) **lie / be lying** on a deserted sandy beach! I'm really looking forward to (23) **do / doing** nothing for (24) **a few / few** days! We really wish you (25) **would be / were** here with us. If you (26) **are / were**, you (27) **'d / 'll** really love it! If only you (28) **didn't break / hadn't broken** your arm! Oh, well. I guess things (29) **could / can** have been a lot worse! Anyway, I hope it (30) **got / is getting** better now.

So, how are things back home? Miguel and Stefan want to know how (31) **are you / you are** coping without (32) **them / they**! We're all expecting (33) **lots of / much** juicy gossip when we (34) **'ll get / get** back next month!

It's late, so (35) **I'll finish / am finishing** now. (36) **Say / Tell** Juliette we'll write (37) **her / to her** a letter soon. Take care and have fun!

Love,

Virginia and Lena xxxxxxxx

Additional material

6 News

The passive voice, 6

Student A

Here are your three stories. Don't show them to anyone.

1 (1) A dramatic chase involved police cars (2) after somebody spotted a sign in the back window of a car (3) saying "Help us, we have been kidnapped." (4) It had been put there by four unhappy children (5) who didn't want to go on vacation to Atlantic City with their parents.

2 (1) An 85-year-old man was asked to leave the Garden State Parkway by the police (2) because he was riding in a wheelchair. (3) His 65-year-old son was pushing the wheelchair.

3 (1) After he spent many hours practicing birdcalls at home, (2) some woods were entered by Maine ornithologist Larry Bloom (3) to try them out (4) and he was shot dead by a hunter.

3 Dating

Twenty-First Century Dating, 2

Student A

Read about couple 1.
When you've finished reading, close your book and tell Student B about the couple.

Couple 1

I've finally found the man of my dreams. We have so much in common; we laugh at the same things and talk for hours. There's only one problem. We've never met. Tom lives in San Diego. I live in Toronto. We met on the Net.

I wasn't looking for Mr. Right; I was just hoping to meet some interesting people. The American singles dating site didn't charge a fee, so I filled in a form with my likes and dislikes and a short paragraph about myself. By the end of the week, I had about 25 responses. Over the next five months, I went on eight dates with men I met on the Net. One I dated for about two months; others I saw a couple of times before I realized there was no real spark. Then, two months ago, just as I was about to take my data off the Net, I received an e-mail from a guy in California named Tom. His note was funny, and he sounded interesting, so I decided to write back.

Soon I found myself rushing back home after work to check my e-mails. Tom made me laugh; he challenged my opinions. We talked about everything. My friends weren't particularly impressed when I told them about him, but I knew this one was different.

We exchanged pictures by e-mail, and we liked what we saw, but at this stage looks didn't matter. Then Tom and I had what we consider our first "date." We talked for 11 hours, and that phone call changed the course of our relationship. We've decided to meet.

7 Party

Phrasal verbs, 4

Dictionary

Dictionary is a game everyone can play. The object of the game is for teams to guess the correct meaning of words.

Team A

1 Invent two false definitions for each of the phrasal verbs below:

get along with. If you *get along with* people, you like them and have friendly relationships with them.
go along with. If you *go along with* someone, you agree with with him/her.

run out of. If you ***run out of*** something, you don't have any of it left. *We've run out of milk. Can you buy some at the supermarket?*
take in. If you *take someone in,* you allow him/her to stay in your house or country, especially if the person is homeless or in trouble.

2 Read aloud your three definitions (one true, two false) for the first phrasal verb. Team B guesses which definition is correct. If they guess correctly, they get a point. If they guess incorrectly, you get a point.

3 Now listen to Team B's definitions and guess the correct one. Take turns. The winning team is the team with the most points.

4 If you want to continue the game, here are more phrasal verbs:

get away. To leave a place or a person's company. *I'm sorry I'm late. I couldn't get away from the office until now.*
get through. If you get through something, you finish it. *I couldn't get through that book. It was really difficult.*

put up with. (something or someone): To tolerate or accept something or someone. *I can't put up with this noise anymore.*
run into. If you *run into* (someone), you meet someone unexpectedly. *I ran into Jim at the station.*

8 Review 1

Sound and Vision, 2

16 Review 2

Who Said What?, 1

Answers

a) John Lennon b) Andy Warhol c) Frank Sinatra
d) Salvador Dali e) Napoleon Bonaparte
f) Rudyard Kipling g) Walt Disney h) Zsa Zsa Gabor
i) Pablo Picasso j) Groucho Marx k) Albert Einstein
l) Oscar Wilde

11 Journey

Conrad's Around-the-World Trip, 3

Answers

Photo 1 Patagonia, Argentina
Photo 2 The Basque country, Spain
Photo 3 Lake Como, Italy
Photo 4 New Delhi, India
Photo 5 Fiji
Photo 6 Petra, Jordan

3 Dating

Twenty-First Century Dating, 2

Student B

Read about couple 2.
When you've finished reading, close your book and tell Student A about the couple.

Couple 2

It was love at first sight for Joel Emerson and Lisa Bunyan, which was lucky because they met for the first time on their wedding day!
As a publicity stunt, a local radio station ran a seven-week contest, which they called "Two Strangers and a Wedding." The radio station voted marketing consultant Joel Emerson, 24, the "most eligible bachelor." Lisa Bunyan, 22, who works in a management training company, was one of 300 single women who rushed to the phone to offer herself as his bride.
The only direct contact they had before their wedding day was when Joel proposed by telephone on the radio. An estimated 50,000 listeners witnessed the romantic (but not particularly intimate) moment when Lisa said yes.
The groom's mother was not amused and told a local newspaper that she was shocked and disgusted. As the couple left for their honeymoon in Cancun, they told the same newspaper, "We know that we're doing the right thing."

1 Friends

Tic-Tac-Toe, 1

Team A

FACTS FOR QUIZ QUESTIONS

Choose ten facts and write questions for them.

1 A spider has eight legs.
2 Greenland is the largest island in the world.
3 The Atlas mountains are in northern Africa.
4 There are nine players on a baseball team.
5 Russian uses the Cyrillic alphabet.
6 The capital of Colombia is Bogotá.
7 Tutankhamen was a king of Egypt.
8 Ringo was the smallest Beatle.
9 Margaret Thatcher was the first woman prime minister of England.
10 Neil Armstrong was the first man on the moon.
11 The Black Forest is in Germany.
12 Hollywood is in Los Angeles, California.
13 Alaska is the largest state in the U.S.
14 Leonardo da Vinci painted the *Mona Lisa (La Giaconda).*
15 Valentine's Day is on February 14.
16 The capital of Algeria is Algiers.
17 Schipol Airport is in Amsterdam.

3 Dating

Dream Date. Vocabulary, 3

Calculating your *Ki* Astrology sign.

Think of your year of birth. The Chinese year runs from February to February, so anyone born between January 1 and February 3 needs to count the previous year as the year of birth.

Add up the last two numbers of your year of birth. For example, if you were born in 1970, add seven and zero (7 + 0) to get seven. If you were born in 1985, add eight and five (8 + 5) to get thirteen.

If the number you have is 9 or less, subtract it from 10 to find your Ki sign. For example, for a person born in 1970, 10 – 7 = 3.

If the number you have is 10 or more, add up the two digits. For example, with thirteen, add one and three to get four (1 + 3 = 4). Then subtract the new number from 10 to find your Ki sign. For example, for a person born in 1985, 10 – 4 = 6.

13 Communication

What Do Men and Women Really Think?, 2

Answers

(1) women (2) men (3) men (4) women
(5) women (6) men (7) women (8) men
(9) women (10) men (11) men (12) women
(13) men (14) women (15) men (16) women
(17) men (18) men (19) women (20) men
(21) women (22) women (23) men

1 Friends

You've Got a Friend. Vocabulary, 3

Answers

a) The Beatles, *I Wanna Hold Your Hand*
b) 'N Sync, *That's When I'll Stop Loving You*
c) Bob Dylan, *It Ain't Me Babe*
d) Destiny's Child, *Bridges*
e) The Rolling Stones, *Satisfaction*
f) Oasis, *Roll With It*

6 News

The passive voice, 6

Student B

Here are your three stories. Don't show them to anyone.

1 (1) Police cars were involved in a dramatic chase (2) after a sign was spotted in the back window of a car (3) saying "Help us, somebody has kidnapped us." (4) Four unhappy children had put it there (5) who didn't want to be taken on vacation to Atlantic City by their parents.

2 (1) The police asked an 85-year-old man in a wheelchair to leave the Garden State Parkway (2) because a wheelchair was being ridden in by him. (3) The wheelchair was being pushed by his 65-year-old son.

3 (1) After many hours had been spent by him practising birdcalls at home, (2) Maine ornithologist Larry Bloom went into some woods (3) for them to be tried out (4) and a hunter shot him dead.

10 Time

To Whom It May Concern, 6

1566b 49th East Street
Santa Barbara, CA

Worldwide Airlines Inc
PO Box 2983
Chicago, IL

February 5, 2002

Dear Sir or Madam,

Application for the position of flight attendant

I am writing in response to your advertisement in the *Los Angeles Times* and would like to apply for the position of flight attendant.

I am 21 years old, and I have just graduated from college. I enclose my résumé for your attention, and I would be pleased to attend an interview at any time convenient to you.

I would be grateful if you could send me an application form and some additional information about the job.

I look forward to hearing from you.

Sincerely,

Anthony Clifford

Anthony Clifford

16 Review 2

The Real You

1 Find out the personality type of your classmate. Take one letter from each section (for example, ESFJ, INFP, etc.).

SECTION 1	SECTION 2	SECTION 3	SECTION 4
If you have answered mostly A's, you are an "E" (extroverted) person. If you have answered mostly B's, you are an "I" (introverted) person.	If you have answered mostly A's, you are an "S" (sensing) person. If you have answered mostly B's, you are an "N" (intuitive) person.	If you have answered mostly A's, you are a "T" (thinking) person. If you have answered mostly B's, you are an "F" (feeling) person.	If you have answered mostly A's, you are a "J" (judging) person. If you have answered mostly B's, you are a "P" (perceptive) person.

2 The following shows the main characteristics of each personality type. Find your classmate's personality type.

ISTJ	Likes to take responsibility and organize things. Orderly, duty-bound, systematic, thorough.
ISFJ	Hardworking, meticulous, patient, responsible. Gives stability to people and projects.
ISTP	Onlooker. Quietly observing and analyzing life. Independent, logical, realistic.
ISFP	Retiring, sensitive, caring, gentle. Dislikes disagreement and does not force opinions on others.
INFJ	Individualistic, intense. Determined and committed to his/her ideals, principles, and work.
INTJ	Has great drive for his/her own ideas and interests. Skeptical and critical of others. Stubborn.
INFP	Reserved, curious and reticent until he/she knows someone well. Warm, loyal, enthusiastic.
INTP	Logical, analytical, precise, likes solving problems. Scientific interests. Doesn't like small talk.
ESTP	Practical, mechanically minded, versatile, tolerant. Good at on-the-spot problem solving.
ESFP	Outgoing, social, friendly, enjoys everything. Athletic and active. Has a lot of common sense.
ESTJ	Likes to organize and control. Direct, impersonal, matter-of-fact, business-minded, systematic.
ESFJ	Warmhearted, helpful, cooperative, hardworking, talkative. Needs harmony around him/her.
ENFP	Able to do almost anything if interested. High-spirited, imaginative, spontaneous, quick-thinking.
ENTP	Quick, outspoken, resourceful, witty. Likes to play devil's advocate. Doesn't like routine.
ENFJ	Concerned about what others think. Considerate, sympathetic, diplomatic, supportive.
ENTJ	Frank, fair, tough, decisive. Intelligent, knowledgeable, confident. Good at reasoning.

(Myers-Briggs Type Indicator)

7 Party

Parties, 5

Are You a Party Animal or a Party Pooper?

KEY

1	a = 1	b = 2	c = 3
2	a = 2	b = 3	c = 1
3	a = 1	b = 3	c = 2
4	a = 3	b = 1	c = 1
5	a = 2	b = 1	c = 3
6	a = 3	b = 2	c = 1

What it means

- If you scored between 6 and 10: You are definitely the life of the party.
- If you scored between 11 and 14: You could afford to let your hair down occasionally.
- If you scored between 15 and 18: You obviously like the quiet life—but you don't have to take everything so seriously!

11 Journey

Coast to Coast, 3

He removed the seat. On the underside was the inscription:

"To Elvis, love James Dean."

16 Review 2

Doing the Right Thing

Answers	What it means
(1) F (2) T (3) F – it's three times (4) T (5) F (6) T (7) T (8) F – but you can with animals (9) F (10) F (11) T (12) F – except on someone's 20th birthday, when you give them 20 (13) T (14) F – in most states, it's 16 or 17 (15) F (16) F (17) F (18) F (19) F (20) T	If you scored between 15 and 20: You're either extremely well-traveled or extremely intuitive. You'll have no problems wherever you go. If you scored between 10 and 15: You should be O.K. in most situations, but be careful! If you scored between 5 and 10: You might make life difficult for yourself from time to time, but you'll survive. If you scored between 0 and 5: Don't go anywhere without a good friend!

1 Friends

Tic-Tac-Toe, 1

Team B

FACTS FOR QUIZ QUESTIONS:

Choose ten facts and write questions for them.

1 John F. Kennedy was assassinated in Dallas.
2 An insect has six legs.
3 The longest river in Europe is the Volga.
4 Picasso was from Spain.
5 Madonna's first name is *Madonna*.
6 The last president of the USSR was Mikhail Gorbachev.
7 Yuri Gagarin was the first man in space.
8 The first modern Olympic Games were in Athens.
9 Patagonia is in Argentina.
10 Roger Moore was the third James Bond.
11 Mount Etna is in Sicily.
12 Quito is the capital of Ecuador.
13 Mickey Mouse has four fingers.
14 The longest river in the world is the Nile.
15 The ancient city of Petra is in Jordan.
16 Riyadh is the capital of Saudi Arabia.
17 Uruguay was the first country to win the World Cup.

6 News

The passive voice, 6

Student C

You are the editor for your group. You will need a pen and a piece of paper.

Explain the activity to your partners.

1 Ask your partners to read their stories aloud.
2 Discuss the two versions and decide together which are the best parts from each one. Sometimes the passive is better, sometimes the active is better, and sometimes it doesn't matter.
3 Ask your partners to dictate the best parts to you, and write the final versions of the three stories.
4 When you have finished, think of a headline for each story.

3 Dating

A boyfriend's worst nightmare, 3

"Pleased to meet you," I lied.
"Hi, I'm Eddie," he said, "and this is my fiancée, Tina. We got engaged last week."
I mumbled something and shook both their hands. At that moment, an enormous weight was lifted from my mind. Eddie is, in fact, a great guy, and we get along really well. But best of all, he's completely devoted to his girlfriend.

7 Party

Phrasal verbs, 4

Dictionary

Dictionary is a game everyone can play. The object of the game is for teams to guess the correct meaning of words.

Team B

1 Invent two false definitions for each of the phrasal verbs below:

cut down on. If you *cut down on* something, you consume or do less of it.
get (one) down. If something or someone *gets you down*, it makes you unhappy.

let (someone) down. If you *let* someone *down*, you disappoint that person.
take after. If you *take after* a member of your family, you resemble him/her in your appearance, your behavior, or your character.

2 Read aloud your three definitions (one true, two false) for the first phrasal verb. Team A guesses which definition is correct. If they guess correctly, they get a point. If they guess incorrectly, you get a point.

3 Now listen to Team A's definitions and guess the correct one. Take turns. The winning team is the team with the most points.

4 If you want to continue the game, here are more phrasal verbs:

get over. To recover from an unpleasant experience or an illness.
put off. If you *put* something *off*, you delay doing it. *The game was put off for a week because of the heavy rain.*

run across. If you *run across* something, you find it accidentally. *She ran across some old letters from a college friend.*
turn (someone) down. If you *turn down* a person or a request or offer, you refuse the request or offer.

Verb structures

Basic structures

		TENSES		MODALS
ASPECT	VOICE	**Present**	**Past**	*will (would, must…)*
simple	active	He **writes** letters.	He **wrote** letters.	He **will write** letters.
	passive	Letters **are written**.	Letters **were written**.	Letters **will be written**.
continuous	active	He **is writing** letters.	He **was writing** letters.	He **will be writing** letters.
	passive	Letters **are being written**.	Letters **were being written**.	Letters **will be being written**.*
perfect	active	He **has written** letters.	He **had written** letters.	He **will have written** letters.
	passive	Letters **have been written**.	Letters **had been written**.	Letters **will have been written**.

* rarer structure

Simple present

See units 1 and 2.

Affirmative	Negative	Question
I / You / We / They **write**.	I / You / We / They **don't (do not) write**.	**Do** I / you / we / they **write**?
He / She / It **writes**.	He / She / It **doesn't (does not) write**.	**Does** he / she / it **write**?

Present continuous

See units 1, 2, and 7.

Affirmative	Negative	Question
I'm (am) writing.	**I'm not (am not) writing**.	**Am** I **writing**?
You / We / They**'re (are) writing**.	You / We / They**'re not/aren't (are not) writing**.	**Are** you / we / they **writing**?
He / She / It**'s (is) writing**.	He / She / It **isn't (is not) writing**.	**Is** he / she / it **writing**?

Present perfect

See units 1, 2, 3, and 4.

Affirmative	Negative	Question
I / You / We / They**'ve (have) written**.	I / You / We / They **haven't (have not) written**.	**Have** I / you / we / they **written**?
He / She / **It's (has) written**.	He / She / It **hasn't (has not) written**.	**Has** he / she / it **written**?

Note: See list of irregular verbs on page 147.

Simple past

See units 1, 3, and 4.

Affirmative	Negative	Question
I / You / He / She / It / We / They **wrote**.	I / You / He / She / It / We / They **didn't (did not) write**.	**Did** I / you / he / she / it / we / they **write**?

Note: See list of irregular verbs on page 147.

Past continuous

See units 1 and 4.

Affirmative	Negative	Question
I / He / She / It **was writing**.	I / He / She / It **wasn't (was not) writing**.	**Was** I / he / she / it **writing**?
You / We / They **were writing**.	You / We / They **weren't (were not) writing**.	**Were** you / we / they **writing**?

Past perfect

See units 1 and 11.

Affirmative	Negative	Question
I / You / He / She / It / We / They**'d (had) written**.	I / You / He / She / It / We / They **hadn't (had not) written**.	**Had** I / you / he / she / it / we / they **written**?

Note: See list of irregular verbs on page 147.

Future forms

Will

See units 7 and 10.

Affirmative	Negative	Question
Simple		
I / You / He / She / It / We / They **will write**.	I / You / He / She / It / We / They **won't write**.	**Will** I / you / he / she / it / we / they **write**?
Continuous		
I / You / He / She / It / We / They **will be writing**.	I / You / He / She / It / We / They **won't be writing**.	**Will** I / you / he / she / it / we / they **be writing**?
Perfect		
I / You / He / She / It / We / They **will have written**.	I / You / He / She / It / We / They **won't have written**.	**Will** I / you / he / she / it / we / they **have written**?

Future (be) *going to*

See unit 7.

Affirmative	Negative	Question
I'm (am) going to write.	I'm not (am not) going to write.	Am I going to write?
You/We/They're (are) going to write.	You/We/They 're not/aren't (are not) going to write.	Are you/we/they going to write?
He/She/It's (is) going to write.	He/She/It isn't (is not) going to write.	Is he/she/it going to write?

Present continuous for future

See unit 7.

Modals

A modal verb has the same forms in all persons.
For example:
I/You/He/She/It/We/They **can come**.

Affirmative	Negative	Question
Can: See units 1, 10, and 11.		
I **can** come.	I **can't (cannot)** come.	**Can** I come?
Could: See units 1 and 11.		
I **could** come.	I **couldn't (could not)** come.	**Could** I come?
Must: See units 1, 10, and 11.		
I **must** come.	I **mustn't (must not)** come.	**Must** I come?
May: See units 1 and 11.		
I **may** come.	I **may not** come.	**May** I come?
Might: See unit 1.		
I **might** come.	I **mightn't (might not)** come.	**Might** I come?
Shall: See unit 1.		
I'll **(shall)** come.	I **shall not** come.	**Shall** I come?
***Shall* is usually used only with questions in the first person (I and we). It is rarely used in American English.**		
Should: See units 1 and 10.		
I **should** come.	I **shouldn't (should not)** come.	**Should** I come?
Will: See units 1, 7, 9, 10, and 13.		
I'**ll (will)** come.	I **won't (will not)** come.	**Will** I come?
Would: See units 1, 5, 11, 14, and 15.		
I'**d (would)** come.	I **wouldn't (would not)** come.	**Would** I come?

Reported speech with backshift

See unit 9.

Present		
"I **write**."		he **wrote**.
"I'**m writing**."	He said/told me...	he **was writing**.
"I'**ve written**."		he **had written**.
Past		
"I **have written**."	He said/told me...	he **had written**.
"I **was writing**."		he **had been writing**.
Modals		
"I **will/would**."		he **would**.
"I **can/could**."		he **could**.
"I **have to**."	He said/told me...	he **had to**.
"I **must**."		he **had to**.*

***_Must_ has no past form. The practical solution is often to use _had to_.**

Questions		
"**Do** you **work** here?"		**if** I **worked** there.
"When **are** you **leaving**?"	He asked me...	**when** I **was leaving**.
"**Have** you **been** to Istanbul?"		**if** I **had been** to Istanbul.
Imperative		
"**Meet** in my office."	He told me...	**to meet** in his office.

Real conditionals

See unit 13.

If clause	Main clause
If you **have** any problems,	**call** me. I'**ll help** you.
If you **aren't going to** the theater,	**can** I have your ticket? **do** you **want** to come out for dinner?
If you'**ve finished** your work,	you **can go** home. **tell** your teacher.

Unreal conditionals

See units 14 and 15.

If clause	Main clause
If you **were** better organized,	you **wouldn't have** so many problems. you **wouldn't have had** that problem yesterday.
If I'**d known** earlier,	I **wouldn't be** in this situation now. I **could have done** something about it.

I wish...

See units 14 and 15.

Fact	Wish
I'**m** not rich.	I **wish** I **were/was** rich.
I **didn't study** hard in school.	I **wish** I'**d (had) studied** harder in school.

Grammar glossary

verb | adjective | conjunction | modal auxiliary | adverb | article | pronoun | main verb

Learn these useful words and you can understand more about the language you are studying.

determiner | noun | pronoun | main verb | preposition | noun | auxiliary verb

Agents are people or things that perform an action in a passive sentence.
For example: *He was brought up by* ***his grandparents.***

Backshift is when a verb moves "one tense back" in a conditional clause or reported statement.
For example: *"I can't come."* ➔ *He said he* ***couldn't*** *come.*

Clauses are groups of words containing a verb.
For example: ***He said*** (main clause) ***that he'll be late.*** (subordinate clause)
Note: Subordinate clauses are introduced by conjunctions.

Combinations refer to words that frequently occur together.
For example: ***common sense…get along well…Happy birthday.***

Complements refer to adjective or noun phrases that give more information about the subject of a clause.
For example: *She was* ***very happy…*** *It's* ***my fault…*** *I look like* ***a complete idiot.***
Note: usually after verbs like *be, seem, feel.*

Expressions are groups of words that belong together where the words and word order never or rarely change.
For example: ***black and white…That reminds me,*** *I have to buy some toothpaste…* ***How do you do?***

Objects usually come after the verb and show who or what is affected by the verb.
For example: *She closed* ***the window…*** *My neighbor hates* ***me…*** *I made* ***a pot of coffee.***
Note: Some verbs take a direct object (DO) and indirect object (IO).
For example: *She gave* ***him*** (IO) ***a kiss*** (DO)*…He sent* ***her*** (IO) ***some flowers*** (DO)*…I teach* ***students*** (IO) ***English*** (DO).

Partitives used with *of* can make noncountable nouns countable.
For example: ***a gallon*** *of gas…* ***a piece*** *of advice…* ***an item*** *of news.*

Relative clauses can be either defining (restrictive) or nondefining (nonrestrictive). A defining relative clause is necessary to identify the person or thing being talked about in the main clause.
For example: *The people* ***who live next door*** *have three kids.*
A nondefining relative clause is not necessary for identification and just gives extra information.
For example: *The Smiths,* ***who have three children,*** *live next door.*
Note: Relative clauses are usually introduced by the relative pronoun *who, that,* or *which* or by the relative adverb *whose, when, where,* or *why.*

Subjects usually come before the verb and refer to the main person or thing you are talking about.
For example: ***Money*** *doesn't grow on trees…* ***My tailor*** *is rich…* ***The biggest rock group in the world*** *has started a world tour.*

Phonetic symbols

VOWELS AND DIPHTHONGS

/ɪ/	big fish	/bɪg fɪʃ/
/i/	green beans	/grin binz/
/ʊ/	should look	/ʃʊd lʊk/
/u/	blue moon	/blu mun/
/ɛ/	ten hens	/tɛn hɛnz/
/ə/	about bananas	/əbaʊt bənænəz/
/æ/	fat cat	/fæt kæt/
/ʌ/	must come	/mʌst kʌm/
/ɑ/	hot spot	/hɑt spɑt/
/ɔ/	fall ball	/fɔl bɔl/
/ei/	face	/feis/
/ɔi/	boy	/bɔi/
/ou/	nose	/nouz/
/ɑi/	eye	/ɑi/
/ɑu/	mouth	/mɑuθ/
/ir/	dear	/dir/
/ɑr/	bar	/bɑr/
/ər/	learn words	/lərn wərdz/
/ɛr/	hair care	/hær kær/
/ɔr/	four sports	/fɔr spɔrts/

CONSONANTS

/p/	pen	/pɛn/
/b/	bad	/bæd/
/t/	tea	/ti/
/d/	dog	/dɔg/
/tʃ/	church	/tʃərtʃ/
/dʒ/	jazz	/dʒæz/
/k/	cost	/kɔst/
/g/	girl	/gərl/
/f/	far	/fɑr/
/v/	voice	/vɔis/
/θ/	thin	/θɪn/
/ð/	then	/ðɛn/
/s/	snake	/sneik/
/z/	noise	/nɔɪz/
/ʃ/	shop	/ʃɑp/
/ʒ/	measure	/mɛʒɛr/
/m/	make	/meik/
/n/	nine	/nɑin/
/ŋ/	sing	/sɪŋ/
/h/	house	/hɑus/
/l/	leg	/lɛg/
/r/	red	/rɛd/
/w/	wet	/wɛt/
/y/	yes	/yɛs/

STRESS

In this book, word stress is shown by underlining the stressed syllable.
For example: water; result; disappointing

LETTERS OF THE ALPHABET

/ei/	/i/	/ɛ/	/ɑi/	/ou/	/u/	/ɑr/
Aa	Bb	Ff	Ii	Oo	Qq	Rr
Hh	Cc	Ll	Yy		Uu	
Jj	Dd	Mm			Ww	
Kk	Ee	Nn				
	Gg	Ss				
	Pp	Xx				
	Tt					
	Vv					
	Zz					

Irregular verbs

Infinitive	Simple past	Past participle
be	was/were	been
beat	beat	beaten
become	became	become
begin	began	begun
bend	bent	bent
bet	bet	bet
bite	bit	bitten
blow	blew	blown
break	broke	broken
bring	brought	brought
build	built	built
burn	burned	burned
burst	burst	burst
buy	bought	bought
can	could	(been able)
catch	caught	caught
choose	chose	chosen
come	came	come
cost	cost	cost
cut	cut	cut
deal	dealt	dealt
do	did	done
draw	drew	drawn
dream	dreamed	dreamed
drink	drank	drunk
drive	drove	driven
eat	ate	eaten
fall	fell	fallen
feed	fed	fed
feel	felt	felt
fight	fought	fought
find	found	found
fly	flew	flown
forget	forgot	forgotten
forgive	forgave	forgiven
freeze	froze	frozen
get	got	gotten
give	gave	given
go	went	gone
grow	grew	grown
hang	hung/hanged	hung/hanged
have	had	had
hear	heard	heard
hide	hid	hidden
hit	hit	hit
hold	held	held
hurt	hurt	hurt
keep	kept	kept
kneel	knelt/kneeled	knelt/kneeled
know	knew	known
lay	laid	laid
lead	led	led
learn	learned	learned
leave	left	left
lend	lent	lent
let	let	let

Infinitive	Simple past	Past participle
lie	lay/lied	lied/lain
light	lit/lighted	lit/lighted
lose	lost	lost
make	made	made
mean	meant	meant
meet	met	met
must	had to	(had to)
pay	paid	paid
put	put	put
read	read /rɛd/	read /rɛd/
ride	rode	ridden
ring	rang	rung
rise	rose	risen
run	ran	run
say	said	said
see	saw	seen
sell	sold	sold
send	sent	sent
set	set	set
shake	shook	shaken
shine	shined/shone	shined/shone
shoot	shot	shot
show	showed	shown
shrink	shrank	shrunk
shut	shut	shut
sing	sang	sung
sink	sank	sunk
sit	sat	sat
sleep	slept	slept
slide	slid	slid
smell	smelled	smelled
speak	spoke	spoken
spell	spelled	spelled
spend	spent	spent
spill	spilled	spilled
split	split	split
spoil	spoiled	spoiled
spread	spread	spread
stand	stood	stood
steal	stole	stolen
stick	stuck	stuck
swear	swore	sworn
swell	swelled	swollen/swelled
swim	swam	swum
take	took	taken
teach	taught	taught
tear	tore	torn
tell	told	told
think	thought	thought
throw	threw	thrown
understand	understood	understood
wake	woke	woken
wear	wore	worn
win	won	won
write	wrote	written

Tapescripts

1 Friends

01

(I = Interviewer; J = Judy Medeiros)

I: Welcome to the *Fame Game*. On tonight's program, we're going to talk about the children of famous people. First, let's talk to Judy Medeiros, a member of the Mick Jagger Fan Club. Hi, Judy.
J: Hello.
I: Judy, you know a lot about Mick Jagger, and you also know about his family, right?
J: Yes, I do.
I: Let's talk about Mick's daughter Jade.
J: Sure. With pleasure. I know a lot about her life.
I: First of all, where was she born?
J: She was born in London, but she has dual citizenship.
I: Why is that?
J: Well, her mother, Bianca, is from Nicaragua.
I: Does she still live in London?
J: Oh, no. Jade's living in Ibiza now.
I: Oh, really? How long has she been there?
J: Not long. She moved from London with her two daughters about a year ago.
I: Is she happy there?
J: Yes, she says she's very happy there. She and her daughters like the outdoor life. And her mother speaks Spanish, so Jade feels comfortable in a Latin country.
I: Does she work?
J: Yes, she's very talented. She's a painter. And she has a jewelry business. She also models occasionally.
I: What does she do in her spare time?
J: She doesn't have much spare time. But she likes to read, and she likes to listen to music.
I: And music? What kind of music does she like?
J: Oh, yeah. She likes all kinds—pop, classical…
I: Does she ever listen to the Rolling Stones? Ha, ha.
J: Ha, ha. She says she doesn't. But don't tell her father.
I: I won't tell him. How often does she see her parents?
J: I don't think she sees them very often. Her mother's in New York, and her father is often on tour.
I: What is her favorite place in the world?
J: Well, I know she loves Brazil. Her children love it there too.
I: One final question—how did she get her name?
J: I think her father named her. Her mother wanted her to have a Spanish name.
I: Thanks, Judy. Now we have with us Roger Case, a friend of Bob Marley's son, Ziggy…

02

a) Where was she born?
b) Does she still live in London?
c) How long has she been there?
d) Is she happy there?
e) Does she work?
f) What does she do in her spare time?
g) What kind of music does she like?
h) Does she ever listen to the Rolling Stones?
i) How often does she see her parents?
j) What's her favorite place in the world?
k) How did she get her name?

03

(B = Balvir; T = Tim)

B: …No, I went out with my friend last night. Well, actually, she's my best friend. Have you ever met her?
T: Uh, I don't know.
B: Lisa?
T: You told me about her.
B: I did. She's the Brazilian girl.
T: Uh, yeah.
B: Really pretty… and she has long, dark hair, and she's uh, she's very petite. Uh, yeah, we had a great time. We met… gosh… we've known each other now… about 15 years. Can you believe that?
T: Oh, wow.
B: Yeah, we met… I was working for her dad. He had a casino. Oh, I tell you, those were wild days but, uh, we met working there together, and uh, she has a sister, a younger sister, and she doesn't get along with her very well, so I always like to say that I'm like her sister. I'm like the sister she never had.
T: Hah, hah, hah…
B: We don't have a lot in common, but, uh… 'cause she doesn't work, she's a full-time mom. She has a little boy.
T: Oh, yeah.
B: He's about… he's about 11 now… difficult age. Uhm, uh, but we still get together about once or twice a month, and it's always good to see her.
T: Nice.
B: Yeah.

04

(See page 11.)

05

***You've Got a Friend*, sung by the Brand New Heavies**

When you're down and troubled
And you need some loving care
And nothing, no, is going right
Close your eyes and think of me
Oh, and soon I will be there
To brighten up even your darkest night

You just call out my name
And you know wherever I am
I'll come running, yeah, to see you again
Don't you know that winter, spring, summer, or fall
All you've got to do is call
And I'll be there, yes I will
You've got a friend
(You've got a friend in me)

Ain't it good to know that you've got a friend
People can be so cold
They'll hurt you and desert you
Take your very soul if you let them
So don't let them

You just call out my name
And you know wherever I am
I'll come running, yeah, to see you again
Don't you know that winter, spring, summer, or fall
All you've got to do is call
And I'll be there, yes I will
You've got a friend
(You've got a friend in me)
You've got a friend
(You've got a friend in me)

2 Relax

06

Barbara

(I = Interviewer; B = Barbara)

I: Do you think you're a relaxed person?
B: Yes, I think so.
I: What do you think of *The Little Book of Calm*?
B: Well, I think it's interesting, but I work from eight thirty in the morning until about seven at night, so I don't have much time to relax. I never have time for a nap during the day. I get a massage from time to time, but I hardly ever take a leisurely bath.
I: Do you ever do any physical exercise?
B: Yes, I go to the gym two or three times a week, and I sometimes walk to work.
I: And how do you relax at night?
B: I have a glass of wine and watch TV.

Robert

(I = Interviewer; R = Robert)

I: Do you think you're a relaxed person?
R: I don't know—I thought I was until I read *The Little Book of Calm*.
I: What do think of it?
R Hah… I think it's stupid. I mean, I like warm water, but only if it has coffee in it. And I've never gotten a massage or taken a nap during the day, but I don't get stressed out very often.
I: How do you relax when you're not working?
R: Well, I go for a walk in the park now and then. I often read at night. I like reading, but I'm so tired after work that I frequently fall asleep with a book in my hands and the light on.

Pete

(I = Interviewer; P = Pete)

I: Do you think you're a relaxed person?
P: Oh yes, definitely.
I: What do you think of *The Little Book of Calm*?
P: I think it's great! It's changed my life.
I: Really? What advice do you follow?
P: I never drink tea or coffee. I drink two glasses of milk every morning and a cup of hot water at night. Uh, I go running every morning before work, and I spend at least 10 minutes alone in a quiet room when I get home at night. Then I relax in the bathtub for about 20 minutes.
I: What does your wife think about that?
P: She thinks I'm nuts.

Sally
(I = Interviewer; S = Sally)
I: Do you think you're a relaxed person?
S: Not really.
I: Why not?
S: I don't think I'm very good at relaxing. I don't like sitting around doing nothing.
I: So what do you do in your spare time?
S: Well, I have three children so I don't have much spare time. But once a month, I get a babysitter and go dancing with my friends. We laugh a lot, and that's what I find relaxing.
I: What do you think of *The Little Book of Calm*?
S: I don't think it was written for people with three children.

07

1
A: Which is your favorite track on the album?
B: The last one—it's amazing. I can't wait to see them live.

2
C: What did you think of it?
D: I thought the acting was excellent, and the photography's superb. Apart from that, the story is really boring.

3
E: Have you finished it yet?
F: Almost.
E: What's it like?
F: Really good. I think it's going to be a best-seller.

4
G: I enjoyed that. What did you think of it?
H: I thought it was so bad—a sentimental tearjerker—and the ending was too predictable.
G: Well, it made you cry anyway.
H: No, it didn't—I have a cold.

5
I: Are you enjoying it?
J: Yeah, I found it kind of difficult to get into, but now that I'm past the first few chapters, I can't put it down.

6
K: What did you think of the special effects?
L: What special effects?
K: It was all done with computers.
L: Oh no…I thought it was real. You've spoiled it now. You spoiled the whole thing!

7
M: Did you have a good time?
N: Not really…I can't stand all that techno stuff. I like it when you can actually hear the lyrics.
M: Old hippie.
N: What did you say?
M: Nothing.

08

[Movie music]

3 Dating

09

Tom and Kathy
(J = Journalist; K = Kathy)
J: Kathy, we last heard from you when you were about to meet Tom for the first time.
K: That's right. It was easier for me to take time off work, so I got a flight to Denver.
J: Wow! That's a long way to go for a date! And kind of expensive, too.
K: Oh, we shared the cost of the flight. Tom's a very generous man. Anyway, he arranged to meet me at the airport.
J: And when was that?
K: It was almost a year ago. I was so nervous, but I couldn't wait to meet Tom.
J: And was he there?
K: Oh, yes. I spotted him immediately. He looked just like his picture.
J: Hah. Was it love at first sight?
K: Uh…no way. I couldn't have predicted what happened, but something turned me off right away. I didn't even leave the airport. I just turned around and came right back to Canada. We haven't been in touch since that day.
J: Wow, what was it that turned you off?
K: Well, it's going to sound really stupid, but I hated his shoes.

Lisa and Joel
(J = Journalist; L = Lisa; Jo = Joel)
J: Lisa and Joel, are you still married?
L: Oh, yes, very much so. We've been married for a year now. In fact, we've just celebrated our first wedding anniversary.
J: Oh, congratulations! How have your lives changed since your unusual marriage?
Jo: Well, my mother hasn't spoken to me since the day we got married! Hah. That's the good news.
J: Hah, hah, hah.
Jo: But, no, I'm kidding. We're really upset about it. But we've moved away from our hometown.
J: Really? Why did you decide to do that?
Jo: Well, everybody knew about the contest and the wedding, and we turned into tourist attractions. We couldn't walk down the street without strangers coming up to us and asking us all these personal questions.
J: So, where do you live now?
Jo: Well, that's a secret. But we love where we are now.

10

a) What's a nice girl like you doing in a place like this?
b) You know, I'm not just an interesting person; I have a body too.
c) I'm in advertising. Would you like to be in our next photo shoot?
d) Do you believe in love at first sight, or do I have to walk past you again?
e) A: Do you have a boyfriend?
B: Yes.
A: Want another one?
f) Your father must be a thief, because he's stolen the stars from the sky and put them in your eyes.
g) I just moved next door, and I was wondering if you could recommend a good restaurant nearby. Would you like to join me?

11

(R = Rose; M = Meg)
R: What do you think of Jake?
M: He's all right.
R: You don't like him, do you?
M: Well, he wasn't exactly friendly.
R: Oh, he's just a little shy, that's all.
M: Shy? You must be joking. Five minutes after meeting me, he asked me to borrow five dollars! That's not what I call shy!
R: O.K., that wasn't very polite, but he's broke.
M: Well, I'm not particularly well-off myself, and I'm trying to save up for my vacation.
R: All right, all right, I'm sure he won't ask you again. He's not bad-looking, though, is he?
M: No, I guess not—but he knows it. I think he's really bigheaded.
R: You're just jealous.
M: No, I'm not. I don't want him. He's mean, bigheaded, and stupid.
R: What do you mean stupid? You're not exactly Ms. Einstein yourself.
M: Shut up!
R: No, you shut up!
M: Mom!

4 Adrenaline

12

A
A: Have you ever skydived?
B: Yes, I have.
A: Was it good?
B: Good? It was absolutely incredible!

B
C: Have you ever gone surfing?
D: Yes, I have.
C: Were you scared?
D: Scared? I was absolutely terrified.

13

Interview with Jane Couch
(I = Interviewer; JC = Jane Couch)
I: Now this is a question that everyone asks you, I know, but,…when…how did you get interested in boxing?
JC: I saw a documentary about women boxing in America about six years ago, it was there, just a li…a little television program, it was about an hour long, and I…I watched the program and it just changed my life, I was just fascinated from there on in, from like a half an hour program, I just went…"I'm going to do that."
I: And were you interested in sports in school?
JC: Nothing. I wasn't even fit or anything. I used to smoke. I used to drink. Uhm, just didn't look after meself at all. Didn't eat very well, and this just changed my life. Hah…
I: How long did it take you to get in shape?
JC: It took me, I'd say, to get to the level that I'm at, it took me…about two years to reach…to reach the level I needed to be at.
I: And do you know how many female boxers there are in Britain?
JC: In the UK, uhm, there's…there's about three hundred women boxing as amateurs, and there's about eight women boxing professionally in the UK at the moment, but throughout the world there's about thirty thousand women, throughout the world.
I: And what do your critics say?
JC: Uhm, at…at the…at the outset it was difficult. It was, like, women shouldn't box, you know…they shouldn't be doing this, and they shouldn't be doing

that, and should be at home looking after the kids, and everything. But, uhm...and she's never be as good as a man, but my last three fights have been live on TV. I've just signed a five fo... fight deal with Bravo Television.

I: What do you think are the uhm... most important skills to have as a boxer?

JC: Uhm, believe it or not, you've got to be... you've got to have a pretty good brain to be a good boxer. Anyone can fight, but to make it to the top you've to know your skills, and you've to have a pretty cute brain, and...and the fitness... the fitness side of it is very, very important.

I: And how do you relax?

JC: I don't. I never do...I...I nev...I don't sleep much. I just...and when I do, I dream about boxing, and when I'm trying to get to sleep it's about my fights. I'm just, I can't...I work really hard. I'm just constantly working, working...

I: How do you get ready for a match?

JC: Uhm, for a... for a ten-round, uhm, world title fight, obviously I go to training camp just outside Bristol, for eight weeks before each fight, and, uhm, once I go to training camp that's it. I don't do anything. I've got a...a very good trainer, I've got a very good team round me, so...

I: Have you ever been seriously hurt in a match?

JC: Uh, not really seriously. Not lasting damage. Things that take a couple of weeks to mend, like broken cheek bone, broken nose, lost a few teeth, but just, uh...

I: Your teeth look great to me from where I'm sitting, I can tell you...

JC: I only lost the back ones. Hah, hah...

I: Jane, do you think you've changed since your success?

JC: Uhm, changed as a person? I...I...I think...I think I've changed as in...in the lifestyle that I live now, is uhm, it's just constantly I'm traveling. I live out of a suitcase. But I think, uhm, as a person, definitely not, no, I've j... my feet are just so firmly on the ground, you wouldn't believe it. Uhm,...

I: I would believe it, having met you. I can assure you. So when's your next big fight?

JC: Uh, the next one's going to be the end of February, beginning of March. I'm going to be defending my world... my three world titles.

I: And where will it be?

JC: In London! Hah, hah.

I: Well, that's great. Thank you very, very much.

14

a

(I = Interviewer; B = Ben)

I: Have you ever gotten injured while you were playing a sport?

B: Yes, I have. I was playing football, and it was just after kickoff. I was jumping up to catch the ball when a player from the other team knocked me over, and I fell heavily on my left leg.

I: Oh, no. Were you badly hurt?

B: Ah, yes, I twisted my ankle and couldn't play football for more than three months.

b

(I = Interviewer; D = Dina)

I: Have you ever been in a dangerous situation?

D: Yes, I...I have. I was walking my dog one day with my sister, and we were crossing this field. There was a horse in the field and it suddenly started running toward us, looking really angry.

I: What did you do?

D: Well, I know you're not supposed to run away from animals because they can sense your fear. But we ran away as fast as we could.

c

(I = Interviewer; F = Frank)

I: Have you ever broken a bone?

F: Yes, I've broken my nose twice. The first time, I was playing soccer and one of the other players kicked me in the face. The second time, I was playing tennis. I missed the ball and it hit me right on the nose.

d

(I = Interviewer; P = Paula)

I: Have you ever been really frightened?

P: Yes, I have. Last summer I was driving on a highway in Mexico, and we were getting close to my exit. So I got into the right-hand lane, ready to turn off, when this car screeched up next to me, pulled in front of me, and slammed on his brakes. I don't know how I was able to slow down fast enough to avoid him. I've never been so frightened in my life.

e

(I = Interviewer; G = Glen)

I: Have you ever thought you were going to die?

G: Yeah. It was when I was eight or nine and I was at the beach with my parents. I was playing in the ocean, but on the edge because I couldn't swim. Suddenly, I realized that I couldn't feel the bottom, and the waves were pulling me farther away from the beach. For a few seconds, I panicked, and I started swallowing a lot of water. Then I felt really calm, as if I were floating away. I was drowning. Fortunately, someone saw me and pulled me out in time.

15

George

(I = Interviewer; G = George)

I: George, is this similar to skiing?

G: Actually, it's slightly easier, and I think it's a lot more exhilarating.

I: Is it cheaper?

G: No, not really. The equipment is just as expensive.

I: What do you need?

G: A board, of course, and that can cost about $700. Then you have to have bindings to attach your feet to the board and you also need special clothes and boots, which are pretty expensive.

I: Is it as popular as skiing?

G: With young people, yes.

Katrina

(I = Interviewer; K = Katrina)

I: Katrina, where did you learn?

K: In Aruba when I was on vacation.

I: I guess you have to learn in the ocean, don't you? I mean, you don't live near the ocean, do you?

K: Uh, no, but I could have learned at home in a lake, although it's much nicer to learn in the Caribbean because it's nice and warm.

I: Did you have to buy all the equipment?

K: No, you can rent it, but it's much better to have your own wetsuit because it's important for it to be exactly the right size.

I: Are the lessons very expensive?

K: Yes, pretty expensive, but it's worth getting lessons from professionals because it's much safer.

I: Were you nervous on your first dive?

K: Yes, but it was one of the most amazing experiences I've ever had.

Paul

(I = Interviewer; P = Paul)

I: Paul, what's your favorite team?

P: I used to follow the Mets, but then I changed to the Yankees.

I: Why?

P: Because they're by far the best team in the sport.

I: Did you watch their last game?

P: Of course. They didn't play as well as usual, and one of their best players was injured in the first inning.

I: How?

P: He hurt his ankle sliding into third.

I: So, did they lose?

P: No way. They won four to two.

Eva

(I = Interviewer; E = Eva)

I: Eva, was it your first time?

E: Yes, and it was amazing.

I: What did you have to do?

E: Well, the first time you do it, they attach the elastic around your waist, and you just jump. At first, you free-fall, and then the elastic pulls you back and you bounce up and down a few times.

I: How did it feel?

E: Incredible...I can't explain the feeling... it's...it's much better than anything else I have ever done. It's exciting, but it isn't nearly as frightening as you would think.

I: What made you do it?

E: It was a birthday present, and it's definitely the best birthday present I've ever had.

16

(V = Vic; R = Ronnie)

V: This is so amazing. It's just the way I imagined it would be—walking along the beach with the one I love.

R: For me, too. I love you more and more every minute. And I know our love will get stronger every day. I mean, I'm not trying to be dramatic or anything, but...

V: But love is bigger than both of us. It makes us poetic. It makes me want to compare it to everything huge and grand and impressive. For example, my love for you is sweeter than the perfume of a thousand roses.

R: That's so sweet.

V: My love for you is deeper than the ocean out there, brighter than the sun shining on the water, taller than those rocks, and stronger than the waves rushing up on the beach.

R: Such beautiful words. Vic, I'm going be faithful to you forever—as faithful as a puppy. And I'll always be there for you.

V: And I'll be there for you, too. I love you like Romeo loved Juliet...

R: …like butterflies love flowers, like kittens love warm, cozy laps…
V: …like I love pizza with mushrooms and green peppers…
R: Huh?
V: Well, all this poetry is making me hungry. Want to get a pizza?
R: Sure. Why not?

5 Kids

17

1
A: Uhm, it's something that lived a l…a very long time ago. It looks very scary.
B: A thing that a lived a long time ago.
C: Uhm,… It's a big monster.

2
D: It's a man, and, and uhm,… he lives in…he lives up in space.
E: It's someone who, uhm…made the world and uhm…he made the animals.
F: He's someone who lives…who died, and he…he,uhm…looks down on people.
G: He's a man up in heaven.
H: A person that helps people in heaven.

3
I: It's something that's uh…uh, very cold, and it's in…it's a…it's a…it's a, uhm… it's a stone.
J: It's something that crashes down on people, and it has ice.
K: It's a sort of big piece of, uhm, ice that cracks off a bigger piece.
L: It's a big ice cube.

4
M: A place where…where animals…have been put up to show.
N: Somewhere where uhm…they show you things that are very old.
O: It's somewhere where uh, people will show things like dinosaurs and olden-days things.
P: A place…a place that uhm…you see loads and loads of…you see bones or things and pictures.
Q: It's in the country, and you see dinosaur bones there.

5
R: It's a person who takes toys away.
S: It's someone that in the middle of the night…and it has uhm…it has a…it has uhm, a…something around his face with, with, uhm…round holes and he's…he's…he has uhm…a T-shirt that's black and white, and he robs things.
T: It's someone who steals things when you're asleep.
U: A person that steals things at night.

18

(See page 46.)

19

Ladybug, ladybug, fly away home.
Your house is on fire, and your children are gone,
All except one, and that's little Ann,
For she has crept under the frying pan.

20

(See page 48.)

21

Her name was Mrs. Pratchett. She was a small, skinny old hag with a moustache on her upper lip and a mouth as sour as a green gooseberry. She never smiled.

Her apron was gray and greasy. Her blouse had bits of breakfast all over it, toast crumbs and tea stains and splotches of dried egg yolk. It was her hands, however, that disturbed us most. They were disgusting. They were black with dirt and grime.

And do not forget that it was these hands and fingers that she would plunge into the sweet-jars when we asked for a pennyworth of Treacle Toffee or Wine Gums or Nut Clusters or whatever. There were precious few health laws in those days, and nobody, least of all Mrs. Pratchett, ever thought of using a little shovel for getting sweets out as they do today.

The other thing we hated Mrs. Pratchett for was her meanness. Unless you spent a whole sixpence all in one go, she wouldn't give you a bag. Instead you got your sweets twisted up in a small piece of newspaper which she tore off a pile of old Daily Mirrors lying on the counter.

So you can well understand that we had it in for Mrs. Pratchett in a big way, but we didn't quite know what to do about it. Many schemes were put forward, but none of them was any good. None of them, that is, until suddenly, one memorable afternoon, we found the dead mouse.

My four friends and I had come across a loose floorboard at the back of the classroom, and when we prised it up with the blade of a pocketknife, we discovered a big hollow space underneath. This, we decided, would be our secret hiding place for sweets and other small treasures such as conkers and monkey-nuts and birds' eggs.

Every afternoon, when the last lesson was over, the five of us would wait until the classroom had emptied then we would lift up the floorboard and examine our secret hoard, perhaps adding to it or taking something away.

One day, when we lifted it up, we found a dead mouse lying among our treasures. It was an exciting discovery.

Thwaites took it out by its tail and waved it in front of our faces. "What shall we do with it?" he cried.

"It stinks!" someone shouted. "Throw it out of the window!"

"Hold on a tick," I said. "Don't throw it away."

Thwaites hesitated. They all looked at me.

When writing about oneself, one must strive to be truthful. Truth is more important than modesty. I must tell you, therefore, that it was I and I alone who had the idea for the great and daring Mouse Plot. We all have our moments of brilliance and glory, and this was mine.

"Why don't we," I said, "slip it into one of Mrs. Pratchett's jars of sweets? Then when she puts her dirty hand in to grab a handful, she'll grab a stinky dead mouse instead."

The other four stared at me in wonder.

Then, as the sheer genius of the plot began to sink in, they all started grinning. They slapped me on the back. They cheered me and danced around the classroom. "We'll do it today!" they cried. "We'll do it on the way home. You had the idea," they said to me, "so you can be the one to put the mouse in the jar."

Thwaites handed me the mouse. I put it into my trouser pocket. Then the five of us left the school, crossed the village green, and headed for the sweet-shop. We were tremendously jazzed up. We felt like a gang of desperados setting out to rob a train or blow up the sheriff's office.

We were the victors now, and Mrs. Pratchett was the victim. She stood behind the counter, and her small malignant pig-eyes watched us suspiciously as we came forward.

"One Sherbet Sucker, please," Thwaites said to her, holding out his penny.

I kept to the rear of the group, and when I saw Mrs. Pratchett turn her head away for a couple of seconds to fish a Sherbet Sucker out of the box, I lifted the heavy glass lid of the Gobstopper jar and dropped the mouse in. Then I replaced the lid as silently as possible. My heart was thumping like mad, and my hands had gone all sweaty.

As soon as we were outside, we broke into a run. "Did you do it?" they shouted at me.

"Of course I did!" I said.

"Well done you!" they cried. "What a super show!"

I felt like a hero. I was a hero. It was marvellous to be so popular.

The flush of triumph over the dead mouse was carried forward to the next morning as we met again to walk to school.

"Let's go in and see if it's still in the jar," somebody said as we approached the sweet-shop.

"Don't," Thwaites said firmly. "It's too dangerous. Walk past as though nothing has happened."

As we came level with the shop we saw a cardboard notice hanging on the door.

CLOSED.

We stopped and stared. We had never known the sweet-shop to be closed at this time in the morning, even on Sundays.

"What's happened?" we asked each other. "What's going on?"

We pressed our faces against the window and looked inside. Mrs. Pratchett was nowhere to be seen.

"Look!" I cried. "The Gobstopper jar's gone! It's not on the shelf! There's a gap where it used to be!"

"It's on the floor!" someone said. "It's smashed to bits and there's Gobstoppers everywhere!"

"There's the mouse!" someone else shouted.

We could see it all, the huge glass jar smashed to smithereens with the dead mouse lying in the wreckage and hundreds of many-coloured Gobstoppers littering the floor.

"She got such a shock when she grabbed hold of the mouse that she dropped everything," somebody was saying.

"But why didn't she sweep it all up and open the shop?" I asked.

Nobody answered me.

After a while, Thwaites broke the silence. "She must have got one heck of a shock," he said. He paused. We all looked at him, wondering what wisdom the great medical authority was going to come out with next.

"Well now," Thwaites went on, "when an old person like Mrs. Pratchett suddenly gets a very big shock, I suppose you know what happens next?"

"What?" we said. "What happens?"

"You ask my father," Thwaites said. "He'll tell you."

"You tell us," we said.

"It gives her a heart attack," Thwaites announced. "Her heart stops beating and she's dead in five seconds."

For a moment or two my own heart stopped beating. Thwaites pointed a finger at me and said darkly, "I'm afraid you've killed her."

"Me?" I cried. "Why just me?"

"It was your idea," he said. "And what's more, you put the mouse in."

All of a sudden, I was a murderer.

At exactly that point, we heard the school bell ringing in the distance, and we had to gallop the rest of the way so as not to be late for prayers.

The Headmaster is the only teacher at Llandaff Cathedral School that I can remember, and for a reason you will soon discover, I can remember him very clearly indeed. His name was Mr. Coombes.

Mr. Coombes now proceeded to mumble through the same old prayers we had every day, but this morning, when the last amen had been spoken, he did not turn and lead his group rapidly out of the Hall as usual. He remained standing before us, and it was clear he had an announcement to make.

"The whole school is to go out and line up around the playground immediately," he said. "Leave your books behind. And no talking."

Mr. Coombes was looking grim. His hammy pink face had taken on that dangerous scowl which only appeared when he was extremely cross and somebody was for the high-jump. I sat there small and frightened among the rows and rows of other boys, and to me at that moment the Headmaster, with his black grown draped over his shoulders, was like a judge at a murder trial.

"He's after the killer," Thwaites whispered to me.

I began to shiver.

As we made our way out into the playground my whole stomach began to feel as though it was slowly filling up with swirling water. I am only eight years old, I told myself. No little boy of eight has ever murdered anyone. It's not possible.

I half-expected to see two policemen come bounding out of the school to grab me by the arms and put handcuffs on my wrists.

A single door led out from the school on to the playground. Suddenly it swung open, and through it, like the angel of death, strode Mr. Coombes, huge and bulky in his tweed suit and black gown, and beside him, believe it or not, right beside him trotted the tiny figure of Mrs. Pratchett herself!

Mrs. Pratchett was alive!

The relief was tremendous.

Suddenly she let out a high-pitched yell and pointed a dirty finger straight at Thwaites. "That's 'im!" she yelled. "That's one of 'em! I'd know 'im a mile away, the scummy little bounder!"

The entire school turned to look at Thwaites. "W—what have I done?" he stuttered, appealing to Mr. Coombes.

"Shut up," Mr. Coombes said.

Mrs. Pratchett's eyes flicked over and settled on my own face. I looked down and studied the black asphalt surface of the playground.

"Ere's another of 'em!" I heard her yelling. "That one there!" She pointed at me now. "You're quite sure?" Mr. Coombes said.

"Of course I'm sure!" she cried. "I never forget a face, least of all when it's as sly as that! 'Ee's one of 'em all right! There was five altogether. Now where's them other three?"

The other three, I knew very well, were coming up next.

"There they are!" she cried out, stabbing the air with her finger. "'Im...and 'im...and 'im! That's the five of 'em all right! We don't need to look no farther than this, 'Eadmaster! They're all 'ere, the nasty little pigs! You've got their names 'ave you?"

"I've got their names, Mrs. Pratchett," Mr. Coombes told her. "I'm very much obliged to you."

6 News

22

(A1 = Announcer 1; A2 = Announcer 2)

A1: And here are the news headlines. As a result of severe droughts in Africa, the president of the U.S. has announced that he is going to send food and provisions to the people of Somalia.

A2: Senator Robert Bailey, member of the Senate Finance Committee, has resigned. The attorney general has ordered an investigation into the mysterious disappearance of a large sum of money. A spokesman for the senator told us that he was out of the country and not available for comment.

A1: High school junior Pauline Gates has not been allowed back in school after the summer vacation, because she had her nose pierced. According to principal Jean Bradley, Pauline knew that piercing was against the school rules. The girl will be allowed back in school when she removes the ring from her nose.

A2: And finally, to end on a happier note, wedding bells are ringing for 81-year-old Max Williams, who won $16 million in the Pennsylvania lottery last month. He is going to marry 22-year-old dancer Sally Lister. The happy couple posed for photographers outside the millionaire's luxury home in Yardley, and Sally held out her hand to show off her $10,000 engagement ring for the cameras.

23

(K = Ken; S= Steve)

K: Hi, Steve. How are you?

S: Oh, not too bad. Actually, it's my wedding anniversary today.

K: Oh, congratulations!

S: But uh, I forgot, and my wife was really upset.

K: Oh, no. That's terrible.

S: But I just called Le Petit Blanc, and they actually had a table free, so we're going out for dinner.

K: Wonderful.

S: Anyway, I have to go.

K: Uh, yeah, me too. See you!

24

a

A: Have you heard about Chris and Shirley?

B: No...what about them?

A: They broke up.

B: That's terrible!

b

C: Hello. You look pretty happy with yourself.

D: I am! I just passed my driving test!

C: That's great! Can I have a ride?

c

E: Guess what. I won a vacation to Florida.

F: Lucky you! Is it a vacation for two?

E: Yes. I'm taking my mom.

F: Oh.

d

G: I just got some bad news.

H: What happened?

G: I failed my final exam.

H: Oh, I'm sorry to hear that. Can you take it again?

e

I: Oh, no!

J: What's the matter?

I: I left my bag on the bus.

J: You idiot! What are you going to do?

I: I guess I'd better call the bus company.

f

K: Have a glass of champagne!

L: Thank you. What are you celebrating?

K: My wife just had a baby.

L: Congratulations! A boy or a girl?

g

M: You don't usually take the bus!

N: No—my car broke down again.

M: Oh, no!

h

O: I didn't know you had a car.

P: My parents bought a new car, and they gave me their old one.

O: Wonderful!

25

That's terrible!
That's great!
Lucky you!
Oh, I'm sorry to hear that.
You idiot!
Congratulations!
Oh, no!
Wonderful!

26

1 We got engaged last week.
2 My bicycle was stolen again.
3 I've decided to move to Brazil.
4 My husband's been taken to the hospital.
5 My daughter just had a baby.
6 I got off the bus, slipped, and fell flat on my face.
7 I won $1,000 in the New York State lottery.
8 My car wouldn't start this morning.
9 When I got to the party, there was someone there wearing exactly the same dress as me.
10 I just got my exam grades, and I passed everything.

7 Party

27

1	/ɪ/	– busy	city
2	/ɛ/	– festival	guest
3	/ɑ/	– holiday	modern
4	/æ/	– band	candle
5	/ə/	– around	different
6	/ʊ/	– full	good
7	/ʌ/	– fund	public

28

(Z = Zoë; S = Sandy)

Z: Hi!
S: Oh, hello.
Z: You don't look very happy. What's the matter?
S: David hasn't called me.
Z: You just saw him yesterday.
S: Yes, and the last thing he said was, "I'll call you tomorrow."
Z: Well, tomorrow isn't over yet.
S: No, but it's eight o'clock. What are you doing tonight? Do you feel like going out?
Z: Uh, I'd love to, but John's coming over and we're going out for dinner.
S: Well, I'm not going to sit here waiting for the phone to ring. I know—I'll call Becky.

29

(B = Becky; S = Sandy; Z = Zoë; D = David)

B: Hello?
S: Hi, Becky, it's Sandy.
B: Hiya.
S: Becky, are you doing anything tonight?
B: Yes. I'm meeting Alex and Suzy in about half an hour.
S: Where are you going?
B: To the movies. Would you like to come with us?
S: Yes, I'd love to. Where are you meeting?
B: At their house, but we could meet you in front of the theater on George Street at eight-thirty.
S: O.K., thanks. See you later.... I'm going to the movies with Becky.
Z: Good idea.
S: And next time I see David, I'm going to tell him to get lost.
Z: Hmm. I'll believe that when I see it.

...

Z: Hello.
D: Is Sandy there, please?
Z: Yeah, hold on a minute—I'll get her for you.... It's David.
S: Oh hello, David.
D: Look, I'm really sorry I didn't call earlier, but I had to work late.
S: Oh, that's all right—I...I forgot you were going to call anyway.
D: Listen, I'm really sorry, but I can't see you tonight. I'm having dinner with my parents.
S: It doesn't matter—I'm going to the movies anyway.
D: Oh, O.K. Well, I'll call you.
S: When? I mean, all right. Bye.
D: Bye.

...

Z: You didn't tell him to get lost.
S: Well, he apologized—and he's having dinner with his parents. Anyway, I...I have to go. See you later.

...

S: Hi, Alex. Hi, Becky. Where's Suzy?
B: Oh, she changed her mind at the last minute. David called her and asked her to go out for dinner at that new Japanese restaurant.
S: What?! Now I'm definitely going to tell him to get lost!

30

(R = Rachel; A = Allison; G = George)

R: So what do you think makes a good party?
A: Uhm...I think the place is really important. It should be big enough, but not too big.
G: Yes, it should be kind of crowded for atmosphere...and dark.
R: Oh, I don't like it when you can't see who you're talking to.
G: No...no, I mean soft lighting. I like it when there are some decorations, too. You know, a few balloons and things, just to make it special.
A: What, like a children's party?
G: Yeah, I suppose so—or candles and things on the wall.
R: Candles are really nice, but you have to be careful the house doesn't catch fire.
G: W...well, you can get those candle holders. But the most important thing is the food and drink.
A: Oh, yes. There has to be enough food. It's terrible when there isn't enough food.
R: What kind of food do you think is good for parties?
A: Uhm, the kind of thing you can eat with your fingers. I mean, you don't want to have loads to clean up at the end of the party.
R: Actually, I think the music is the most important thing. Loud, but not too loud, and the kind of music you can dance to.
G: I think the best thing is to make party tapes with all the best dance tracks; then you don't have to worry about it.
A: But what about people? That's the most important, isn't it?
G: Uhm, yes, you do need people for a party!
A: No, I...I mean the right people. You need some party animals who get up and start dancing.
R: And you need a mix of men and women. I went to a party recently where there were five women for every man.
G: Sounds good to me.
A: Oh, shut up. So what do we think are the three most important things?
R: Food and drink, music, and the right mix of people.
G: Right.

31

***It's My Party,* by Lesley Gore**

It's my party and I'll cry if I want to,
Cry if I want to, cry if I want to.
You would cry too if it happened to you.

Nobody knows where my Johnny has gone,
But Judy left the same time.
Why was he holding her hand,
When he's supposed to be mine?

It's my party...

Play all my records, keep dancing all night,
But leave me alone for a while,
'Til Johnny's dancing with me,
I've got no reason to smile.

It's my party...

Judy and Johnny just walked thru' the door,
Like a queen with her king.
Oh, what a birthday surprise,
Judy's wearing his ring.

It's my party...

8 Review 1

32

Sue
We met at college—we were both studying music, and I guess we hit it off right away. Afterwards, I went away traveling for a year, and we lost touch for a while, but really we've been friends since we were at Princeton. We see each other, say, three or four times a week I guess. We're both very outgoing and energetic, which I guess is why we get along so well in the band...

Juan
It was an amazing coincidence, to tell you the truth. Not only to meet like that, but to get along so well and have so much in common. We also helped each other with our studying. And there was no time at all to feel homesick or anything. From the minute we got on the plane, we had lots to talk about. And when we finished, we had a great time seeing the place and, well, it was just one big party till it was time to come back home. I wish we could see each other more often these days.

Elisa
It was in Brazil, just after college. I'd already been there for a few months. At first, we didn't get along too well, but we kept bumping into each other, like you do when you're traveling, so we, uhm, well, we ended up traveling together. We found we had similar interests...you know, we like the same music and like going to music concerts, and we had similar opinions, and so on. I guess we've been friends for about, well, three or four years now.

Enrico
We have similar interests, especially music. We like to see as many bands as we can. We like going out a lot. We, uh, don't get to travel as much as we used to, but we're planning to go back to South America together for a few weeks next year. That's where we met in the first place, about four years ago.

Cindy
We've known each other for a few years now, and we still get along well— most of the time anyway! We see each other a lot. Of course, we're together twice a week when the band rehearses, and we often go to clubs or to friends' houses and just, kind of, hang out and chat. Yeah, we both love a good party!

Jim
We first met in the, uh, airport. We just bumped into each other at the check-in counter. It turned out we were both going to the same place to study, and we ended up living on the same floor in the dormitory. It was pretty amazing! We got along from day one. It just happened naturally, you know, two people away from home and all that. We did almost everything together, and then after graduation we traveled around for a month or so before coming home. Now, I guess we see each other only about three or four times a year.

33

(See page 69.)

9 Soaps

34

(See page 74.)

35

Pacific Heights, **Scene 2**
(P = Penny; E = Ella; Ph = Phil; M = Mara)
P: So what have you been up to today?
E: We went to the travel agency to get some brochures.
Ph: I thought we talked about that.
M: But Dad…
Ph: Look, I've told you once, and I'll tell you again—you are not traveling by yourself. You're too young.
E: But Becky's parents let her travel without them last year.
Ph: Yes, but she went with her brother.
M: Well, let's ask Charlie. Where is he, by the way?
P: Oh, he's participating in a big surfing competition out of town.
Ph: But his surfboard's here.
P: Oh, that's strange. I must have made a mistake.
M: Come on, Ella…let's go over to Becky's.
P: Uh, don't be late for dinner.

Pacific Heights, **Scene 3**
(M = Mara; E = Ella)
M: I think I know where Charlie is.
E: Where?
M: He went to see Clare. I'm sure there's something going on.
E: Oh, between Charlie and Clare?
M: Yes.
E: But Clare's married to Uncle Dave.
M: So? Lots of married people have affairs.
E: Well, I don't think it's right. Anyway, how do you know?
M: Well, I heard him talking to her on the phone yesterday. He asked her if Dave had left for Mexico, and then he said he couldn't wait to be in her arms again!
E: Oh, what a creep. Poor Becky.
M: Oh, don't worry, she'll get over it. But listen, I have an idea.
E: If it's about Charlie coming on the trip with us, forget it. He already said he doesn't want to.
M: Yes, but if we catch him with Clare, we can blackmail him to come with us.
E: Oh, yeah. I see what you mean. But don't you think we should tell Becky about him and Clare?
M: No, stupid. If we tell her, we won't be able to blackmail him. Come on, let's make a plan.

Pacific Heights, **Scene 4**
(A = Amy; M = Mark)
A: I don't know what to do. If I don't participate in the demonstration, I'll have to leave the group.
M: Just think about those poor little animals. Do you have any idea what they do to them?
A: I know, but it's my stepfather's company.
M: Well, it serves him right for experimenting on animals.
A: Are they going to do any damage?
M: No, it's a peaceful demonstration, that's all. Anyway, it's up to you.
A: Uhm, O.K. I'll come, but my mom will kill me if she finds out.

10 Time

36

(PR = Paul Roesch; RW = Roberta Wilson)
PR: That was Sonny Best with "Midnight in Vermont." Now, do you make the best of your time? In the studio today, we have Roberta Wilson, who's a time-management consultant. Good morning, Roberta.
RW: Good morning, Paul.
PR: Roberta, what exactly do time-management consultants do?
RW: Well, Paul, it's all about helping people to organize their work in an effective way; maximum efficiency, minimum stress.
PR: Hah, sounds like something I need. So, who are your clients?
RW: Uh, mainly business people, but I've also worked with politicians, city employees, and college professors.
PR: Oh, so quite a range. And what kinds of things help people organize their time? I suppose punctuality is important?
RW: Uh, yes and no. It's easier to finish a meeting on time if it starts on time. But in international contexts, you do have to be aware of cultural differences.
PR: For example?
RW: Well, in Britain, big, formal meetings usually start on time, but less formal meetings often begin a few minutes late. In Germany, on the other hand, people expect all meetings to begin on time. In some countries, uh, for example, in Latin America, there's a more…relaxed attitude. So, you do have to adapt to circumstances.
PR: When in Rome…
RW: Uh, to some extent, yes.
PR: Uhm, it sounds like even if you manage your own time very well, you still can't control what other people do.
RW: Well, you can set limits. If you're meeting a friend who always arrives late, you can say, "Well, I'm going to wait for 15 minutes. If my friend isn't there by then, I'll leave."
PR: Hmm. I have one friend who's always late. I don't think I'd ever see her if I did that.
RW: Sure, but people who are always late are the ones you need to set limits with. If they know that you won't wait, then maybe they'll make an effort.
PR: Isn't that harsh?
RW: No, not really. Someone who constantly shows up late is putting a low value on your time. Let them know you have other things to do. And I'm not suggesting you do that with everyone—just the persistent latecomers. But, again, different cultures do have different viewpoints on what constitutes serious lateness.
PR: What about interruptions? A lot of times I come into the studio with something important I need to do. Then the phone rings or someone comes to see me… Before I know it, the day's over and I haven't done what I planned.
RW: Uh, you need to watch your time. If you're working on something important and people drop in to see you, get your datebook out. Politely tell them you're busy, and make an appointment for another time. If it isn't important anyway, they'll just go away. If it is, they'll make an appointment and you can deal with it properly.
PR: That sounds practical.
RW: Yeah, but again, you have to be careful. In some cultures, particularly Latin ones, this technique can upset people. But here in the United States, almost no one will be offended.
PR: Hmm. So, does everything depend on culture?
RW: No. Attitudes toward time are one of the big differences between cultures. But how you organize your own work is up to you. And there are lots of techniques here. For example, imagine you have two important things to do. One of them is pleasant and the other isn't. Always try to do the unpleasant task first. That way, the pleasant task is a reward for finishing. If you do it the other way around, you'll tend to slow down the pleasant task because you don't want to do the unpleasant one.
PR: Hah, hah. I'll remember that. Finally, what, to you, is a hardworking person?
RW: Oh, I'm not very interested in hardworking people. You can spend twelve hours a day at the office without doing very much. I'm interested in productive—and happy—people.
PR: And on that note, I have to say we've run out of time. Thank you, Roberta. Now here's Jasmine Dahar with the news…

37

1 /s / – Sunday
second
Saturday
weeks
first

2 /z / – days
Tuesday
Wednesday
hours
weekends

3 /θ / – three
thirty
month
Thursday
third

4 /ð / – then
there
weather
that
these

38

(J = Julie; M = Martin)
M: O.K., so what dates did you get?
J: I have February 20, 1997.
M: O.K., I'll write that down…'97.
J: Uh, May 24, 1972.
M: O.K.
J: Then I have November 5, 1999.
M: O.K.
J: Then there's July 31, 1991.
M: …'91. O.K., and the last one?
J: The last one…July 15 of next year.
M: Great. O.K., well, let's go for the oldest one. May 24, '72. What's that?
J: That's my birthday.
M: Hah, hah, hah.
J: Hah…and I'm a Gemini.
M: Oh, right. O.K. Uh, February 20, '97?
J: That is my cat's birthday.
M: …I don't even know my cat's…
J: Her name's Sparkle.
M: Hah, hah, hah. July 31, '91?

J: Ah. That's the date that I graduated from college and got my first job, in a Virgin Megastore.
M: Uh, let's see... November 5... November 5, '99.
J: Well, that was the day I met Miguel.
M: Miguel?
J: Yeah. My personal trainer. He's amazing.
M: All right... And finally, what's July 15 of next year?
J: Well, I'm going on vacation.
M: Oh, where are you going?
J: I'm going to Australia, Sri Lanka, to India, the Far East, then to Russia.... All over the place.
M: Oh, lucky you. It sounds great.

39

1
We're supposed to start work at nine, but I often come in later because I have to take my children to school first, but then I stay a little later. Of course, if I have an early meeting or if I have to be in court first thing in the morning, my wife has to take the kids to school. We're supposed to work a 40-hour week, but I think most people actually work more than that. We're supposed to dress professionally, especially if we have contact with clients, so I always wear a suit and tie to work. Female lawyers aren't allowed to wear slacks. They have to wear skirts that are knee-length or longer—no mini-skirts. The secretaries can wear tailored slacks, but no jeans. And now we have casual Fridays, which means that we don't have to wear business clothes on Fridays. Personally, I have no desire to come into work wearing khakis and a polo shirt. I like to differentiate between work and home, and I can wear casual clothes at home. I think people should dress professionally for work—it makes a good impression. Smoking, eating, and drinking are strictly forbidden in the office. There's a nonsmoking cafeteria downstairs, and smokers have to go outside. Personally, I think smoking ought to be banned in all public places.

2
As you can see, it's a really busy office and we have to work long hours. Everybody works different hours because people are coming in and out all the time. We can drink coffee or water at our desks, but we're not allowed to bring food into the offices. There's a little, like, café downstairs. We're supposed to have a break every two hours, but when you're working on a deadline, you can't afford to take time for a break. Sometimes I work right through my lunch hour—it's kind of crazy. In fact, you have to be crazy to work here. We're not supposed to smoke in the office, but some of the reporters and journalists do when they're working late. You know they've been smoking because the place smells horrible in the morning. As far as dress is concerned, it depends. The editors and senior staff dress professionally. I think our senior editor has two suits and about twenty identical striped shirts, because I've never seen him wearing anything else. The younger men are more fashion-conscious, and they don't have to wear suits. The women can wear slacks or skirts, but we can't wear jeans. Neat, casual clothes are O.K.

3
As you can imagine, people who work here are pretty fashion-conscious. They can wear whatever they like, but people usually choose to dress pretty well for work. They're the kind of people who like to look good, and they're very competitive. Most people wear black—it's a bit like wearing a uniform. Black turtlenecks, black jeans, black leather jackets and boots—and that's just the women! The men tend to be more imaginative with their colors. They wear nice bright-colored shirts...and then color their hair to match! Personally, I go for a more elegant look—suits and high heels. Unfortunately, a lot of the young models who come to the agency are smokers—but they're not allowed to smoke in the building, in fact, they can't smoke anywhere near the building. It gives such a bad impression when you see people smoking in the entrance. The agency is open from ten o'clock in the morning, but the employees arrive anytime after eight. They have to work a nine-hour day, but the starting and finishing times are flexible. Coffee is available whenever you want it, but food isn't allowed in the office. Nobody here eats anyway!

11 Journey

40

(F = Friend; C = Conrad)
F: It must be really weird to be back home after such a long time.
C: Yes, it is. I... I mean, it's great to see everybody, and I really appreciate my bed.
F: So, let me see your pictures.
C: Well, they're all mixed up. Just let me sort them out.
F: Uhm, this looks nice. Where is it?
C: Where do you think it is?
F: Oh, well... it must be somewhere really hot. It looks like paradise. I guess it could be Thailand or Bali. Or it could even be Puerto Rico.
C: No. I'll give you a clue. It's an island in the Pacific Ocean.
F: Hawaii.
C: No, I didn't go to Hawaii.
F: You didn't? I thought you'd been everywhere! Then it's probably Fiji.
C: That's right. Oh, it was so incredible. This man wanted me to marry his daughter. She was beautiful.
F: Oh, a Fijian wedding... that would've been fun.
C: Yeah, that's what I thought. But I don't think my mom would've been very happy about it. Anyway, what about this one?
F: Hmmm... this one is completely different. Well, must be Switzerland, or somewhere in the French Alps?
C: Nope.
F: Who's the girl, by the way?
C: Oh, yes... that's, uhm, what's-her-name. She's Argentinian.
F: Oh. Was she traveling around Europe too?
C: No. In this picture, she wasn't far from home.
F: Well, it can't be Argentina, can it? Maybe it's Chile?
C: No, it is the southern part of Argentina... Patagonia.
F: Oh...
C: They call it the Switzerland of the southern hemisphere.
F: Really? That's amazing. It really does look like Switzerland. So anyway, did you meet a girl in every country you visited?

41

Liz
(I = Interviewer; L = Liz)
I: So, who would your ideal companion be?
L: My friend, Anna, who's getting a master's degree in Asian studies.
I: And how would you get around?
L: We'd probably use one of those very fast bullet trains to get there, and then walk or take a taxi.
I: And what would you wear?
L: It depends on the time of year. I'd want to go there in spring for the cherry blossoms, so probably just jeans and a sweatshirt. I'd make sure I had a clean pair of socks and some slip-on shoes, because I think you have to take them off when you visit the temples.

...
I: What would you buy?
L: Nothing touristy. I might buy an electronic gadget, like a calculator. They are supposed to be cheaper there.
I: Uhm, and what would you eat and drink?
L: I'd look for Western food, and I'd probably end up eating at McDonald's. I can't stand raw fish, and I don't like rice much, either.
I: Hmm. What essential items would you take with you?
L: My camera would be essential—the temples, the...the shrines and the gardens. They're all supposed to be stunning.

...
I: Who would you most like to meet there?
L: I'd like to meet a geisha who speaks English and ask her lots of questions.
I: What sights would you want to see?
L: I'd visit the Golden Temple and the Ryoan-ji temple, I think it is, where they have that amazing Zen rock garden.

...
I: Uh, who would you send a postcard to?
L: My ex-boyfriend, to show him what a good time I'm having without him.
I: Hah. What would spoil your perfect weekend?
L: Bumping into somebody from work. Although I don't think it's likely on the other side of the world in Kyoto!

Cristina
(I = Interviewer; C = Cristina)
I: Who would your ideal companion be?
C: My mom and her credit cards!
I: And how would you get around?
C: I'd walk or take the subway. Or the metro, as the locals call it.
I: What would you wear?
C: I'd wear all the new clothes my mom's going to buy for me there.
I: And what would you buy?
C: Apart from clothes, maybe a painting from one of the artists who sell their stuff along the river.

...
I: What would you eat and drink?
C: I'd sit and drink lots of coffee and watch the world go by.

I: Um, and what essential items would you take with you?
C: Sunglasses. Not for the sun, but because they look cool.
I: Who would you most like to meet there?
C: Jean Paul Gaultier—I love him.
I: What sights would you want to see?
C: Well, I've been to all the obvious places, so I'd just like to hang out in the Latin Quarter.

...

I: Who would you send a postcard to?
C: My dad.
I: What would spoil your perfect weekend?
C: If the shops were closed. Paris is a beautiful city, but for me the main attraction is the shopping.

Rick

(I = Interviewer; R = Rick)
I: Who would your ideal companion be?
R: Uh, definitely not my wife. She can't stand the sun. So... probably my brother, because I don't see him very often.
I: Uhm, how would you get around?
R: I'd walk. I'll only be going from the hotel to the beach.
I: What would you wear?
R: As little as possible.
I: And what would you buy?
R: I'd probably buy some souvenirs for my wife and kids at the airport.
I: What would you eat and drink?
R: Uh, what's that special dish?... Uh, moussaka?

...

I: Right. Who would you most like to meet there?
R: Oh, nobody at all. I like peace and quiet.
I: And what essential items would you take with you?
R: Uhm, a couple of good books and plenty of sunscreen.
I: And what sights would you want to visit?
R: The beach in the daytime and a taverna at night.

...

I: Who would you send a postcard to?
R: Nobody. Writing a postcard would be too much like hard work.
I: Hmm. And what would spoil your perfect weekend?
R: Rain. Oh, and if the island were full of other tourists. Greece can be really touristy in the summer.

12 Basics

42

(M = Matthew; D = Dawn; W = Waiter)
M: Well, here we are at last. Do you like it?
D: Yes, it's very nice. The music's not too loud. I hate it when they have loud music in restaurants.
M: Me too.
D: Hah.
W: Good evening. Uh, are you ready to order?
M: Oh, no. We haven't looked at the menu yet. Could we have something to drink first?
W: Certainly. Uh, what would you like?
M: Uhm, would you like some wine?
D: Oh, yes, that would be nice. Uhm, red, please.
M: Two glasses of red wine, please, and uh, could we have a few crackers, too?
W: Of course. I'll be right back to take your order.
M: Great, thank you. We'd better look at the menu. What kinds of food do you like?
D: Uh, well, uhm, I don't eat any kind of meat or fish, so anything without meat or fish, I guess. Hah...
M: Oh, no... I didn't know you were a vegetarian. I don't think there are any vegetarian dishes on the menu.
D: Oh. Oh, yes, there are. Look, there are lots of things. Uh, well, they have salads, anyway. I'll have a house salad and a bowl of vegetable soup.
M: Are you sure?
D: Yes, that's fine. I love salad.
M: O.K. Uh, do you mind if I have meat?
D: No, o... of course not. That's up to you.
W: Are you ready to order now?
M: Yes, we'll have a house salad and a bowl of vegetable soup, and, uh, the steak with French fries, please.
W: How would you like your steak done, sir?
M: Medium rare, please. And could we have some bread and a water, please?
W: Mineral or tap?
D/M: Mineral./Tap.
D: Oh, that's all right, It doesn't matter.
M: No, no, it's O.K., uh, let's have mineral. Mineral, please.
W: Anything else?
M: No, that's all for now, thank you.

43

(M = Matthew; D = Dawn; W = Waiter)
M: So, how long have you been living in Cincinnati?
D: Uh, a couple of years. How about you?
M: Only a few months. I moved out here for my job.
D: Ah.
M: There weren't many jobs available in my town.
W: Your bread, and here's some water. Uh, can I get you anything else?
M: No, I'm fine, thank you. How about you?
D: I'm fine too, thanks.
M: And, uh, where are you from originally?
D: Oh, uh, from a small town just outside Wichita. The job market was terrible there, so I moved to Cincinnati.
M: And do you like living... Oh no—I'm so sorry. Oh, no, did it get on your skirt?
D: Uh, just a little. It's O.K.
M: Excuse me, waiter! Uh, can you bring a napkin... Uh, I spilled some wine.
D: It's O.K., honestly. Hardly any of it got on my skirt. Just a drop.
M: I'm really sorry. I'll pay for the dry cleaning.
W: A napkin, sir.
M: Thank you. Here, let me wipe it up.
D: No, I'm fine really. Don't touch me!
W: Who's the salad?

44

(I = Interviewer; M = Michael)
I: Michael, you've had the opportunity to taste some of the more unusual dishes from around the world. Can you tell us something about them, and in particular, what they taste like?
M: Yes, well, I've just come back from Thailand, and in the winter, huge bags of grasshoppers and locusts are brought into Bangkok from the countryside because the Thais love them. They make a really crisp and tasty snack. In fact, most people think fried grasshoppers are delicious, as long as they don't know what they're eating. They eat crickets in parts of North America, and they taste just like them.
I: Hmm. I'm not sure I'd like to eat insects.
M: Well, you'd better not go to Indonesia then. Last time I was there, I had a feast of insects. The main course was roasted cockroaches.
I: Oh my gosh. What did that taste like?
M: They're kind of chewy on the outside, and then there's a rich liquid on the inside which tastes really sweet and fruity.
I: What other insects have you eaten?
M: Well, did you know that in Colombia, movie theaters serve roasted ants instead of popcorn?
I: Really? What are they like?
M: Sweet and crisp... delicious, actually. I also ate barbecued lizard in South America, but that was pretty disappointing. It was a little bland... not particularly tasty. On the other hand, iguana eggs were surprisingly good. After being boiled in very salty water for ten minutes, they made a very tasty evening snack. A little too salty for my taste, but very good.
I: I've heard that they eat worms called grubs in Australia. I can't believe that. Is it true?
M: Yes. I've never eaten them raw, but I have eaten them fried. They're O.K.... a little chewy... crunchy on the outside but chewy on the inside.
I: I'm sorry, I don't even want to think about it. Can we change the subject. How about shark fin soup? Have you ever tried that?
M: Only once, in China. It's very expensive and takes forever to make. But it's delicious. The taste depends on how the chef prepares it, but when I ate it, it was really spicy and not particularly fishy. Anyway, what about you? Have you ever eaten anything strange?
I: Well, I'm not as adventurous as you, and the only foreign country I've ever been to is Scotland, but I had something really revolting there.
M: Oh, you mean haggis?
I: No, no. Haggis is delicious. No, it was a deep-fried candy bar.
M: What? You mean, like fish and chips... a candy bar and chips?
I: That's right. Greasy and much too sweet. Disgusting!
M: Oh.

13 Communication

45

Welcome to the Inside Out helpline for students of English. Here are some useful numbers and addresses for your information. For news and current events, the Associated Press Web site is a good starting point at www.ap.org. An alternative is CNN at www.cnn.com.
You can get the latest news and reviews on the music scene at www.mtv.com. Or, if it's

sports results you want, then the ESPN site at http://espn.go.com will keep you up to date. For travel information, try one of the major search engines like Yahoo at http://travel.yahoo… that's all one word… Y A H double O… .com. If you need to plan a train trip in the U.S., call Amtrak at 1-800-USA-RAIL.
AccuWeather has lots of up-to-the-minute weather forecasts. You'll find them at www.accuweather… all one word… .com. And if you want to contact the president, you can call the White House switchboard at 1-202-456-1414.

46

1
Hi, Rich. It's Jeff, six thirty Wednesday night. I'm in Boston for a few days. Give me a call if you're around. It's 723-4934. Talk to you soon.

2
Hi there! This is Stan from Tim's Travel Company. We finally have your tickets for ten days of scuba-diving in Key West. Come by and pick them up anytime. We're open from nine to five every day. Bye.

3
Richard… it's Andrew. I just got a call from Ian Watson at Smith Insurance. They have a problem with the program we installed on their computer network last week, so I told him I'll get somebody out there as soon as possible to figure it out. Could you call him first thing tomorrow morning and arrange to go out there and see what you can do? The… the number is 555-9876. Give me a call at the office to let me know what you set up. Thanks.

4
Uh, this is Alex at Virgin Megastore. The new computer game you ordered has come in. You can come by and pick it up anytime. Thank you.

5
Hello, it's me… Maggie. You may remember me. I'm supposed to be your girlfriend, although you wouldn't think so. Get off your computer for five minutes and give me a call. By the way, have you heard anything about the tickets for Key West?

6
Hello. This is Alison Moore from the Southwestern Bank. Could you call me to discuss your overdraft? The number is 555-7200, extension 300. Thank you.

47

1
(J = Jane; R = Richard; M = Maggie)
J: Hello.
R: Oh, hi. Is Maggie there?
J: Is this Richard?
R: Yes, hello, Jane. How are you?
J: Fine, thanks. Hang on. I'll get her.
…
M: Hello.
R: Hi! It's me.
M: So you got my message. I thought you'd forgotten about me.
R: Don't be silly. Of course I haven't forgotten you. I've just been busy, that's all.
M: Busy playing computer games, probably.
R: No, not all the time. Anyway, how are you?
M: Uhm, not too bad. A little tired. Too much work, as usual. Which reminds me—have you heard anything from the travel agent?
R: Oh, yes. They have the tickets.
M: Great! Oh, I really need this vacation.
R: Listen, I can't talk now, but what are you doing later?
M: I have to work tonight, but I thought we could go to a movie tomorrow.
R: O.K., I'll come by at about seven.
M: See you tomorrow.
R: Bye.

2
(Re = Receptionist; R = Richard; A = Alison)
Re: Good morning. Southwestern Bank. Can I help you?
R: Yes, I'd like to speak to Alison Moore, please.
Re: Who's calling, please?
R: My name's Richard Swainston.
Re: O.K., hold on, please. I'll transfer your call…. Oh, Mr. Swainston, I'm afraid she's on the other line. Would you like to hold?
R: Yes, thank you.
…
A: Alison Moore.
R: Oh, hello. This is Richard Swainston.
A: Oh, yes. Mr. Swainston. Thank you for getting back to me so promptly. There seems to be a problem with your account.
R: Really? What kind of problem?
A: Well, you're over your limit by more than $800. You really need to come to the bank to take care of it. Are you available later on today?
R: Actually, no, I'm kind of tied up today. Uh, would tomorrow be convenient for you?
A: Uhm, yes, that's fine. Ten thirty?
R: Yes, ten thirty's fine for me.
A: Well, thank you for calling. I'll look forward to seeing you tomorrow.
R: Good-bye.

48

(MS = Mrs. Swainston; R = Richard)
MS: Hello?
R: Mom, it's Richard.
MS: Oh, is everything all right?
R: Yeah, everything's fine. How are you?
MS: Oh, not too bad. Your father's playing golf, so I'm enjoying the peace and quiet. How's Maggie?
R: She's O.K. Working hard. Mom, I was wondering… do you think you could lend me some money until the end of the month?
MS: Oh, Richard, have you gotten yourself into debt again? Because if you have…
R: No, no. It's just a bit of an overdraft.
MS: Where does all your money go, Richard? I mean, you have a good job…
R: But Mom, living in Boston is expensive.
MS: Well, of course it is. What do you expect if you go out every night? And you just bought that expensive computer, too.
R: It's not a computer. It's a PlayStation.
MS: Oh, well, whatever. I mean, your sister never calls up asking for money.
R: But you spent a fortune on her wedding.
MS: Yes, and when you get married, we'll do the same for you.
R: Well, I'm not going to get married, so you might as well give me the money now!
MS: Richard! What would Maggie say! Now come on, this is silly. How much do you need?
R: Eight hundred dollars.
MS: Oh, honestly, Richard, you have to learn to budget.
R: Look, Mom, if you can just help me out this time, I promise I'll try to be more careful in future.
MS: Well, we'll see about that. Listen, I… I'll do it this time, but this really is the last time. If you get yourself into trouble again, you'll just have to figure it out yourself.
R: Oh thanks, Mom.
MS: But I'm doing this on one condition…
R: Yes?
MS: You never say you're not going to get married again.
R: O.K., I promise. Thanks, Mom. Bye.
MS: Bye… and next time, you could call up just to chat!

14 Style

49

1
I think my favorite thing right now is my white turtleneck sweater. It goes with everything, and it's really easy to wear.

2
I love my flowery silk vest. I wear it only on very special occasions, and I usually wear it with a suit. It cheers me up.

3
My favorite thing is my black leather jacket, which I bought in Spain. It's really old, and it gets better as it gets older.

4
My baseball hat is my favorite thing. I have very short hair, and I'm really cold without it. The colors are great: bright orange and pink.

5
I really spend a lot of money on clothes, but my favorite things usually aren't the most expensive. For example, I love my old short-sleeved T-shirt with a big banana on the front. I got that on sale for less than $10.

6
My favorite thing is definitely my leopard-print fake fur coat. I got it from a secondhand store, and it looks terrific with my high-heeled boots.

7
I tend to like comfortable clothes best. My favorite outfit is my baggy green pants and my plaid shirt.

8
My grandmother sent me a beautiful plaid cashmere scarf for my birthday, and I love it.

50

***Ugly*, by Jon Bon Jovi**
If you're ugly, I'm ugly too!
In your eyes the sky's a different blue
If you could see yourself like others do
You'd wish you were as beautiful as you

And I wish I was a camera sometimes
So I could take your picture with my mind
Put it in a frame for you to see
How beautiful you really are to me

Ugly, ugly
All of us just feel like that some day
Ain't no rainbow in the sky
When you feel U.G.L.Y.
And that's ugly

Yeah yeah yeah
Yeah yeah yeah

Ugly, ugly
All of us just feel like that some day
Ain't no rainbow in the sky
When you feel U.G.L.Y.
And that's ugly, ugly
All of us just feel like that some day
Ain't no cure that you can buy
When you feel U.G.L.Y.
And that's ugly

So, if you're ugly, I'm ugly too
If you're a nut, then I must be a screw
If you could see yourself the way I do
You'd wish you were as beautiful as you
I wish I was as beautiful as you

51

(See page 124.)

15 Age

52

(M = Man; W = Woman)
M: You look worried. What's on your mind?
W: Well, there is something I've been meaning to tell you…
M: Look, if it's about last night, it really doesn't matter. I shouldn't have said anything.
W: No, no, it has nothing to do with that. Or…well, maybe it does, in a way.
M: I knew it. If only I'd kept my mouth shut.
W: Look, I agree with you. The Rolling Stones are old-fashioned, and I wish I'd never played that album.
M: It's not a bad album. It's my fault. I shouldn't have called them boring old dinosaurs.
W: No, it's my fault. I shouldn't have reacted like I did. It's just that that music brings back special memories for me.
M: Hey, I understand. My parents used to play the Rolling Stones too.
W: No, you don't understand. I was in my teens when that album first came out.
M: Oh, of course. I see what you mean. Well, you look very good for your age.
W: Oh, shut up.
M: No, no, no. What I mean is that I don't care how old you are…and anyway, I have something to tell you. I'm not 31, I'm 26.
W: What?!

53

a
Of course I didn't say anything…I mean, the cashier should have asked to look in her purse, shouldn't she? If it had been a small store, I probably would have said something, but a big supermarket like that can afford it.

b
Well, I picked it up, brushed the cat hair off, and served it. Well, what you don't see you don't worry about, do you?

c
So I said, "It looks great!" and then spent the rest of the day wishing I'd told her the truth.

d
I was so shocked. It took me a few days to decide what to do, but once I'd made up my mind, I was sure it was the right thing. I cashed the check and went straight to the travel agency, where I bought tickets to Egypt for myself and a couple of friends. At least they love me as I am. The divorce will be final next month.

e
I don't know if he saw me, but I didn't want to embarrass him, so I just kept walking. I often think about him and wonder how he ended up on the streets.

54

Fred
(I = Interviewer; F = Fred)
I: How old are you now, Fred?
F: Twelve.
I: Is that a good age to be?
F: Yeah…you're grown-up enough to be a little independent, but you're still young. At school I've just gone from being one of the oldest in my old school to being one of the youngest in junior high school.
I: Oh, and which do you prefer?
F: Well, it was good being the oldest because I could boss people around, but it's cool being the youngest, too. And having an older brother in the same school helps.
I: What are the advantages of being 12?
F: You're not a teenager yet, so you're not all crazy and uptight about everything.
I: How old's your brother?
F: Sixteen.
I: What differences are there between being 12 and being 16?
F: He smells, and I don't. Hah. And he has more homework than I do.
I: Do you ever wish you were older or younger than you are?
F: Yeah…I'd like to be old enough not to have to clean my room.
I: Hah. But you have to clean your room whatever age you are.
F: Yeah, but if I were old enough to leave home and have my own place, I wouldn't have to clean my room.

Jerry
(I = Interviewer; J = Jerry)
I: How old are you, Jerry?
J: Sixteen.
I: What's it like being 16? Is that a good age to be?
J: Uh, well, I'd prefer to be 18.
I: Why?
J: Because I'd be a legal adult. I could vote.
I: Are you looking forward to voting?
J: Yeah.
I: Do you mind if I ask you who you might vote for?
J: Well, I really don't know. Uhm, it could all change in two years.
I: What do you think is the best age to be?
J: Uh, probably when you're really young, before you go to school. You don't have anything to worry about.
I: You have a brother who's 12, don't you?
J: Yes, unfortunately.
I: Hah. In what way are your lives different?
J: I have a lot more responsibilities. I have a part-time job on weekends, and I'm learning to drive, and I have a heavier workload in school. But I also have a lot more freedom. He's not allowed out after six o'clock.
I: Ah. Do you mind if I ask you whether you have a girlfriend?
J: Uh, not really.

Yvette
(I = Interviewer; Y = Yvette)
I: You just had an important birthday, right?
Y: Yeah—the big two-one.
I: So, how does it feel to be 21?
Y: Oh, exactly the same as 20. I really don't drink, so being 21 is no big deal.
I: Is there anything you can do now that you couldn't do before you were 21?
Y: Besides drink alcohol? Uh, no, not really. But I guess when you're 21, you have more responsibilities. You're supposed to be more independent, and uh, you can't depend on your parents so much. Uh, like I have to pay for all my own stuff now, so that's a disadvantage. And uh, people expect grown-up behavior from you.
I: Yvette, what do you think is the best age to be?
Y: Oh, maybe five years old. You go to kindergarten and you play all day. Everybody spoils you, and life is just fun.
I: Have you ever wished you were older or younger?
Y: Oh, yes. When I was about 15, my brother was allowed to go out late and I wasn't. He's three years older than me, and I wanted to be the same age as him.

Carla
(I = Interviewer; C = Carla)
I: Do you mind if I ask you how old you are?
C: Well, I'd rather not say. But put it this way—I'm the wrong side of 30.
I: Is that a good age to be?
C: Uh, yes, pretty good. But it's a lot older than 25, which is how old I feel.
I: What's life like when you're in your thirties?
C: Well, not very different from my twenties, except that I'm seriously thinking of buying more expensive moisturizers, and wondering if they really work.
I: What do you think is the best age to be?
C: I think anywhere between 25 and 30 is a good age, because you've kind of figured out what you want, and you know how to get it, and you have some experience trying to get it. At that age you don't think about the consequences of what you do, whereas when you're older, you do tend to worry about the consequences.
I: So do you wish you were still 25?
C: No, I'm happy at the age I am now. I mean, I had a good time in my twenties, but I wouldn't necessarily want to relive them.
I: Uh-huh!

16 Review 2

55

(I = interviewer; KT = Kim Thomas)
I: …so, if we could turn to the origin of language? Uhm, do we know when, where, and how language originated?
KT: Oh, that's a difficult question to answer. The answer is no one really knows. What we do know is when language was first written down.
I: I see. And that was…
KT: That was about five and a half thousand years ago, in about 3500 b.c. The Sumerians, who lived in Mesopotamia, were the first people to write down their language. They used symbols called pictographs to represent

everyday objects—a little like Egyptian hieroglyphics—and the first actual alphabet was developed around 3,500 years ago by the Phoenicians, who lived on the eastern coast of what is now Syria. Today there are about 65 alphabets in the world. Interestingly, the shortest of them, the one used in the Solomon Islands, has only 11 letters.

I: That's amazing. And the longest?

KT: Uh, the Cambodian, I think. I believe it has 74 letters.

I: So how many languages are there in the world today?

KT: Somewhere in the neighborhood of 4,000. I don't think we'll ever find out the exact figure.

I: Uhm, and which of these are the most spoken?

KT: Well, Mandarin Chinese has about a billion speakers. English is next, with about half a billion speakers, and Hindi, Spanish, and Russian are not too far behind. These five languages account for half of all the conversations in the world!

I: Wow. And is it true that Mandarin is the biggest language? I mean, the one with the most words?

KT: Again, it's difficult to say, but the latest thinking is that English is actually the biggest, largely due to the number of technical and scientific words it contains. There are at least a million words in English. Most native speakers use only about 10,000 words—that's one percent of them.

I: No kidding—only 10,000?

KT: Yeah, and can you guess which are the most common of these? The most frequently used words in English.

I: Huh. Let me think. Uh, maybe *be*?

KT: Well, according to recent research, where tens of thousands of hours of conversation have been fed into computers and analyzed, the most common word is *the*.

I: Oh, and *be*?

KT: Well, *be*, we think, is the most used verb in English. But of course there are different forms of these verbs. Uh, what do you think the most common noun in spoken English is?

I: Hmm. The most common noun? Uh,... maybe something like..., oh, I have no clue. You're going to have to tell us.

KT: Ha-ha. Well, you just said it, actually. Apparently, it's *thing*.

I: Hmmm... O.K.... ha. What about the origins of words? Where does English come from?

KT: Well, modern English, which is about 500 years old, is a mixture of mainly Romance and Germanic languages. Greek and Arabic have also provided English with many words. Uh, did you know that *sugar* comes from Arabic? And, surprisingly, so does *alcohol*. In fact many, many words have been borrowed from other languages. For example, did you know that *coffee* comes from Turkish and that *chess*, the game, is a Persian word?

I: Oh, no.

KT: Where do you think *ketchup*, as in tomato ketchup, comes from?

I: Uhm, I've never really thought about it. I have no idea. Ha-ha. The U.S.?

KT: Ha-ha. It's from the Malay language. A traditional Malaysian sauce, I believe.

I: Interesting.

KT: How about *shampoo*?

I: Hmmm... It sounds like it might be from an Asian language. Maybe Japanese?

KT: It's actually a Hindi word, from India.

I: Uh, speaking of India... Isn't that a country with hundreds of languages?

KT: Well, I don't know about hundreds. I think Papua New Guinea has the most, with over eight hundred fifty separate languages, but India has dozens of languages. The bank notes there have thirteen languages written on them. I suppose they're the main languages. Uh, most people there speak at least two or three languages.

I: Speaking of which... I have one more question. To speak two languages fluently is difficult enough, but do you have you any idea what the highest number of languages spoken by one person is?

KT: There is, or was, a Frenchman, I, uh, can't remember his name, but he spoke 31 different languages—all of them fluently!

I: Oh. On that note, Professor Thomas, we'll say thank you very much and, uh, au revoir, auf Wiedersehen, arrivaderci, sayonara, adios...

Published by Macmillan Education
Between Towns Road, Oxford OX4 3PP
A division of Macmillan Publishers Limited
Companies and representatives throughout the world.

ISBN 140500262X

First published 2000
American Edition 2003

Designed by Keith Shaw, Threefold Design
Illustrated by Kathryn Adams p. 67; Peter Campbell pp. 85, 86; Tim Davies pp. 62, 67; Tim Etheridge pp. 29, 43, 111, 117, 137, 140; Ian Kellas p. 7; Julian Mosedale pp. 28, 36, 42, 45, 83, 88, 95, 100, 103, 106, 113, 122, 127, 130; Andrew Peters pp. 46, 47, 48, 93, 98, 105, 116, 128; Peter Richardson pp. 64, 78.
Cover design by Andrew Oliver
Cover illustration © Howard Hodgkin

Authors' acknowledgments
We would like to thank all our colleagues at the Lake School, Oxford for their help. In particular Peter Maggs, whose thoughtful comments on work in progress were much appreciated. A big thank-you to our wonderful intermediate classes, who unwittingly helped shape much of the material. We are especially grateful to Jon Hird for the excellent review units, help on the Teacher's Book, and otherwise tireless support. Similarly, we would like to thank Philip Kerr (*Inside Out* Workbook), Helena Gomm (*Inside Out* Teacher's Book), and everybody involved in the *Inside Out* Resource Pack: a great team!
And finally, the biggest thanks go to our families, without whose support and understanding none of this would have been possible.

The authors and publishers would like to thank the following institutions for their help in piloting the material and making comments:
Alejandra González, Florencia Lambertini, and Gustavo Seminario, Northside School of English, Buenos Aires. Ana Belén Montero, Carmen Arévalo, EOI Bilbao. Andrea Giulano and Alicia Valle de Ghiorzi, Instituto ITELS, Buenos Aires. Armando de León-Sotelo, EOI Alcorcón. Austin Core, Greylands School of English, Southampton. Carlos Trueba, EOI San Sebastián de los Reyes. Carmen Santos Maldonado, EOI Santander. Catherine Downey and Jan Kingsley, ESADE, Barcelona. Ceri Jones, International House Serrano, Madrid. Charo Martínez, Herminia Blat, José Carte, José Miguel Galarza, and Mari-Cruz Iribarren, EOI Pamplona. Claudina Lovalvo, ICANA, Buenos Aires. Dan Austin and Ian Stuart, St. Joseph's Hall, Oxford. Dave Willis. Elisa Jiménez, EOI Fuenlabrada. Freda Miller, International House Livorno. Gabriella Lacza, International Language Studio, Budapest. Genoveva Barsanti, LEA Institute, Buenos Aires. Gergó Farkas, Spell Language School, Budapest. Henny Burke, British Language Centre, Madrid. Idilia Bernadeu and Isabel Tornero, EOI II, Barcelona. Jason Worsnop, British Institute, Bilbao. Jennifer O'Brien and Mike Sayer, Regent's School, Oxford. Jim Scrivener, International House, Budapest. Juan Francisco Silgado, EOI Jesús Maestro. Judit Biró, Európai Nyelvek Studiója, Budapest. Judit Csepela, Globe Language School. Katalin Schmell, Globus Language School, Budapest. Kate Threadgold, the British Council, Bilbao. Kit Cree, Glen College, Pamplona. Laura Romero and Miguel Angel Almarza, EOI San Blas. Luis Suárez and Niam Glenn, EOI Alcorcón. Macarena Rodulfo, EOI Getafe. Maite Sanjuan, Miquel Bretón, and Núria Godoy, EOI I, Barcelona. Marek Doskocz, Lingwista, Warsaw. María Angeles, EOI Ciudad Lineal. María Galbis and María Piteira Troncosa, EOI Gandía. María Lorente and Michael Hellmer, London Institute, Montevideo. María Silvia Stagnaro, Profesoras Asociadas Egresadas del Instituto Lenguas Vivas, Buenos Aires. Marian Cruz, EOI Mostoles. Mónica Harvey de Campisteguy and Patricia Alvárez, Dickens Institute, Montevideo. Mónika Marton, KOTK, Budapest. Nancy Cortell, Info English, Buenos Aires. Nicholas Sheard, English@Oxford, Oxford. Pablo Arroya, EOI Zaragoza. Paola Ferrari and Kate Jones-Page, Centro Linguistico di Ateneo, Parma. Pascual Pérez Paredes, EOI Cartagena. Peter Hall, Alboraya English Centre, Valencia. Philip Kerr and Vince Desmond, International House, London. Philip Rickett, International House/Academia Lacunza, San Sebastián. Rebecca Place, International Centre, Bilbao. Rosina Otegui de Perrier, Geraldine Poole, and María Ema Mira, Instituto Cultural Anglo-Uruguayo, Montevideo. Russell Stannard, CLIC Seville. Ruth Sánchez García, EOI A Coruña. Sándor Csupor, Budapest International Language Studio. Sara Klughaupt de Lieberman, Susana R. Margoniner, María Rosa Sánchez, José Luis Formoso, Queen Victoria Institute, Montevideo. Silvina Campagnoli, Leeds School of English, Buenos Aires. Sonia Casal, EOI Alcalá de Guadaira-Seville. Steve Bush, British Institute of Florence. Sue Bailey, University of Strathclyde. Tania Bastow. Teachers at Atlanta Language School, Budapest. Teresa Blanco, EOI Fuenlabrada. Virginia López Grizolia, Silvana Ioli, Interaction Language Studio, Buenos Aires. W. Arnold and Julian Wright, Instituto de Idiomas Universidad Deusto, Bilbao.

A special thank-you to María Galbis and her colleagues at EOI Gandia, Spain and to our great intermediate class of summer 1998.

The publishers wish to thank Nick Blinco, St. Thomas More RC Primary School, Kidlington, and Jane Couch.

The authors and publishers would like to thank the following for permission to reproduce their material:
Brand New Heavies *You've Got A Friend* Words and Music by Carole King © Screen Gems-EMI Music Inc, USA and London, WC2H 0QY, reprinted by permission of the publisher and International Music Publications Ltd. All Rights Reserved.
Paul Wilson Extract from *The Little Book of Calm* (Penguin Books Australia, 1996), reprinted by permission of the publisher.
Extracts from *Collins Cobuild English Dictionary* (HarperCollins Publishers Ltd., 2001), © HarperCollins Publishers Ltd. 2001, reprinted by permission of the publisher.
Michael B. Vederman Extract from "My Name is Mike, and I'm a Sky Diver" from deadmike@deadmike.com, reprinted by permission of the author.
Jon Bon Jovi *Ugly* Words and Music by Eric Bazilian and Jon Bon Jovi © Human Boy Music and Bon Jovi Publishing/Polygram Music Publishing Incorporated, USA 1997, reprinted by permission of Music Sales Ltd. All Rights Reserved. International Copyright Secured.
Richard and Helen Exley Extracts and illustration from *To Mum (The Kindest of Ladies)* (Exley Publications Ltd.), reprinted by permission of the publishers.
Roald Dahl Extracts from *Boy* (Jonathan Cape and Penguin Books Ltd., 1984), reprinted by permission of David Higham Associates Limited.
Nicholas Taylor Extract from "Valencia Burns and the People Come Out to Play" published in *Independent on Sunday* 02/08/98, reprinted by permission of the publisher.
Maxton Walker Extract from "Global Myths No.6" published in *Independent on Sunday* 02/22/98, reprinted by permission of the publisher.
Interview with Jane Couch, reprinted by permission of Jane Couch.
Sarah Blake Extract from "Ageism Has Withered Her" published in *Independent on Sunday* 12/8/96, reprinted by permission of the publisher.
Lesley Gore *It's My Party* Words and Music by John Gluck, Wally Gold, and Herbert Weiner, © Arch-Music Co. USA, Warner/Chappell Music Ltd., London, W6 8BS 1982, reprinted by permission of International Music Publications Ltd. All Rights Reserved.
Alice Hart Extract from "I've Got a List" published in *Weekend Telegraph* 12/13/97, reprinted by permission of the publisher.
Alex Garland Extract from *The Beach* (Viking, 1996), © Alex Garland 1996, reprinted by permission of Penguin Books Ltd.
Extract from "Holidays in Hell" published in *Focus* Magazine January 1999, reprinted by permission of the publisher.
Chart "Aspiration and Reality" published in *The Economist* 10/9/99, © The Economist Newspaper Limited, London, 1999, reprinted by permission of the publisher.
Josie Lloyd and Emlyn Rees Extract from *Come Together* (William Heinemann), reprinted by permission of the Random House Group Ltd.
Extract from "Interview with Jon Bon Jovi" published in *Candis* Magazine October 1997, reprinted by permission of the publisher.

Although every effort has been made to contact copyright holders before publication, this has not always been possible. If notified, the publisher undertakes to rectify any errors or omissions at the earliest opportunity.

The authors and publishers would like to thank the following for permission to reproduce their photographs:
Advertising Archives p. 124; Art Directors & Trip pp. 40 (fr, r), 55 (br, tl), 93 (3,4), 104, 133 (r); Big Pictures p. 50; J. Birdsall p. 27 (c); Bridgeman Art Library pp. 25, 80; Bubbles pp. 27 (b), 30, 54 (2, 4), 60; Colorific p. 58; © Bettmann/Corbis (Casablanca) pp. 22, 23; Corbis pp. 73; Warren Morgan 93 (1); Galen Rowell 93 (2); Julian Cotton pp. 15 (c); 27 (d), 62 (l), 68 (5,6), 73 (br, fbl, fbr); Corbis Sygma, © Trapper Frank (Destiny's Child) p. 12; courtesy of Harley-Davidson p. 126; James Davis pp. 93 (5); Eye Ubiquitous p. 100; Jimmy Gaston p. 14; Robert Harding p. 13; Image Bank p. 53, 54, 62 (r), 77 (tr), 108, 129 (b); Images Colour Library pp. 68 (2, 3, 4), 73 (mr); London Features International pp. 4 (1, 3, 5), 5 (f); Pam McNee p. 9 (l); Mark Peterson/Saba/Network Photographers p. 129 (c); © Nova Development Corporation and its licensors. p. 52, 53; P.A. News p. 35; People in Pictures p. 5 (d); Popperfoto p. 5 (b); Redferns pp. 11, 41; Rex pp. 4 (2, 4, 6), 5 (c, e), 47, 55 (l), 79, 122, 123, 129 (t), 134 (t, b); Telegraph Colour Library pp. 24, 40 (l), 50, 54 (1), 77 (bl), 89 (r), 118, 133 (fl, l, fr); Topham Picturepoint p. 63; Frank Spooner pp. 27 (a), 59, 93 (6), 103; Tony Stone pp. 15 (tr, m), 31, 32, 40 (fl), 68 (tl), 73 (ml, bl, t, br), 82, 83, 89 (c), 93 (t), 95, 97, 138; Superstock p. 89 (l).
Commissioned photographs by Haddon Davies pp. 20, 119, 121; Chris Honeywell p. 9; David Tolley p. 43; John Walmsley pp. 15, 17.

Cartoons on p. 26, p. 30, p. 49, p. 75, p. 88, p. 107 reproduced with permission of Punch Ltd.; p. 18, p. 37, p. 44, p. 81, p. 83, p. 96, p. 108, p. 109, p. 110, p. 124, p. 125 reproduced with permission of Private Eye; p. 10 reproduced with permission of Harry Venning.

Printed and bound in Thailand

2007 2006 2005 2004 2003
10 9 8 7 6 5 4 3 2 1